THE BEGINNER'S GUIDE TO
SWIMMING AND WATER SPORTS

Books by the same author:
Young Person's Guide to Nature
Concise Encyclopaedia of Herbs
Textbook of Botanic Medicine (8 vols)
Herb Growing for Health
Herbs for Cooking and Healing
Herbal Teas for Health and Pleasure
How to Defeat Rheumatism and Arthritis
How to Keep your Hair on
Degree Course in Philosophy
Handbuch der Heilkräuter
Luonnonvaraista Terveysteetä
Astrology, Palmistry and Dreams
Beginners Guide to Sailing (1974)

THE BEGINNER'S GUIDE TO SWIMMING AND WATER SPORTS

DONALD LAW

Illustrated by Patty Johns

DRAKE PUBLISHERS INC.
NEW YORK · LONDON
1975

ISBN 0-87749-825-3

Published in 1975 by
DRAKE PUBLISHERS INC.
381 Park Avenue South
New York, N.Y. 10016

Library of Congress Cataloging
in Publication Data 74-25160

© Donald Law
All rights reserved

Printed in Great Britain

Table of Contents

Introduction to Swimming Section	*page* vii
Swimming	1
Canoeing	159
Sailing	189
Fishing and Subaqua	198
Rowing, Punts and Rafts, Outboard Motors	213
Water Polo, Water Skiing, Diving for Delight	222

DEDICATIONS

Carl Olaf Homen
> *Kenpä puuta etsimähän, tammea tavoittamahan,*
> *Väinämöiselle venoksi, laulajalle pohjapuuksi?*

Bernd Ebel
Manfred Lang
Rudi Peters
> *Hilpt mi, Sünn un Wind, hilpt mi bit Fischen*
> *Ik heet Klaus Mees un bün van Finkwarder*

To the memory of Carel Tirion of 's Gravenhage
> *Wie gaat mee, gaat er mee over zee?*
> *Houd het roer recht!*
> *Fris blaast de wind langs de ree*
> *Blijft ge in 't nest met de rest—*
> *Houd het roer recht!*

Dr. Jordi Mallafré y Morel

es la santa amistad, virtue divina, que no dilata el premio de tenella,

pues ella misma es de si misma el fruto.

ACKNOWLEDGEMENTS

Firstly, I wish to record my sincere gratitude to my friend David Luxon, a very fine teacher of swimming, who has painstakingly checked the technical data and text of this book with much patience, and who made many helpful suggestions. For this and many fine swims together— Thanks Dave!

Next, my sincere thanks and good wishes to

REG BRICKETT—THE GREATEST!

Jim Essex—a fine sportsman,

Brian Elton—who has done a lot for swimming,

and to Rudi Peters of Aachen, a great swimmer and teacher from whom I learnt much.

Also Joan Harvey, Ivy Ing, Avril Mitchell and Dawn Zajak.

I wish to acknowledge with sincere thanks the hard work of Louis Small, of Benoni, who checked through the proofs.

> *Sal ons ons vriende ooit vergeet,*
> *die vriende van ons jeug.*

INTRODUCTION TO SWIMMING SECTION

Here in simple language is everything you need to know to become a very good swimmer. If you never learn to swim you will miss all the fun of the beach; it is a social art like dancing or driving; it can save your life, build a physique which others admire; strengthen your staying power or stamina, fortify your internal organs and help them work more efficiently.

Swimming restores many invalids to radiant good health. It builds up self-confidence, and is an enjoyable form of therapy.

Adults and young alike solve their problems better after a healthy swim. Research undertaken by American psychologists proved that swimmers and athletes develop a much higher intelligence quotient and greater academic potential than do any non-sportsmen.

Here you will find the most scientific and up-to-date facts about swimming given in an easy-to-understand fashion. The four major strokes are fully explained with detailed lists showing you how to correct any weak points and become a really fast super-swimmer. Several valuable, easy-to-learn lesser-known strokes are described in detail.

Advice is given on how to teach the physically-handicapped, blind, deaf-and-dumb, educationally sub-normal and so on. Few sports offer such pleasure, recreation and success to these who so easily feel cut off from other sports and pursuits.

This goldmine of information tells you how to look after complete beginners on their first visit to the baths, how to coach, how to save life, how to behave in case of accidents, with special advice on diet to help champions achieve deserved success. Professional advice is given on racing, with a guide to the psychological aspects and how to master them.

Techniques which have never before appeared in print are provided to help you become a champion—the theory of balance and poise, a special part on breathing in the water—just as you would get them from a coach training world-beaters.

For most readers it is best to read the part for beginners, dealing with the First Visit to the Baths, and from there read up the fully-detailed section on the stroke you want to learn first. Most racing is done in Front Crawl, Back Crawl, Dolphin (Butterfly) and Breast Stroke.

I have used *he* throughout this book instead of writing *he and she* all the time; also *his* instead of *his and/or hers*.

Swimming is something you must think about and understand. Using this book will help you check and correct your own stroke during practice. No amount of practice in the world can make you a world-beater if you do not understand *why* you perform the exact movements in an exact way.

Nobody gets too old to enjoy swimming, it is a sport whose joys remain with you forever.

I have been swimming ever since my mother persuaded my father to learn so that he could teach me. He was trained by the Olympic coach Walter Brickett; many years later I was trained by his son, famous international coach, Reg Brickett.

DONALD LAW
Ph.D., D.B.M., Dip.D., Psy.D.,
D.Litt., M.N.T.A., phil. med.D.

Swimming

THE FIRST VISIT TO THE BATHS (*Teaching Beginners*)
Start as you mean to carry on. Check the hygiene regulations which ensure that swimming is a pleasure for you and the other users of the pool.

All beginners, regardless of age, are conscious of splashing caused by other swimmers. Get the novices to make a big splash themselves, which helps them surmount the difficulty. They must avoid wiping their faces, after a splash or two ('Your face is only going to get wet again') and must not shut their eyes.

(1) Sit the beginners down on the edge of the shallow end of the bath, with their knees curled over the edge and feet dangling in the water. On the word 'Go' everybody kicks their feet up and down as hard as they can. Stop for a breather and start again, having a competition to see who can kick fastest.

(2) When this is over, all the beginners are asked to put up their left hands and wave them above their heads. They then put their left hand down on the left side of the body palm downwards on the side of the bath. When this has been done they cross the right hand over the body and put it down firmly side by side with the left, so that the trunk is now turned sideways towards the water. A slight twist of the body still more to the right and the body slips gracefully into the water firmly supported by the arms on the side of the bath—and they didn't even need to use the steps.

(3) Every bath has a metal rail or a scum channel which provides hand-hold. The beginners transfer their grip to the rail, holding tightly with two hands, and walk along the width of the bath, taking small, well-balanced steps.

(4) The same exercise is repeated, holding on only with the left hand, then returning holding on only with the right hand.

(5) Now, led by the teacher or a competent, older swimmer the beginners form a straight line, one behind the other. Each puts his or her hands on the shoulder of the learner in front and a walk across the bath width is made without touching the side of the bath at all. This is also repeated with the learners holding on with one hand at a time, giving the free hand an opportunity to push the water down at the side of the body 'as if we are all paddling a big canoe'.

(6) With the teacher or a swimmer alongside, the learners now march across the bath without holding on to one another or the bath side. When this has been achieved the water will no longer seem a strange or hostile element.

(7) At this stage the techniques on floating should be applied because, having become accustomed to movement, we now have to convey the idea that movement in the water must be horizontal, not vertical.

INTRODUCTORY NOTES ON FLOATING

Nearly everybody has a natural body buoyancy, depending upon how they let their body balance on the water. Movement in the water must be like a fish along the surface.

By learning a few floating tricks we can learn to swim more quickly. The deeper the parts of the body sink into the water the harder it is to swim. Watch fish in an aquarium and see how easily they make their streamlined movements. Try to keep your movements smooth and streamlined. Don't be afraid to stand in water that reaches up to your neck; the deeper the water the better it can carry your weight.

There is an important psychological factor involved in learning how to let the water carry one's body. All movements must be made calmly and positively—half-hearted movements are useless.

(8) To start with, the learner should enter the water and hold on with both hands to the rail. This is best held by turning the palms round to face yourself, taking a strong hold on the rail. The elbows are placed against the bath's wall, slightly below the surface—this gives a strong grip, one cannot fall. Then let the legs drift up slowly behind you; relax them slightly and don't be frightened when you feel

them floating up into their natural position. Do this several times.

(9) This is the same as the above exercise but the learner places his face down in the water (with the eyes open) and blows out a mouthful of air before lifting the head to breath in. Start with one blow out, then with two, three—up to five before standing down again. There will be a natural tendency to move the legs slightly when they are on the surface—this is to be encouraged.

(10) When the teacher or a competent swimmer is in the water the learner can hold on to the rail with one hand only, pointing the free arm in the direction of the helper, about six feet (two metres) away. The knees are bent up like a coiled spring and a foot or two off the floor of the bath. On the word 'Go' the pupil lets go of the tension and glides towards the helper, bringing the holding arm to point in the same direction as the pointing arm—towards the helper.

(11) When the above technique has been mastered the pupil can start from a hold in which both arms hold on but are brought out in front sharply at the start of the glide.

(12) This is the same as the above but is performed lying on the back, the arms being swung smartly over the head; it involves getting the face wet from the resulting splash, which helps the pupil practise presence of mind.

Few pupils will master so many techniques in one lesson. Experience shows that it may take up to four lessons before confidence and success manifest themselves. There is a story of an old negro preacher whose sermons were so eminently successful that he was asked how he achieved such progress. His reply is very apt: 'First, ah tells 'em what ah's going to tell 'em; then ah tells 'em what ah tells 'em; then ah tells 'em what ah's told 'em'. If you cannot repeat instructions patiently again and again don't expect to be a successful teacher.

EXPLAINING RELAXATION
At a fairly early stage in preliminary teaching explain to the learners that tightly-contracted muscles sink more quickly than loose, relaxed muscles.

Get the class to stand on the side and contract the bicep muscle on one arm as tight as possible—this will prove that a contracted muscle tires quickly—especially if they try to hold the contraction for one minute. Then after a short pause tell the class to contract and relax the same muscle, repeatedly for one minute. Take care that this is done properly and they will soon convince themselves that this is more comfortable and less painful.

The goal is to learn how to relax muscles during the recovery movements, i.e. when the muscles are not actively propelling the body forward through the water.

In the Front Crawl, Back Crawl, Dolphin/Butterfly and Side Stroke recovery is made wholly or partly above the surface of the water. If the recovery movements are not relaxed they will exert an unnecessary pressure forcing the body deeper into the water than is good for balance and buoyancy, which upsets the breathing rhythm. The beginners are encouraged to make all movements above the water loosely, quickly and precisely: This gives the muscles a chance to recuperate and makes breathing easier.

The more the pupils understand the technique the easier it becomes for them.

THE SECRET OF SUCCESSFUL TEACHING: TELL THE PUPILS WHAT TO DO AND WHY THEY MUST DO IT THE WAY YOU SAY.

The more they understand the reason behind the rules the more they will try to apply that technique, and this eliminates a lot of fear—which as a psycho-physio reaction inhibits proper breathing and easy muscle movement.

NOISE

Some beginners, especially children, are dreadfully disturbed by the noise of a swimming pool, where the simplest shout may produce a great volume of sound and echoes. This can be greatly offset by the teacher avoiding shouting himself and showing a very calm demeanour.

The presence of the teacher in the water with the nervous learner is very helpful in such cases.

WHICH STROKE SHALL WE LEARN?

This depends upon the individual pupil.

It is widely taught today that the Front Crawl is the easiest stroke to learn. The author hastens to rewrite this dogma: 'Front Crawl is the easier stroke for the instructor to teach'. Whether it is the easiest for every learner is debatable. When the initial floating tests are carried out at the bar the teacher can find out which of the leg movements the learner makes most naturally. In the case of children it is often the Front Crawl, but few are given much opportunity to show any choice. For the difficult case it would be advisable to try out tests for all the three main strokes (Dolphin is not a learner's stroke) and even for the lesser-known strokes. Many children can swim a Trudgen well before they ever get round to the Crawl—much to the instructor's despair; Trudgen is a stroke with a very natural movement.

SWIMMING AIDS—A CRITICAL SUMMARY

(1) *The Pole and Belt*—one of the oldest known swimming aids in the world. The teacher holds a stout pole, stands on the bath side (it used to be the river bank) and the pupil is supported in some belt, tyre or any harness which keeps his head above the surface. It is usually passed round the chest, leaving the arms free to move. It is still valid for very nervy pupils, but unsuitable for a class, as one aid is required for each learner.

(2) *Pole alone*—Useful for an uncertain adult who is learning the Front Crawl rather late in life. The teacher first pulls the pupil—who holds the lower end of the pole with his hands—all the width of the pool while the learner kicks his legs. When the movements are good the teacher makes the pupil move both legs and one arm ('Three-quarters of you is swimming already'), then the other arm; after holding on with one arm many a pupil feels that the holding arm could be better employed pushing and pulling in the water. Very good for instructors who have a propensity for weightlifting. Many of the pupils who seem to want this are those who weigh heaviest. Suitable for individual tuition only. If used with children they tend to play about and make little or no effort to learn.

(3) *Rings and fancy-shaped rings*—Once when I was with the National School of Swimming we were asked to test out some strange animal-shaped ring which would from its appearance prove attractive to children. We put our star turn in it. The girl turned turtle within a few minutes, and although a good swimmer had difficulty in righting herself. A nonswimmer would have drowned if speedy help did not come along. Whether of rubber or plastic, fancy-shaped rings or just plain rings (old inner tubes etc.) have all the inherent danger that while they do float on the water they simply don't mind which way up they float, and if you put your baby in one they may float just as well with him head down as head up! Occasionally inner tubes full inflated can be used by a teacher with an awkward squad, to make them get their feet off the bottom. Not to be used without supervision. Avoid all fancy shapes.

(4) *Inflatable Jackets, etc.*—These may inhibit the arm action of the swimmer—while useful to save life in accidents they are not suitable for learners, in the opinion of the author.

(5) *Swimsuits with pouches for floats*—Although becoming popular these are liable to be laughed at for their ungainliness. But they have the advantage of being able to have the support decreased by removing one or more of the polystyrene cylinders which fit in the pouches.

(6) *The Armbands (inflatable)*—These probably represent one of the greatest advances in the teaching of swimming for centuries, so much so that any teacher who has taught with them rarely reverts to any other method. The learner cannot capsize; arm and leg movements can be made freely. If the pupil stops moving the armbands force the body into a safe, confidence-inspiring vertical position. They are worn above the elbow. I have seen an eight-month-old baby, who could neither walk or talk, crow with delight when he bobbed along the water with inflated armbands on. His parents lived on a Thames-moored barge and wanted to make sure that when he toddled about he wouldn't fall into the river and drown. Arm bands can be gradually deflated as confidence increases.

(7) *Polystyrene or Cork Floats*—This is definitely the most

ancient swimming aid in the world; bas reliefs from Assyria show men swimming with floats. They can be used for beginners and for advanced pupils perfecting their technique.

Inflated rugger ball bladders make very useful floats, and provided that they are properly dried after use give years of service. Even a large tin with the lid soldered on will contain enough air to float with satisfactorily. A ball is too hard to hold on to, it gets slippery and is no use as a float.

(8) *Flippers*—I oppose them for beginners because they hinder correct leg development. They are essential for sub-aqua swimmers etc.

What about the old idea of supporting a swimmer by holding a hand under the tummy? Well, anything that creates a false sense of security is to be avoided. If you have no alternative but to hold a beginner support them from the back by holding their costume.

The sooner the learner can get the feel of spreading his weight over the entire surface the happier he will be.

The beginner should be taught to swim in to the side of the bath—towards firm support and safety. Don't expect miracles! Until the swimmer can make half the bath width going in to the side do not force him to swim outwards.

The experienced teacher will be able to intersperse all of these initiatory stages with a play element and by using lively and skilful patter make the exercises sound like a game for children.

LAND DRILL FOR BEGINNERS

You either believe in land drill or you don't. It has more value for large classes and the less bright pupils than for individual learners or adults, in the author's opinion.

FRONT CRAWL

(1) Loosening exercises for the shoulder girdle.
   (a) Windmill motion. Arms circling across the body, both fully stretched, hands meeting above the head and coming down.

(b) Reverse action.
(c) Windmill action sideways from front to rear, left arm, then right arm, in front, going backwards.
(d) The same action with arms coming from rear to front.
(2) Breathing check.
(a) Hold a rail or chairback with left arm. Pull right arm down as described in section on Front Crawl and breathe on the right hand side. Release left hand and pull, keeping head downwards blowing out hard, as left hand finishes elliptical movement recommence with the right arm.
(b) The same as above but with the feet shuffling or kicking four or six kicks to the cycle.
(3) Leg kicking, heel to toe, heel to toe all the time. Trying to avoid unnecessary knee bending.
(4) Repeat the leg kicking while lying face down on the floor; support the head.

BREAST STROKE

For the following exercises the body should lean forwards so that the learner's head may look straight along the arms when they are raised to shoulder height.

(1) The arms stretch out and then in this position press down with no bending at all between fingertips and shoulders; at the wrist the palms turn slightly outwards. They descend about 15 inches, not wider apart than a handspan on each side of the shoulders. The elbows bend backwards against the ribs, then they push the arms forward again.
(2) Seated on the floor, lying back on the elbows. The legs close together, toes pointed. The knees bend upward and outward. The legs kick open wide, toes pointed, and then sweep together again without bending.
(3) The same movement as before, but performed in a sitting-up position. The legs are together and the arms together, all limbs pointed and straight. The arms sweep downward as in exercise 1. The arms bend, the legs bend. The legs shoot outward as the arms recover and shoot forward.

BACK CRAWL

(1) Stand and make a windmill motion with alternate arms going up, backwards and round.
(2) The legs make a gentle kicking motion, keeping as straight as is comfortable. They must be kept close together.
(3) Combination of exercises one and two.

Land drill is fairly useful for this stroke to reinforce the exact position of the hands as they reach a point which in the water is behind the head but on land above the head.

DOLPHIN STROKE

A double windmill motion both arms *thrown*—not lifted, forward simultaneously with inhalation, pulled down and brought to point of recovery during exhalation.

The full leg movement of Dolphin cannot be performed on land. If the swimmer is practising Butterfly which has the Breast Stroke leg movement, the land drill exercises described under that heading can be used.

GENERAL REMARKS ON THE EARLY STAGES OF SWIMMING

The beginner must be encouraged to crouch down to keep the shoulders under the surface of the water; this helps to keep the pupil warm, since the air facilitates the evaporation of the water in the wet skin.

For the first few lessons it may help to have the class shout out as loud as they can '*Swimming is to save my life*' or some similar phrase which impinges upon their memories.

Finish every lesson with a game or a free choice period of a few minutes so that you can observe what the trainees do with it. When they start swimming of their own free will Success is on its way.

If the class is too young for games or a free period let them have a little sing-song in the water.

THE FRONT CRAWL

When you have some place to go in a hurry, or wish to swim purely for the sheer joy of it, there is probably no stroke which gives the swimmer and the beholder so much pleasure as a good Front Crawl. The low horizontal position of a good Crawl swimmer minimises the resistance of the water; well performed, it is a stroke which enables the swimmer to make a swift, gliding dart over the surface of the water without any retarding jerks.

In the case of a racing swimmer the flat body has the shoulder girdle and part of the head emerging slightly to break the pure streamline, so that there is only a minimum frontal plane acting on the water, producing little bow wave. The buoyant swimmer who achieves a high speed in this stroke appears sometimes to be riding so high on the surface that he or she might be said in the words of Matt Mann, to be 'swimming downhill'.

It was an unforgettable event when in August, 1906, C. Healy, an Australian, ran away with the Imperial prize at a Hamburg swimming contest by using the hitherto unknown stroke to obtain a record of 1:07.4 over 100 metres. Then Prince Kahanomoku from Hawaii popularised the stroke throughout Europe, and for 10 years took nearly every prize going for 'free style' racing.

In 1922 Johnny Weissmueller, the American who became a film star—famous for his Tarzan roles—swam 100m. in 58.6 seconds, using a modified form of the Crawl stroke which was based upon his personal powerful shoulder girdle. Much time has been spent trying to imitate his style, but without his very powerful shoulder and chest development it is extremely difficult to master.

THE USES OF CRAWL

(a) Use when you are in a hurry.
(b) Use when you are in the sea and worried about sharks; the commotion and violent splashing tend to frighten them away.
(c) The splashing of the legs can attract the attention of of a pilot in an aircraft on rescue detail.
(d) For sport, racing and enjoyment.

ARM ACTION IN FRONT CRAWL

We start with the body buoyant and poised along the water; the right arm is back along the thigh and the left arm is stretched out in front and just above the surface.

SECRET: KEEP THE SHOULDERS SQUARE, DON'T LET THE STRETCHING-OUT OF THE ARM DISTORT THE SQUARE SHOULDER POSITION.

If the arm, as it comes forward, distorts the position of the shoulder girdle this will distort the position of the body and pull the legs deeper down into the water, ruining poise, relaxation, balance and breathing.

The thumb of the left hand is lowermost and the hand slants slightly down from the wrist; we try to aim at an angle of 45 degrees. The left hand and arm drop into the water relaxedly on a line midway between the swimmer's nose and shoulder; at a certain depth below the surface of the water an increase in resistance will be met by the travelling arm; this is between eight and twelve inches below. As the hand and arm feel this, sometimes called the *catchpoint,* the pupil stiffens the arm by contracting the muscles and exerts as much effort as possible to pull propulsively upon the water. The famous Johnny Weissmueller kept his arm straight, relying upon unusual muscular girth and mind-muscle co-ordination to establish with the pointed hand a fulcrum along and over which he would propel his body forward. The majority of swimmers must be content with bending their arm in towards an imaginary centre line down the length of the body as they pull, making a different leverage in the arm pull.

The bending of the arm is done in this way—the elbow bends and the forearm moves inwards to the centre-line of the body in a downwards, semi-circular motion (the more muscular the forearm the more water it can move against). During the action the hand is slightly cupped with the fingers closed together to increase the purchase on the water.

The movement of the bent arm ends in a slight push, the hand moves outwards slightly (beginners are often taught to brush the thumb deliberately against the external surface of the thigh to make sure of the correct position). Following the natural upwards direction of the swinging arm the hand and then the arm emerge limply and relaxedly from the water and describe a low ellipse over the water until ready to repeat the motion.

SECRET: THE ARM OUT OF THE WATER FOLLOWS AN EGG-SHAPED LINE NOT, A CIRCLE. Beginners who may have considerable difficulty with their arm movements used to be taught to make a circle with a stiff arm. This has two drawbacks: (i) The stiffness of the arm does not give the exercised muscle time to relax. (ii) The weight of a tensed muscle group high above the surface of the water forces the rest of the body deeper into the water; balance is lost, and breathing becomes very difficult.

How high should the recovery arm be above the surface of the water? Aim at about three inches (8 cm) above the surface; if in doubt practise making the movement with the thumb hanging limply downwards, so that the tip of the thumb is barely skimming the surface (if the thumb tip actually does skim the surface there will be a loss of speed because this will initiate *drag* by increasing the resistance to propulsion).

This arm movement takes a long time to perfect; it requires very skilled mind and mucle co-ordination, especially in regard to the alternate contracting and relaxing of the muscle groups in the arm. To make the movement without the right contraction of muscles is a waste of energy and effort.

The movement of the right arm is, of course, identical to that of the left arm described above.

The speed of the arm moving through the air is much greater than that of the arm moving through the water, because air presents less resistance than water does; this may result in a breakdown of rhythm and breathing technique.

SECRET: TO COMPENSATE FOR THE DIFFERENT RATES OF MOVEMENT OF BOTH ARMS MAKE THE RECOVERY ARM PAUSE SLIGHTLY AT *CATCH* (where you 'catch' the resistance of the water).

The recovery arm is, of course, the arm moving above the surface of the water. By waiting at *catch* before pulling it allows the other arm to reach a position of rhythm and balance before beginning its pull downwards as described above. The effect of the waiting by the recovery arm is rather like than of an outrigger on a South Sea island canoe, preventing rolling and making buoyancy more easy. Rolling of the body from side to side during the Front Crawl wastes energy and effort, because it allows an increase of the body area below the surface of the water. This acts as a brake, and also requires an extra output of energy to correct it. Energy used to make corrections of poise could (and should) be employed to produce forward propulsion.

FAULTS TO WATCH OUT FOR IN CRAWL ARM MOVEMENTS

(1) The arms swerve or zigzag during the pulling down.
(2) The pulling down is too slow to bring balanced forward movement.
(3) The arm is pulled out of the water too soon.
(4) The exact position of entry of each hand is found in this way: imagine a straight line going down the middle of the nose, and another line going through the middle of each shoulder muscle. The hand enters out in front between these two lines. If the hand enters outside the shoulder line or too far across towards the other line the body will roll, breathing will become difficult and buoyancy will be lost.
(5) The hand is not slanted downwards from the wrist. This means that the hand may actually increase resistance on entry—so point your wrist and fingers downwards, to make them enter like a spear. A very slight inclination of the back of the hand towards the centre line of the body is often found helpful, this inclines the palms slightly outwards. Weak wrists mean a loss of power.
(6) Use of a straight arm pull by a sprint swimmer or a bent arm pull by a distance swimmer. The best results are obtained when the sprint swimmer uses a bent arm pull, and the long distance swimmer using crawl uses the straight arm (Weissmueller) pull, pushing that arm almost up to the thigh before it emerges from the water.
(7) Too high a swing of the recovery arm over the water: this pushes the swimmer down too deep in the water.
(8) Moving the shoulders while the arms are moving. Make the arms move independently without wriggling

the body itself.
(9) Inability to move the propulsion arm along the centre line—easily corrected by float exercises.
(10) Opening of the fingers during the propulsion—loss of power in the pull.
(11) Whipping the hand through the water. There must be conscious exertion of force on the water, using the water resistance to obtain progress and speed. Try to grip an area of water until the chest has moved over the 'handful'. The hand must be inclined downwards on entry and not enter the water flat.
(12) Do not over-reach. This will not make your stroke any faster, only pull your body out of balance.
(13) Over-cupping the hands; if the hand makes an angle inwards beyond 120 degrees (two thirds of capacity) this reduces the actual surface which can *grip* the water and effect propulsion.
(14) All Crawl arm movements must be smooth and not jerked; this disturbs poise and destroys rhythm which is essential for breathing.
(15) Flat hand emerging from the water. When the hand comes out of the water to begin recovery through the air the little finger should be uppermost so that the hand behind it *slices* the surface, reducing the resistance to the minimum.
(16) Asymmetry of arms. The arms do in effect stay in a line of 180 degrees. As one arm enters the water the other emerges; this is the result of waiting at catch point; not waiting is a fault with slowing down of progress as its consequence.

My father always told me: 'If you hurry in the water you can't swim so fast'; hurried movements are always wrong until the swimmer has perfected the movement, then *the economy of perfected movement gives the illusion of speed*.
(17) Arm not synchronised with the breathing. Common among careless beginners. Corrected by float work.
(18) Arm action without intelligent thinking: A sheer waste of time.

Refer to the text above to correct these faults.

It is important to remember that the legs of human beings differ greatly. The action of a muscular 6 ft. 6 in. man's legs in the water give a totally different result to the flutter of a small man's thin legs. A Malaysian friend who swam in the Asian Games, and two Chinese and a Japanese, all of whom I swam with or against at some time, all had extremely small fluttering leg movements in the Front Crawl. What is the answer?

SECRET: USE YOUR LEGS IN PROPORTION TO THEIR SIZE, BUT NEVER LET THEIR MOVEMENTS RETARD YOUR PROGRESS.

Too much leg movement can brake your forward propulsion and make the efforts of your arms less effective.

Most of the propulsion in the Front Crawl comes from the arms, but the legs do provide some forward propulsion if correctly used.

The body should be stretched out at its full length along the surface of the water, in which position it will be slightly submerged. The stretching should be achieved without undue distortion of the thorax and abdomen. If the legs are to function at their maximum efficiency there must be movement from the hips without any corresponding movement of the body. The legs kick up and down vertically with as insignificant a movement at the knee as the swimmer can manage.

If there is bending at the knee this brings more of the swimmer's leg down into the lower strata of the water where there is a correspondingly more powerful resistance to forward progression.

So how far down should the kick extend into the water? I usually tell my swimmers to make a heel-to-toe movement as a good general rule. This means that no heel extends down into the water beyond the depth of the toe of the other foot when that foot is suspended on the surface; this limits the foot movement to a stratum not more than 20 inches (50 cm.) deep; in individual cases it may not descend more than 12 inches (30 cm.).

The movement should end in a very loose whiplash action by the ankles. Experiments have shown that stiff inflexible ankles act as brakes when they recover from the downward thrust.

Owing to the natural resistance of the water that which is kicked down must come up.

How far up should the leg come above the surface of the water on the return journey? This is governed by the fact that the raising of any tensed muscle group of the swimmer's body above the surface of the water acts as a powerful weight, depressing the whole more deeply into the water. The swimmer should aim to raise scarcely more than the heel itself above the surface. Generally speaking, it is easier to make the most effort on the downbeat of the leg and let the muscles relax during the naturally resistant buoyancy return upwards caused by the reaction of the water. An upward thrust is favoured by some for sprints.

The legs must work close to each other if there is to be the fully-effective piston movement on the water which produces the remarkable propulsion from the backwards-directed swirling created by the whiplash flutter of the feet.

Tell pupils that they must imagine they are in a hurry to wipe their feet in order to get in to tea. 'We're not playing football; we're not in the ballet; we don't want *big* kicks, we want little kicks and lots of them'.

Although there is a lot of serious and interesting academic discussion among experts about the exact depth to which the feet should descend, all are agreed that they should not rise high out of the water.

If the legs splay apart from one another horizontally they provide two minor motions at different angles to the line of progress and so slow down the forward propulsion of the body.

If the legs *thrash* the water the effort of lifting them high is wasteful, unproductive and slows down progress. This action should only be undertaken if attempting to frighten away sharks (mercifully absent from swimming pools!).

There must be rhythm in the leg movement if there is to be efficient propulsion forward; lack of rhythm slows people down.

How many beats to the bar? How many beats of the fluttering legs to one ellipsoidal cycle of the arms? The great

Australian Murray Rose made only two kicks to an arm cycle (this means from an arm starting the downwards pull, completing it the opposite arm doing likewise and then the first arm returning to the starting position) but when Murray Rose kicks he kicks strongly and has extremely flexible ankle movements. Furahashi and one or two other great swimmers used four beats to the cycle.

I usually instruct beginners to aim at six beats, and often go as far as eight kicks, depending on their overall physique and the power of their legs. Some Japanese and other swimmers have gone as far as 10 beats to the cycle.

The reason for the diversion of opinion is that from time to time some champion appears on the swimming scene, winning races as easily as his compeers lose them. Very often the new champion has some extraordinary quirk in style and swims better in spite of it! Competitive swimmers and coaches, ever on the look-out for something new, attribute his ability to this peculiarity and search for reasons to explain it. Sometimes there is a reason, sometimes their logic is open to doubt.

Allow me to turn aside from swimming for a moment. The world-famous tenor Caruso had a slightly abnormal throat; his fantastic ability as a singer was achieved in spite of this—not because of it! The will to win and the ability to work hard achieve more than many changes of style.

FAULTS TO WATCH OUT FOR IN FRONT CRAWL LEG MOVEMENTS

(1) When something it clearly wrong with the leg kick, check on the breathing first; if the shoulder girdle is being swung right round to breathe in (instead of the head being moved independently of the shoulders) this will twist the legs badly. Correct the breathing technique.

(2) The body may not be in a correct, extended, level position on the water: this depresses it down into deeper water where there is heavier resistance; this is particularly noticeable in the movements of the legs, and slows them down.

(3) Excessive knee action, producing the same result as in (2) above.

(4) Excessively-wide leg action so that the feet are splayed out across the water and little or no whipping motion is achieved. Try to bring the feet together 'as if you want the ankles to touch when they pass one another'. This fault is often linked with bad breathing techniques.

(5) The kick is too deep into the water, causing a retarding action rather than adding to the propulsion of the swimmer.

(6) The kick is too shallow to be really effective. This depends entirely upon the individual swimmer, upon his physique and upon the power-drive of the arms of the swimmer. What may be a fault in one may be a virtue in another. This is often a fault with a lazy beginner.

(7) Toes not pointed. This is a debating point for experts, but generally I strongly recommend the Crawl swimmer to point the toes; it finishes off the streamlining of the body.

(8) Feet rising too high out of the water—related to the point in (5)—the higher they rise the deeper they fall, producing rolling and general distortion. Only the heels should break the surface.

(9) Stiff ankles. Although the intention is that the toes should be pointed this is to give a sense of direction rather than imply stiff, contracted muscles. If the ankles are stiff this tends to slow down the return beat of the foot as it rises upwards, in so much as it is forced against the water above it rather than drifts upwards by the force of water's natural resistance. This means that the leg muscles are not getting sufficient relaxation after the deliberate effort of a controlled downwards kick.

(10) If the swimmer is being coached (that is beyond the beginner's stage) and it is found that this individual must use the upbeat theory (popular still in America) the relaxation must occur on the downbeat. I personally prefer the effort to go into the downbeat, but refer

the readers to Forbes Carlile, the great Australian expert, who said of his pupils: 'no two of them kick in quite the same way'. It has been said of Forbes Carlile that he almost *eliminated* kicking from the Front Crawl. The less conscious the advanced swimmer is of his legs the more he will attend to the propulsion from his arms. (See (12) and also the additional notes below).

(11) Leg-consciousness. A good Front Crawl swimmer is arm-conscious, because it is reckoned that 75 per cent of all propulsion comes from the arms. Work the arms harder to get rid of this fault.

(12) Inadequate use of the ankle-instep area as pressure planes bearing downwards upon the water—usually caused by stiff ankles. Clearly the larger the surface presented to the water the more water can be moved.

(13) Head too low in the water. This depends on the physique of the individual. If the head is forced too low the legs will come up higher on the surface; this is only a fault if the legs are already high enough.

(14) Vertical leg kick. This means that the legs actually turn slightly inwards at the ankles to produce a slight parallel placing of the instep on each foot. Its value has been disputed, but it is a small refinement which many swimmers in the top ranks prefer.

Refer to the text above to correct these faults.

ADDITIONAL NOTES ON LEG BEAT: *For advanced swimmers.*

The foot kicks in the opposite direction to the knee and bends in the opposite direction, therefore it exerts it maximum force during a downwards kick, employing the minimum energy to do this. Although the seeming logic of bending the knee and putting strength into the upbeat is attractive, this approach encourages excessive knee bending, and uses more energy on a movement which produces at its maximum 25 per cent of a swimmer's propulsive power.

Yet another approach to the leg kick is the introduction of a deliberate and controlled pause into the leg action— in effect this is a glide, counting 'one, two, three, pause, four, five, six'. I do not recommend this because it makes a swimmer leg-conscious. The sooner a Crawl swimmer concentrates on the arms the better.

BREATHING IN FRONT CRAWL

Successful breathing, and indeed the entire success of the stroke, depends upon the ability to turn the head sideways without turning the shoulders with it.

The SECRET: BREATHE IN WITH YOUR CHIN TURNED ROUND TO YOUR SHOULDER. Which shoulder is of little importance except that, having found out which is the best side for the individual to inhale on, this side should be kept to by that swimmer, thus ensuring the build up of a successful rhythm. Exaggerated turning induces rolling of the body.

In the position of poise the hairline is usually on the water level. In this position the moving swimmer is breathing out hard, one arm is moving through its fulcrum under the water, the other arm is midway in the recovery position. The recovery arms moves forward to the point of entry and to *catch* point, the arm that has been working in the water is approaching emergence. Assuming that the swimmer breathes in on the left shoulder, the head turns to the left shoulder while the left arm is emerging at the rear of the head and the swimmer inhales. As the left arm recovers the head turns forwards, resumes the hairline on the waterlevel position and the swimmer exhales by the methods described.

SECRET OF CO-ORDINATION: IMAGINE YOU HAVE A PIECE OF COTTON THREAD TIED TO YOUR THUMB AT ONE END AND TO YOUR TOOTH AT THE OTHER. Every time the left arm moves back the head turns back, chin on shoulder; when the arm moves forward the head must move forward and the eyes look ahead, slightly downwards. Breathing is the key to good rhythm in the Front Crawl. No swimmer can practise breathing exercises too often.

DO NOT BREATH ON BOTH SIDES; this makes you giddy. I sometimes describe this as 'watching tennis', with the head clip-clopping from one side to the other, like a ball over a tennis net.

There is nothing that slows a swimmer down so much (in the Front Crawl) as badly-integrated breathing, in the Front Crawl apart from which unco-ordinated breathing means the beginner in particular has no time to concentrate on any other fact of Crawl swimming.

The first thing to aim at is the inhaling of breath at the identical moment in each arm cycle, the more exact this becomes the better the speed attain. Try 1 breath to 2, 4 or 6 arm movements.

VARIATIONS OF BREATHING TECHNIQUE IN FRONT CRAWL

(a) Continuous breathing.
   This is the method which the author tends to favour because it is logical, extremely easy to learn, and *it requires the minimum of thought* by the swimmer who has a very large number of things to think about; it is easily turned into a habit, an automatic reflex. Breath is inhaled by the mouth while the face is turned sideways, as described above, and then is continuously breathed out while the mouth and nose are under water, being blown out through both nose and mouth, slowly and continuously.

(b) Plosive breathing.
   This involves inhaling a breath and holding it tight until the very last fraction of a second before you are due to breathe in again. Some coaches insist upon it because they maintain that it (i) increases the buoyancy of the body (for a fraction of second?) and thus increases speed; (ii) prevents water being taken into the mouth (something no racing swimmer should ever have to worry about) and thereby prevents panic; (iii) Makes the thorax (lungs etc.) a firmer base from which head and arms may move during propulsions; this is the most legitimate and logical reason for the use of the plosive technique, and it is usually used only in short distance races (sprints 30 metres, 50 metres, 100 metres). But there is an increasing tendency to allow far more individuality in *racing* swimmers these days, and rolling is now no longer so frowned upon *if the swimmer can*

cut down seconds or even fifths of seconds by using it.
(c) Bilateral breathing.
During racing a swimmer who uses this method can watch out of the corner of his eye other swimmers in lanes on either side of him or her. Whether this is an advantage I am inclined to doubt. From the psychological point of view I think it is often more disturbing to see opponents streak ahead (disheartening) or lag behind (when like the tortoise and the hare legend the racer may ignore the furious last minute spurt of a swimmer more desperate than himself). It involves a more complicated counting by the swimmer because he uses this technique usually twice in three arm cycles, occasionally in four. I think the use of the technique should be learnt only from a coach who will advise it in special conditions only. It is occasionally employed as a temporary measure to correct faulty head movements.
(d) Retention of breath.
Matt Mann, a famous authority on swimming, once said that if swimming 100 yards in a 25 yard long pool the first length from the start should be swum entirely on the first breath after emerging from the start, during the second length only two breaths need be taken, three during the third and four during the fourth. For a really fit and trained swimmer this is absolutely true; the author has often done this himself—even in his midforties. In short distance swims the less the need to breathe the less the retardation of the propelled body through the water on account of the head movements. It builds up a slight lack of oxygen, but one which can be quickly made up if the swimmer stops at the end of the 100 yards. If swimming the same distance over a $33\frac{1}{3}$ yard pool the swimmer must try with two breaths, five breaths, and seven for the third length.
This is not to be used outside racing training. Do not use retention beyond 100 yards distance.

FAULTS TO WATCH OUT FOR IN FRONT CRAWL BREATHING
(1) Badly timed breathing rhythm: Poor co-ordination can be corrected by using the practice exercises.

GUIDE TO SWIMMING AND WATER SPORTS 23

(2) Trying to breathe through a throat constricted by tense muscles; this is caused by lack of practice and fear; relax the throat.
(3) Jerky, spasmodic breathing. Lack of mind and muscle co-ordination.
(4) Wrong breathing technique for a specific event (racing): this must be observed by the coach or instructor and corrected as early as possible.
(5) Inhaling too much air for comfort. A mistake of the beginner. Read up the general notes for breathing.
(6) Trying to keep water out of the mouth instead of avoiding its entry into the lungs by checking it with the muscles at the rear of the throat.
(7) Breathing on both sides (this is not bilateral breathing but the spasmodic, panicky breathing of the undisciplined or poorly instructed beginner. See details in this chapter, above.
(8) Technique faults. Read again the instructions about the various techniques described in this chapter.

To correct these faults read text above.

EVERY RACING SWIMMER USING FRONT CRAWL SHOULD MASTER AT LEAST TWO TECHNIQUES OF BREATHING

POISE IN FRONT CRAWL

To appreciate the full impact of poise in this popular stroke the reader should refer to the chapter on Balance.

The body is extended along the water, slightly submerged, the head rises out of the water and the hairline rests on the surface of the water. The theory is to keep the entire body from shoulders to hips as still as possible, while moving the head, arms and legs from this base. In practice this is nigh impossible, and, in the light of modern research, from Australia in particular, of dubious value. Nevertheless the beginner will *never* reach an advanced stage of swimming the Crawl unless vigorous efforts are made to keep as near poise as possible. Only mastery of the elementary theory will enable the budding champion to modify it to his or her own personal requirements, under the advice of a coach or instructor.

To a significant degree good poise in the Front Crawl is maintained by speed of execution of correct movements of arms and particularly of the legs, and anybody who practises diligently with a float the arm, leg and breathing techniques under guidance will not find the acquisition of good poise difficult.

FAULTS TO WATCH OUT FOR IN FRONT CRAWL POISE

(1) Overreaching with the arms; it never makes you faster.
(2) Bad breathing of any sort.
(3) Irregular arm movements.
(4) Irregular leg movements.
(5) Nervousness, feeling of lack of security, inevitable in beginners.

To correct these faults refer to the text of this chapter.

EXERCISES TO TEACH YOU FRONT CRAWL

(1) The beginner sits down on the side of the bath, places the right hand across the body by the side of the left hand, twists the body round, slips down gently over the edge into the water, and holds on to the rail.
(2) Hold the rail with both hands. Put the head down into the water and blow out bubbles under the water, raising the head to breathe in, then repeating the exercise. Blow out harder under the water.
(3) Repeat this exercise, carefully controlling the breathing out, counting up to ten while blowing out, then to twenty, thirty, etc.
(4) Holding on to the bath rail just above the surface of the water by gripping it with the hands, bringing the elbows against the bath wall. In this position let the legs float up to the surface and begin to move them up and down. *Try to get a regular rhythm.* Only the heels should break the surface of the water, and the foot should not go down beyond 12 to 20 inches depth. The legs should remain close together, the toes slightly pointed. Make 20 kicks with each leg then rest; make three series of 20. At subsequent lessons increase the number to 40, 60, 80 and 100 or extend the actual time spent in leg kicking, starting with two minutes,

going up to ten minutes: don't forget to allow intervals between longer sessions.

(5) Either hold the hands of a teacher or partner. Or hold on to a pole held by the teacher at the side. HOLD ON FIRMLY WITH BOTH HANDS. Kick your way across the bath and back, several times in each session, allowing a short pause for the swimmer to make the mental adjustment and regain breath. BEGINNERS GET OUT OF BREATH QUICKLY BECAUSE OF PSYCHOLOGICAL STRAIN RELATED TO EFFORT OF WILL AND PHYSICAL EXERCISE. This exercise can be repeated so that one partner holds on with his hands to the back of the pupil in front and kicks with his legs while the pupil walks forwards pulling with his hands. In a busy class this ensures that both partners are fully occupied.

(6) The same exercise is repeated as in five, but only one hand holds the partner or the support; the free hand of the learner is moving down into the water making the same movement as the old steam engine trains' pistons used to do—downwards then backwards returning on a higher swing round to press down again. AT THIS STAGE KEEP THE ARM *UNDER* THE SURFACE OF THE WATER. Repeat, using the other arm. Exercise this movement until the arm action is loose, easy and without any strain. All the time the legs keep kicking a regular, shallow and rhythmic beat—at this stage the learner has three out of four limbs actually swimming!

(7) All the exercises from 4 to 6 above should be repeated with the head *turning* on the left or right shoulder (whichever is most comfortable for the learner but NOT BOTH) and breathing in with a wide open mouth while chin is on shoulder, and then breathing out calmly and quickly *under* water. Aim to keep the eyes (in advanced stages the hairline, not the eyes) on the surface of the water. DO NOT PROCEED FURTHER UNTIL THIS HAS BEEN ACHIEVED, because further exercises require a modicum of breath control.

(8) The pupil stands two paces away from the rail, feet slightly apart. On the word 'Go' he launches himself at the rail and kicks the feet quickly, pressing one arm down in the water, and reaching for the rail with the other.

(9) This is a repeat of exercise 8, but the pupil stands four paces back, and this time presses down with both arms moving alternately. A partner or a teacher with a pole—ready for the pupil to grab—should be near. This stage is mastered easily. From here onwards progress can be remarkably quick. One pace back all the time, and suddenly the pupil finds that half the width of the bath has been swum! The pupil with *character* will never rest until he has covered the whole width of the bath. The author has had a large number of pupils who have swum the whole width of the bath in their first or second lesson of 20 minutes each lesson!

DO NOT PROCEED FURTHER UNTIL THIS STAGE HAS BEEN REACHED.

All the previous exercises described have enabled the learner to swim *Doggie Paddle*, so called because the arm movements are exactly like those of a dog pawing the water. Some purists insist that this was the origin of the front crawl. Even for adults the same procedure is highly recommended because it prepares the learner psychologically for the more advanced full Front Crawl movements.

Unlike some writers, I prefer that an effort be made to use the full Crawl breathing even in doggie paddle, because this cannot be learned to soon.

(10) The arm movements described on page 11 can be practised on land. If the learner is a child the instructor can check whether the pupil is concentrating hard enough by getting the learner to repeat the arm motion *with closed eyes*. This land exercise involves raising the arms in one of the recovery methods described, usually with the elbow emerging first.

(11) The land drill above is repeated with the deliberate

control of breathing, to co-ordinate it exactly with the arms, so that the learner breathes in, *chin on shoulder,* only when the arm on the breathing side is at the rear of the body (in the emerging position). We must remember that the shoulder muscle consists of anterior and posterior deltoids; it is sufficient for the chin to reach the anterior deltoid, and superfluous for it to twist round to reach the posterior deltoid.

(12) The exercises in 10 and 11 are repeated in the water.

(13) The exercises in 10 and 11 are repeated with the arm alternating in holding a polystyrene float (an inflated rugby football bladder will substitute). During these exercises the legs must kick in the usual rhythmic flutter.

(14) Holding a float with one hand, kick the legs, and breath constantly on one side to master control of breathing. If it is difficult, do this with both hands on the float before using only one hand and moving one arm to effect propulsion. This is not always easy because the nervous learner is upset by the splashing caused by a slow-moving arm recovering above the water surface.

(15) The same exercise as in 14 above, but concentrating on streamlining the body in the water.

(16) As above, concentrating on eyes (the hairline in advanced stages) on the surface of the water and ensuring that the head is always facing front when breathing out. This is a co-ordination exercise.

(17) Both hands on the float, concentrating on the exact depth of the leg kick and its rhythm.

MASTER THE ABOVE TECHNIQUES BEFORE TRYING OUT NEW REFINEMENTS.

(18) Leg kick as in 17 with precise breathing control.

(19) As in exercise 14, concentrating on the exact point of entry of the hand between the two lines described previously.

(20) As in 19, aiming at precision in the angle of the elbow and wrist slant; practise alternate widths, then lengths, changing arms at each end.

(21) As above, controlling the exact depth to which the arm of the individual must descend to obtain maximum purchase on the water for the best effect with least effort.

When there are several learners together it is better to pair them off and get one to help control and guide the movements of the other.

There are innumerable other refinements which can be brought into the exercises, such as flexing the ankles, turning the instep slightly inwards, and the instructor or learner at this stage should consult the sections dealing with faults to watch.

For the more confident learner there are a number of exercises which can be performed with the float clasped between the knees, keeping the legs afloat and enabling the pupil to concentrate solely on the arms. This is psychologically very frightening to a nervous pupil who has not mastered the breathing technique.

GENERAL GUIDANCE FOR LEARNERS

(a) Master the technique of breathing as early as possible. And I mean MASTER IT, not just practise it.

(b) Work hard at your leg movements during the early stages so that you never have to work on it so much again.

(c) Make the arm movements most precisely, take care to co-ordinate breathing and arm movements—arm movements learnt without proper co-ordination get in your way and don't help you.

(d) Ensure that you control every movement you make. Never make movements haphazardly; learn to force certain groups of muscles to relax and contract quickly.

(e) Speed develops when the movement is perfect. Using brute force to 'bash' your way along will tire you out and ruin your style.

(f) Aim at increasing the distance swum without stopping. One width, two widths, five, ten; lengths, lengths, until you reach 440 yds., half a mile, one whole mile.

(g) It is essential to see a good Front Crawl swimmer performing.

FRONT CRAWL RACING TECHNIQUES, STARTS, AND TURNS

There are some limitations to the speed attainable by any group of swimmers within a certain age group and trained by similar methods; the fact that these limitations change now and then is immaterial. Consequently it is inevitable that many races are lost and won by small details such as starts and turns. The author has seen many races decided in this way.

STARTS

A swimmer whose start is poor will be at an inevitable psychological disadvantage when he sees a number of other swimmers slightly ahead.

A good swimmer should instinctively make every start the same as he would at a race because it is good training for the real event. Of less concern for the watcher, a bad, splashy start is often uncomfortable if not slightly painful.

In racing, the general procedure is that the swimmer stands slightly behind his allotted place which may be a raised starting block or just the edge of the bath. While he is under starter's orders the swimmer should spend his time in deep breathing, which calms the nerves and prepares his body for its best efforts by minimising the oxygen debt which occurs temporarily towards the end of any racing event. Usually one or two paces from the 'marks' suffice. When the command 'On your marks' (or 'Take your marks') is given the swimmer steps quietly and quickly on to the block or to the edge of the bath and (HERE IS THE SECRET) gets into a *well-balanced* position, gripping the edge of the block or bath with curled toes. Generally speaking there are only two suitable stances for a good racing start, although individual champions make minor modifications to whichever is their own favourite.

(i) The swimmer bends his knees, bends slightly at the waist, and the ankles can bend slightly, provided that the swimmer does not look down at the water but holds the head sufficiently upright to look where he is going. If the head is held down looking at the water then do not bend the ankles, for this would threaten good balance. The feet are slightly apart, but either below the shoulders or within their compass. To have them too far apart lessens the capacity for a good spring. Getting the feet comfortably and profitably placed is the most important and significant element in any racing start. Make quite certain that the weight of the body is equally balanced—never try to stand on tip-toe, you will overbalance and might thus disqualify yourself. Having correctly placed the feet, the swimmer then brings back his arms behind the body. There is much discussion among coaches as to whether the arms should be higher than the inclined body or the same height as the body; whether the arms should extend like wings slightly to the side of the shoulders or sweep back directly in a straight line from the shoulders. There is further debate about the value of the palms facing each other or the backs of the hands facing each other. I personally prefer palms facing each other across the back of the swimmer, with the arms raised slightly above the level of the inclined body. This leaves the position of the body like a letter 'S' with arms extending behind it and very slightly above. The signal to go is given perhaps by a gunshot, a whistle, a shout or a loud clapperboard. The arms swing *forwards and upwards* and in one continuous rhythmic movement the swimmers' legs come out of their coiled-up spring position; the take-off is effected by a movement which from ankles to upward-thrusting arms is a flowing ballistic effort.

ANOTHER SECRET: The resistance of the air is less than that of the water; the more distance you cover in your entry flight the quicker your racing time will be. In view of the foregoing it is clear that the swimmer must aim to travel as far as possible out over the water and to be in no hurry to dive down into the water, a mistake common to all beginners. Keep the body as streamlined and straight as possible; avoid some of the strange concave and convex body shapes which beginners make. At the highest point of the flight the swimmer inclines hands and head very slightly to permit of a clean entry into the water, endeavouring not to submerge more than two feet (60 centimetres) in depth, keeping the body sufficiently rigid and arrowlike to establish a powerful gliding propulsion, while he prepares to swim. This initial glide for a fraction of a second is still at a greater speed than his own propulsive motions will induce, and the racing novice is urged not to rush straight away into his stroking movements when he hits the water.

Do not let the force of the water deflect the hands by bending the arms at the elbows because this considerably retards progress. The first stroke is allowable under water, which is a good technique not forcing the body too rapidly to the surface; care must be taken to see that the first stroke is made in such a way that by the time the arm which makes that first stroke is recovering the body is sufficiently high on the water to avoid a struggling movement to raise the arm out of the water. This is done by turning the hand during the first stroke to give a directional uplift at the final stage of the propulsive pull. Clearly it is wholly undesirable to breathe during the first stroke, which by even the slightest movement could add to retardation. Efforts must be made with beginners to prevent them raising their head like questing ducks when they surface from the starting dive because this slows down their progress.

(ii) The second common method of starting, while in essence following all the general rules of the above, varies in stance. The body bends at the waist only, the knees are flexed but not bent. The arms descend loosely from the shoulders (or are held forward). The head is held in an elevated way to look across the water. This second method has a slight disadvantage for some swimmers who do not get the violent upthrust of a full arc swing from the arms but only get the arms moving about 90 degrees instead of the 180 degrees specified in the first method. But there is also an advantage: the arms are more ready for the point of entry. In the long run it depends upon the physique and temperament of the individual which methods produces most success. Details about flight and the movement of the legs are much the same for the first method, but it is debatable whether the legs give such a strong spring—the answer depends upon the length of the legs. A lot of tall swimmers seem to prefer the second method.

FAULTS TO WATCH OUT FOR IN FRONT CRAWL STARTS
(1) Slovenliness in getting on your marks.
(2) Bad balance when on the mark.
(3) Failing to grip the edge of the bath with the toes.
(4) Feet insufficiently apart or too far apart.
(5) Badly balanced arm position.
(6) Lack of co-ordination or arm swing and drive from the ankles.
(7) Dropping the head too soon.
(8) Arching the body during flight, concavely or convexly.
(9) Too deep an entry into the water.
(10) Forgetting the initial glide after entry.
(11) Arms apart at moment of entry, increasing resistance of water.
(12) Relaxing arms or legs during flight.
(13) Bad surfacing so that the arm meets too much resistance from the water when recovering from first underwater stroke.
(14) Breathing during the first stroke.
(15) Confusion of styles in starting.

Refer to the above text to correct these faults.

TURNS

There are four distinct turns which can be used by the Front Crawl swimmer.

(A) *Front Somersault*

This is the fastest turn, and one which is favoured by most racing swimmers, particularly in the shorter distances. This is the most difficult turn, and one which requires most practice. If it is not performed absolutely perfectly it is not only useless but a cause of slowing down. It must be learnt with both hands, and so well practised that it can be applied *instinctively* whichever hand touches the side first. Properly applied, this turn increases the momentum of propulsion. While practising, it is performed slowly, and speeded up only when the movements are perfected.

The following description is of the turn performed completely.

(i) The swimmer strokes on in front crawl with one arm leading towards the wall of the bath where the turn is to be made.

(ii) Just a fraction of a second before the leading hand contacts the wall the head and shoulders fold down towards the knees, the hips thrust upwards to the water surface, the knees tuck into the chin. Contact is made with the back of the hand about a foot (30 cm.) below the surface of the water. (In learning this turn slowly it is necessary to place the back of the hand against the wall, follow it by the forearm, and the back of the head which gives a good feel of the turn.)

(iii) As the turn proceeds the two feet, kept closely together, make contact with the wall of the bath. At this moment the feet give a very powerful thrusting kick against this wall while the body comes out of its tucked-up position, and by twisting the shoulders in a slight turn the body resumes a face downward gliding position on the surface of the water, swimming back in the direction whence it came.

Generally speaking the chief fault is raising the head just before the turn. Another is not balling up the body into a tuck soon enough. It is a turn which has to be learnt slowly and correctly or else not at all. Avoid until the beginner can turn a controlled somersault in the water using the simple momentum of a head-down swing with a tucked-up body in the middle of the bath, this should be practised before work begins near the wall.

(B) *Back Somersault*

The approach is with an outstretched leading arm; this turns at the wrist, palm touching the wall, fingers pointing downwards to the bottom of the bath; following the direction of the turning palm the body twists, the knees fold up under the chin, the head snaps back directly towards the vertebrae of the back. Performed at speed the sheer momentum of the swimmer's progress carries the body round into the back somersault. The face goes down looking at the wall where the turn is being made; the body in its balled-up position remains close against the wall, the tucked up feet touch the wall and are used again as a coiled-up spring which on contact unlocks to give a powerful thrusting kick; at the same time the arms shoot out forward with a slight twist of the shoulders bringing the body into a face-down frontal glide as the swimmer resumes swimming in the direction whence he came. This turn is preferred by many racing swimmers, and is equally useful for less speedy turns.

(C) *Grip Turn*

Advisable for long or medium distance swims. *The author advises against the use of this turn for racing.*

The lead arm and hand contact the wall of the bath, the hand grips the side of the bath, scum-rail, etc. As soon after the moment of touch as possible, and if possible, simultaneously, one or both feet are brought up just below the hand which touches. The hand which is not affecting the touch sweeps in under the body to increase streamlining of the movement and avoid slowing down the turn. The balled-up position from which a spring can be made has been completed, the contacting hand lets go of the rail and is flung directly over the head in a rigid straight line at the same time that the underwater arm snakes out from under the body to join it as closely as possible, pointing in the same direction. The coiled-up spring of the legs is released and the swimmer returns down the bath.

(D) *Spin Turn*

This can be used very effectively by racing swimmers who are not comfortable making the somersault-turns.

The swimmer approaches the wall with the fingers

of the leading hand directed slightly inwards and upwards so that the external edge of the hand makes contact). The legs ball up quickly into a tucked position. The free arm makes a sweeping movement into the body and then snakes out towards the desired direction. As the feet make contact with the wall (while the head and free arm move under water) the body straightens out into a streamlined position, the contacting hand completes a semicircular, gliding motion and comes out to join the straightened arm as the swimmer returns down the bath.

A QUESTION OF ARMS AND BREATHING—*For the more advanced swimmer.*

How many arm strokes can you do on one breath? And over how long a distance?

These two questions will help you to increase your speed. Think about them carefully, and begin to experiment over a short distance, say half a length of the bath to start with. You should obviously be quite comfortable breathing every other stroke—so that you always breathe in on even arm counts, 1, 3, 5, etc. before you start. Then try: 'Breathe in, puff, puff, puff—below water'. So there are three distinct puffs, accompanied by an arm movement for each puff.

I find it comfortable to do 440 on one breath to six arm movements, and I can do 880 at this rhythm, but there is no point in achieving this unless you have very strong lungs and are unlikely to build up a serious oxygen debt.

Both one-in-four and one-in-six make for a very smooth and elegant style of Front Crawl.

Do not try any of this technique until you have mastered a very efficient breath control.

I RECOMMEND NASAL EXHALATION ONLY FOR ONE-IN-SIX RHYTHM. Purely nasal exhalation may also be found helpful for a one-in-four stroke.

Vis-a-vis the relationship of leg-thrash to arm movement it is fairly common to expect a theoretical movement (often barely perceptible) of two kicks to one arm movement; that is to say four to any one given arm cycle.

THE BACK CRAWL

This is a charming, relaxing, stroke which has the advantage of giving free vision, easy breathing and comparatively good speed. It is a popular racing stroke.

It is a relatively modern stroke, first appearing in the second decade of this century. It depends greatly upon precise timing, cultivated relaxation and should give the onlooker an impression of effortles, continuous rhythm.

DESCRIPTION OF ARM MOVEMENTS

(1) The body is lying supine in the water; the head is slightly raised but not beyond 45 degrees, the eyes looking at the ceiling rather than at the toes. The left arm makes a speedy arc from the side of the left thigh over across the head to a point which on a clockface would represent roughly 12 o'clock. In fact, few beginners can place their hands so accurately, and ten to two and five to one are more usual positions—depending upon the flexibility of the shoulder muscles. Many coaches have learned arguments as to which of the positions is the best.

To start with an approximation will serve. When the left hand is at the rear position just described so the right hand and arm lie alongside the right thigh.

(2) As the hand enters the water following the flinging arm the thumb points limply to the ceiling and the little finger makes first contact with the water. Never contact with the back of the hand. Once in the water the hand takes and keeps a cupped position ('you can't use a fork as a paddle').

(3) Catchpoint is usually obtained not more than 15 inches below the water, depending greatly upon the swimmer's individual physique. Beginners may need to be advised to keep their thumbs up like a submarine periscope just breaking the surface, to prevent them from dropping their arms too low. There is a very slight pause. The arm now pulls round powerfully until it reaches a place alongside the left thigh. During the pull of the left arm the right arm is being thrown backward. In theory the

arms remain 180 degrees apart (i.e. a straight line).
(4) Unless both arms are in continual motion the body will sink or roll so much that breathing becomes difficult. The arm movement should be learnt in land drill, and then practised with the feet tucked under the rail usually present in a bath while the body floats in a moored position.
(5) It is essential that each arm reaches a balanced, symmetrical position behind the head, and that neither arm descends to a deeper position in the water than the other. A moment's thought will show how unbalanced movements can distort the stroke.

FAULTS TO WATCH OUT FOR IN BACK CRAWL ARM MOVEMENTS

(1) Over-reaching with the arms. No swimmer will ever be faster just because he is reaching out that little bit farther; he will only roll more, lose poise and breathe less efficiently.
(2) One arm pointing to one place on the 'clock' behind the head, the other arm pointing elsewhere. If the arms are not symmetrical there will be loss of energy, —loss of propulsive progression, and some rolling, and difficulty with breathing will follow.
(3) Failure to relax arm muscles during the throwing action; if the arm is kept stiff throughout the stroke the muscles tire more quickly—this is found often in nervous beginners who need the relaxation so much!
(4) Dropping the back of the hand into the water instead of the side of the hand. This slows down the swimmer by increasing resistance.
(5) Too great a depth during the pull, causing imbalance.
(6) Unequal depth of one arm; in other words the arms move in different strata of the water. Causes rolling etc.
(7) An arm pull with opened fingers, losing energy, very uneconomic.
(8) Slow arm movements. *Don't lift, throw!*

DESCRIPTION OF THE LEG MOVEMENTS IN BACK CRAWL

(1) The leg thrash is very similar to that of the Front Crawl with one major stipulation—the knees should never move above the surface of the water. Too much kicking slows you down!

(2) Only the toes come above the surface during the upkick of the leg thrust. The origin of the power is exactly the same as described for the Front Crawl (see page 15).

(3) The movement comes from the hips, the ankles must be kept very flexible, and the toes pointed positively upwards. The knees must finish the upwards kick straight otherwise the entire surface of the front of the leg is not being fully utilised to shift the water by pressure.

(4) In more advanced legwork the leg turns very slightly inward to the centre line; big toe leaning towards the opposite big toe.

(5) The legs do not usually kick deeper than 15 inches, but this depends upon the length and power of the individual swimmer.

(6) Several arguments have taken place about the number of kicks which should be given to one completed arm cycle. The lowest number suggested is four, the highest ten (reducing the leg movement to a mere flutter), and the six and the eight beat kickers cover the general run of Back Crawl swimmers.

(7) For a swimmer with well-muscled shoulders, back, pectorals etc., it is possible to achieve 75 per cent propulsion from the arms alone, but for girls and the less powerful the utmost propulsive capacity of the legs must be extracted to compensate for the corresponding lack of arm power.

(8) The legs must keep close together while kicking, close enough for the ankles almost to touch each time they pass. The kick is downwards. Recovery is upwards.

GUIDE TO SWIMMING AND WATER SPORTS 39

FAULTS TO WATCH OUT FOR IN BACK CRAWL LEG MOVEMENTS

(1) Too much knee-bending while the legs descend during the thrash, this takes the leg into deeper strata of water where resistance is heavier.
(2) Too much knee-bending while the thrash moves upwards; this is exhausting and produces little or no propulsion.
(3) Leg kicking with the legs wide apart, a waste of time and energy.
(4) Kicking that does not originate in hip movement.
(5) Kicking that is neither deep nor high enough to produce propulsion. This may not be a fault in a broad-shouldered, powerfully-armed swimmer.
(6) Uncontrolled, wooden, movements without smoothness or continuity.
(7) Failure to relax the legs when they come up from the powered downwards kick.
(8) Using a bicycle kick instead of an up and down thrash.

DESCRIPTION OF BREATHING FOR BACK CRAWL

As the mouth and nose are wholly clear of the surface of the water during this stroke there is little or no difficulty to be expected for the breathing, but I recommend that the swimmer makes a habit of breathing in always during the movement of the left arm and breathing out always during the movement of the right arm.

In swimming, breathing must be learnt for every stroke as a conscious habit. Only in this way can the swimmer safeguard against sudden mouthfuls of water and accidents.

If the poise is wrong then the head position will be such that breathing cannot be effected properly.

FAULTS TO WATCH OUT FOR IN BACK CRAWL BREATHING

(1) The swimmer is sitting up in the water—not lying back; as a result the head is deeper in the water than it should be.

(2) If the arm movement produces over-reaching there will be a distortion of the breathing rhythm.
(3) Stiff throat muscles—due to nervousness. RELAX!
(4) Unbalanced arm movements vertically or horizontally produce instability, disturb poise and ruin breathing rhythm.
(5) Inattention to breathing rhythm.
(6) Holding the breath, due to nervousness.
(7) Slow arm movements (lifting the arms instead of throwing them) produce splashing which can go on to the face and disturb breathing.
(8) Splashing caused by faulty hand entry behind the head.
(9) Bobbing up and down on the surface of the water, caused by irregular arm movements below the surface.
(10) Sinking of the head below the surface, caused by the arms being placed in the water at shoulder level instead of behind the head.
(11) Sinking caused by the rhythm of the stroke being too slow so that there is an unsupported gliding motion between one movement and the next. This is the cause of the childrens' heartrending cry: 'I can't do it'. Land drill helps in this case.

DESCRIPTION OF POISE IN BACK CRAWL

The body lies in a relaxed position, as free from effort and strain as possible. The head should lie happily on the water as if lying down on a pillow in bed. The body slopes slightly downwards to make it possible for the legs to have operating room for their thrash; i.e. there must be sufficient water above them to allow them to displace it.

There is a considerable difference between the poise of the beginner and the experienced swimmer using the stroke for racing. The beginner may feel an intense need to have his head up more than does the advanced swimmer.

FAULTS TO WATCH OUT FOR IN BACK CRAWL POISE
(1) Too flat on the surface; this interferes with the breathing. It also lessens the effect of the leg move-

ment for beginners more than for the advanced swimmer.
(2) Knees breaking surface; this upsets the poise and makes the stroke less effective.
(3) Moving the head during the execution of the stroke.
(4) Slow arm moving, destroying poise and buoyancy.
(5) Incorrect placing of arms behind the head causes loss of direction of balance. Zigzag swimming is tiring.
(6) Head too high, increases resistance to propulsion. Avoid a 'sitting' position.
(7) Too tense. Stiffened muscles sink more easily.
(8) Uneven kicking destroys balance.

EXERCISES TO TEACH YOU BACK CRAWL

(1) The learner will almost certainly have learnt how to enter the water and how to swim one other stroke. If not refer to 'The First Visit to the Baths', page 1.
(2) Land-drill as indicated on page 7.
(3) Tuck toes into the bath rail; if there isn't one get an instructor or friend to tuck both your legs under their arms and support you while you make the back crawl arm movements described above.
(4) When these are fast enough the swimmer can proceed to let go from the supported position and add a gentle leg movement to the efforts being made by the arms.
(5) Concentrate on repeating exercise 4 with correct breathing.
(6) Place a float behind the head; hold firmly with both hands, pushing back slightly with the head. Practise the leg kick to attain the more precise movements set out in this chapter under 'Legs'. Repeat with a float held on the chest.
(7) Practise full stroke until the width of the bath has been swum.

BACK CRAWL START AND TURN

The start is made in the water. When the words 'On your Marks' are given the racers seize the rail with both hands at a *comfortable* distance apart, then raise their knees up towards the chest, placing their feet against the wall. The toes and feet should not come above the water line this would lessen the spring of the start. When the command goes the body uses the resistance of the wall and springs backwards, throwing *both* arms to the rear making a slight arc with the back, the head dropping into correct place, and as the flight ends the body glides into the water, the legs begin kicking, and the left arm pulls first. Do not pull until the body has surfaced if it has gone below the surface on completion of the arc. (Some racers descend nearly 18 inches after the start.)

BACK CRAWL TURNS

(1) *Back somersault turn.* This is the fastest turn. The approach is with an outstretched leading arm which turns at the wrist, palm touching the wall, fingers pointing downwards to the bottom of the bath, sliding down the wall immediately after contact. At about 24 inches down the knees fold up towards the chin, the head presses backwards and downwards, the free arm moves out sideways. As the tuck position closes up the slightly-apart feet slap against the wall while the body twists a little on to the side and continues turning until the swimmer is face up but below the surface. The arms swing out backwards, the coiled-up legs release themselves from the spring position and the swimmer glides out on his back into the direction whence he came, rising to the surface and pulling with one arm.

It is very graceful and very fast. It needs long weeks of practice to get perfect.

(2) *Swivel turn.* Slower but much easier for beginners. The lead hand establishes contact with the wall. Simultaneously with the touch the knees bend in towards the chest. The head rises and the body sinks slightly, swivelling round the touching hand, the free arm sculling slightly to aid the turn. The feet slightly apart, slap against the wall, and having touched uncoil the spring position. The body glides backwards at the same time as the head twists back and the feet uncoil. It is possible to perform this with the head

above water or below water; generally speaking it is more likely to be a faster turn if performed under water.

(3) In races it is customary to string a line of flags over the water to advise back crawl swimmers that they are approaching a turn.

RACING NOTES

(1) Generally speaking, the fingers should be kept loosely closed.
(2) Many racing swimmers prefer to use a bent arm recovery. The pros and cons of this are widely debated. The bent arm pull is most useful to swimmers with weak arm muscles—especially if they have long limbs. It allows strong leverage but doesn't guarantee speed to all.
(3 The arms are theoretically at 180 degrees and movement must be continuous.
(4) Work with a stop watch in the hand of a reliable timekeeper.
(5) Concentrate on strong, efficient, arms movements.
(6) Beginners in racing should have themselves tested over many distances. Practise for your best event.
(7) Work hard at starts and turns; these may win you the race.
(8) Read up the racing notes for the Front Crawl; many of them apply here.

THE BREAST STROKE

This seems to be the stroke described in Isaiah xxv, verse 11. In any case, its antiquity stretches back into the mists of time.

Other strokes have developed which are faster, which look more elegant, but the Breast Stroke has always survived because it is the ideal form of swimming for health, the ideal form of swimming for a long swim. A friend of the author used it to save his life, swimming over 20 miles after being torpedoed off Malta.

The Breast Stroke enables a swimmer to swim long distances with very little physical strain, with clear breathing and vision straight ahead. It is the easiest stroke to swim in a choppy sea because one can just dive straight through the wave without losing rhythm or breath. It is a quiet stroke for tropical waters and will not disturb sharks etc. (If they do come up thrash the legs loud and make a LOT of noise to keep them at bay).

In the hands of an expert it can still be a fast and streamlined stroke. In contrast to the Front Crawl, this stroke derives most propulsion from the legs and least from the arms.

Its performance is rigidly controlled by rules, and it is easier to merit a disqualification during a race in this stroke than in most others.

DESCRIPTION OF THE ARM MOVEMENTS

Arms move with graceful symmetry at the same time. Having made the forward movement there is a slight glide in a streamlined position, during which the body darts forward like a canoe. The shoulders stay in a balanced straight position throughout the stroke, deviating neither to left nor right.

Starting from a glide, in which hands and toes are both pointed for and aft respectively, the body more or less rests slightly below the water line. At precisely the same moment both arms move outwards slightly and downwards to a position not more than 15 inches below the water, where the hands may still be seen without turning the head; the hands are slightly cupped and the arms form approximately the sides of a right angle, although often not quite so wide in a fast stroke. Having swept through to the end of this arc, the arms bend at the elbow, bringing the upper arms against the ribs and slightly abeam, shooting forwards to the original gliding position at surface level.

The wider the angle which the downspread hands and arms attain, the lower the head will sink in the water; if the swimmer prefers a stable and steady head position keep the arms at a narrower angle than 90 degrees when at maximum depth in the water, *during which stage the swimmer breathes in*. A wide-angled arc of the arms leads to a 'duck' style of swimming, the head tending to bounce up and down like that of a questing duck searching for food.

There are several variations of this movement, well within competition rules, which will be described later on.

FAULTS TO WATCH OUT FOR IN BREAST STROKE ARM MOVEMENTS

(1) Bringing the arms too far back behind the line of the shoulders in their downwards and outwards arc; this, instead of aiding propulsion and balance, brings retardation and lower the head too far down into the water.
(2) Failing to bring the arms deep enough or down enough into the water. This makes a wholly ineffectual movement (common among children beginning the stroke) and produces little or no propulsion at all, only a tendency to sink!
(3) A slow recovery movement so that the surface of the forearms meets and creates resistance.
(4) Badly asymmetrical bending of elbows during the recovery movement, produces wobbling and instability, makes breathing difficult and destroys balance and buoyancy.

DESCRIPTION OF THE LEG MOVEMENTS

The stroke may have originated from observation of frogs; the kick is virtually identical with the movement of a frog's legs. From the straight position of the legs during the glide the legs bend at the knees and move forwards and slightly outward avoiding extremes, the object being to keep the heels together during this manoeuvre. From that bent position the legs kick out backward and outward and downward, executing a swirling motion which is followed by a powerful sweeping together of the legs, squeezing a wedge of water out backwards (similar to jet propulsion).

Racing swimmers have developed many refinements of these movements, these are discussed later.

FAULTS TO WATCH OUT FOR IN BREAST STROKE LEG MOVEMENTS

(1) The legs do not come together with a smack but float like limp seaweed. (Loss of leg power, propulsion and poise are the result).

(2) Leg action lacks horizontal balance, the legs move at different levels.
(3) One leg coming higher in the water than the other.
(4) Badly-turned knees, making the correct drawing up of the legs impossible.
(5) Lazy leg action, failing to complete the actual close of the inwards sweep after the kick.
(6) Knees being drawn inwards more than outwards before the kick. For the racing stroke this may be desirable; generally it is not. A swimmer who cannot fully control the limbs will not make a good racer.
(7) Jerky leg action instead of a smooth continuity.
(8) Wrong leg action altogether. Occasionally a beginner brings the legs up only to return them in the same way to where they started, so that there is no kick or buoyancy.
(9) The feet which are brought upwards in the preparation for the kick come too near the buttocks; this produces a strange, undulating movement by disturbing the distribution of the weight over the surface.

Note: Apart from land drill most errors in the leg movements can be corrected by earnest use of a float and *legs only* exercises; with the head and arms supported by the buoyancy of the float the learner can concentrate wholly on the point he is studying.

DESCRIPTION OF BREAST STROKE BREATHING

If a swimmer cannot breathe comfortably in a stroke he has little chance of concentrating on any other point at all.

(1) In a wide-arm propelled Breast Stroke the head will necessarily move up and down in the water, in which case the swimmer breathes out when the head is below water, and breathes in when it is above water. If the angle is too wide the swimmer will find it a longer time before the head emerges from the water.
(2) In a narrower arm movement exhalation takes place with the mouth on or just below the surface.
(3) In all cases breathing out finishes when the arms have established the straight-out-in-front position.

Breathing in is completed by the end of the downward sweep which pulls the swimmer forward.

FAULTS TO WATCH OUT FOR IN BREAST STROKE BREATHING

(1) Bad synchronisation of arm movements with breathing.
(2) Head too deep when inhalation is required.
(3) Breathing in while the arms are stretched out front, or breathing out when the arms are pulling.
(4) Neck too stiff and the body tense (usually due to nervousness) constricting the muscles of the throat and making breathing very difficult.
(5) Incorrect breathing out. Nobody can breathe in if the mouth is already full of air.

DESCRIPTION OF POISE AND GLIDE IN BREAST STROKE

(1) The shoulders should be maintained squarely against the direction of propulsion.
(2) The body must be kept straight in the glide position when arms and legs are straight out fore and aft. Arching the back is to be avoided.
(3) The head should be above the water throughout the movements. The body is just below the water surface. If the head is too low in the water the feet can flap around the surface and prove a less effectual means of propulsion.
(4) As the arms shoot forward after the recovery there is a short motionless glide in the general stroke, but in the faster racing version this becomes purely theoretical.
(5) Good poise and an efficient glide depend on the correct distribution of the swimmer's weight over the water.

EXERCISES TO TEACH BREAST STROKE

(1) The beginner sits on the side of the bath, places the right hand across the body by the side of the left hand, twists the body round, slips down gently over the edge into the water and holds on to the rail.

(2) Hold the rail with both hands. Put the head down and blow out bubbles under the water; raising the head to breathe in. Repeat the exercise several times.

(3) Grip the rail with the backs of the hands against the wall. Allow the legs to float up behind you. Keep them straight out aft, and then draw them up bending at the knees, moving forwards and slightly outwards, keeping the heels together. From this position the legs kick out backwards, outwards and downwards, then sweep together in a strongly-made smack. Repeat.

(4) This exercise can be done next with a teacher or another swimmer walking backwards, holding the learner's hands.

(5) The same exercise with the hands holding on to a float.

(6) The learner stands facing the side, about three or four feet away. Feet balanced and slightly apart. The arms are stretched out forward and then move outward slightly, down to a position not more than 15 inches below the water; they bend at the elbow, draw into the ribs and shoot forward again.

(7) The same exercise performed bent down with the trunk leaning forward. Eyes looking straight along the arms; shoulders under the water level. Concentrate upon synchronised breathing.

(8) The same as above. Performed three to four feet from the side. A teacher or competent swimmer is near the learner, otherwise a teacher on the side should have a pole to reach the beginner. The learner moves the arms and practises the leg kick. The distance covered by the learner is increased until the width of the bath is achieved.

THE BREAST STROKE START

The swimmer stands slightly behind his allotted place, which may be a raised starting block or just the edge of the bath. While he is under starter's orders the swimmer should spend the time breathing deeply. This calms the nerves and prepares the body for its best efforts. When the command

'Take your marks' is given the swimmer steps quietly and quickly on to the block or to the edge of the bath and gets into a *well-balanced* position, gripping the edge of the block or the bathside with curled toes.

The swimmer bends his knees, bends slightly at the waist, and bends the ankles slightly. Generally speaking it is better if the swimmer can hold the head up somewhat rather than look down at the water—if he tends to look at the water cut out the bend at the ankles. The feet are parted a little but not more than the width of the shoulders. The weight of the body must be perfectly balanced. The arms are usually placed behind the body, their ideal height is debated hotly, but slightly higher than the inclined body is usual. They should be almost like wings extending back from the shoulders. Generally the palms face inwards towards one another. The signal to go is a gunshot, whistle blast, shout or a loud noise from a clapperboard.

The arms then swing *forward and upward* and in a rhythmic and continuous movement the legs are released from the coiled-up spring position. Take off is effected by a movement which from ankles to upward-thrusting arms is a flowing ballistic effort.

The competitor must aim to travel as far as possible through the air because the resistance of air is less than that of water. During the flight the body should be as straight and streamlined as possible. At the peak of the flight the swimmer inclines head and hands slightly to permit a clean entry into the water. Try not to submerge deeper than two feet (60 centimetres). Practice is required to avoid surfacing too soon, which would bring the body up at a steep angle, creating resistance to forward progression. On submerging the swimmer brings the outstretched arms round powerfully to the bent position before the glide forward (and inclined upward) which is effected on the top of the water, surfacing at the same time as the head; the first kick is usually made *below* the water before surfacing, and it is the force of this which gives the swimmer momentum to surface.

THE BREAST STROKE TURN
Contact with the wall must be made with both hands to-

gether. As contact is established the swimmer whips his head round in the direction to which he is turning, bends his arms so that the elbows sink in towards the rib cage, and lets his legs sink motionless. Then his legs twist round in time with the spin of the head while the spine arches concavely, so that for the briefest moment the body is practically hanging downward in the water; next a swift bending at the knees whips the feet up to a fairly high position on the wall, the upper body glides forward slightly submerged, and one full arm movement and leg kick are permitted below water before surfacing to resume the stroke.

This modern variation of the turn originated in America and is extremely fast, but it requires a great deal of practice, dividing each individual action of the complex movement into parts and practising each part until perfect. It may take a good swimmer from a week to 10 days to do it faultlessly —longer if the racer is not up to high standard.

The same type of turn may be made without verticalisation and concave spinal movement, but it is much slower.

Do the slow turn in a race unless you are sure that you have the fast turn perfect! A slow turn made well is faster than a fast turn which is bungled!

Usually the racer breathes in immediately the hands contact the wall before doing the other movements.

BUTTERFLY-DOLPHIN

The Butterfly stroke was introduced shortly after 1930, and I remember reading a hair-raising report by a medical *authority* demanding that it should be banned as it would overstrain the heart and eventually bring the swimmer to a speedy and untimely end! In those days serious-minded coaches were recommending their adventurous pupils to keep it for 100 metres or at the most 200 metres. In my 45th year I swam one mile Dolphin non-stop before witnesses and felt all the better for it.

I give the original Butterfly details first, because they make the understanding of the more highly developed and complex Dolphin stroke easier to follow. *Properly swum neither form of stroke should prove tiring.*

The competition rules governing Breast Stroke swimming

demand symmetrical movements of arms and legs, but used to leave the precise manner in which the respective limbs moved less clear than today. It was not too long before some enterprising swimmers developed a fast recovery movement above the water (decreasing resistance) instead of below water (heavier resistance). It was at one time called *'Racing Breast Stroke'* but the name was quickly changed to the more picturesque one which it now bears. After the 1952 Olympics the Butterfly/Dolphin was officially declared to be a distinct stroke and could not be swum under the rules for Breast Stroke swimming.

THIS IS NOT A STROKE FOR BEGINNERS

The leg movements for Butterfly are exactly the same as those for Breast Stroke. During the glide which occurs in the Breast Stroke proper the Butterfly swimmer tended to make what was at first an involuntary wriggle with the legs as they were together, but although this is important vis-a-vis the later development of the stroke this is not really necessary because a racing swimmer using the Butterfly stroke would normally cut out the glide altogether.

A powerful Breast Stroke kick is made as the legs swing together, the arms and shoulders emerge from the water in an upsurge above and across the water, and the hands enter the water in a slightly cupped position, the thumbs slightly more down than the fingers; they are roughly shoulder-width apart. The hands drop to the catch point and then press downwards and slightly to the side not more than 18 inches. The arms may then be swung up to the surface in one of two methods: (a) The original straight arm swing, requiring considerable strength; (b) By bending the elbows, a more modern adaptation and an easier movement.

During the bending of the elbows the legs bend to execute another kick, and the motion is repeated. The beginner will find it easier to put in a glide immediately after entry while the hands are at catchpoint.

The breathing for the Butterfly should be made as follows: Inhale as the head rises slightly above the surface during the flying arm movement and exhale while the head is below the surface. The beginner needs one breath per stroke, although more practised swimmers will often take one breath for two or more.

The Dolphin is a very attractive stroke when it is well performed. We noticed that in the original form of the Butterfly the legs tended to make a wriggle during the period that the arms effected a glide—the object was to maintain the fullest buoyancy possible. This wriggle developed into a positive downbeat of both legs moving together, and then into a double downbeat which was so highly successful that the actual Breast Stroke leg movement was found to be not merely unnecessary but a hindrance to the swimmer in that it increased retardation.

The basic movement of the Dolphin is a progressive wriggle along the surface of the water; the older theory of undulatory movement is wholly abandoned in the light of modern research. Undulation does not add to the forward progression, but tends to increase the drag caused by presentation of opposed planes to the water.

THE USES OF DOLPHIN

(a) Racing stroke.
(b) Ornamental, but very satisfying for the swimmer.

ARM ACTION IN DOLPHIN

The major part of the propulsion should come from the arm action, and it is in effect the Front Crawl performed with both arms at once. Breathing was once performed to the side because of this but I recommend against this technique; it is liable to disturb poise, and is not easier.

The object of the arms moving through the water is to avoid lifting them too high because this depresses the body down into the water. Consequently the arms should be swung low in an ellipsoid (not a circle) across the surface, the downward-pointing thumbs only a few inches above the water, speed is the essence of this movement—the slower the movement the deeper the body will sink. Flexibility of shoulders is essential. The arms are limp and relaxed during the fling which is the recovery motion. The modern tendency is to bend the arms slightly at the elbow just prior to entry—this is fairly consistent with the relaxed recovery, and then the arms spear the water, fingers, wrists and arms pointing very slightly downwards, slightly cupped hands, and wrists at a very slightly inclined angle so that the thumbs touch a fraction before the fingers do; the point of entry tends now to be hands in front of the shoulders. In the fast version there is no delay at catchpoint and the arms pull down with the elbows bent, and the sweeping motion is like that of two powerful paddles or fins which sweep backwards behind the body, the hands only move towards each other as they sweep back below the body and prepare for recovery during the next ellipsoid swing. Some coaches recommend a keyhole movement. The arms on entry describe a small circle before pulling back under the shoulders to begin the recovery.

FAULTS TO WATCH OUT FOR IN DOLPHIN ARM MOVEMENTS

(1) Too great a downward inclination of the thumbs on entry, bringing a waste of energy and loss of power. If the hands are entered back to back (regardless of width apart) they cannot effect a desirable pull to produce propulsion.

(2) Too little inclination of the thumbs on entry, producing a flat-handed entry which increases water resistance. In theory the twist of the wrist is barely 30 degrees, and is adjusted by the swimmer after sufficient experience.

(3) Long pauses while the legs are being kicked, producing sinking movements, rather like a submarine preparing to surface. Slows the swimmer down and increases drag.

(4) Asymmetrical movements by the hands or arms, produce rolling; a fault found only with beginners. Corrected by a little land drill on the arm movements, followed by the same movements made while standing in the water.

(5) Stiff shoulder movements, cramping the arm movements. Physical exercises and land drill are needed.

(6) Bringing the arms too deep down into the water. Produces a drag by heavily increasing resistance at deeper strata of the water.

(7) Entry of arms in front of the face instead of in front

of the shoulders (or even wider apart).
(8) Too short an arm pull before the recovery.
(9) Too slow a recovery, causing sinking of the body, increased drag.

Refer to the text above to correct these faults.

LEG ACTION IN DOLPHIN

Much has been written about the leg action of the Dolphin, but since the undulatory movement went out of fashion most details written before 1966 can be ignored.

The steady movement of the hips is increasingly important, and the less the hips bend the better. The legs provide barely 25 per cent of the propulsion; they are used basically to maintain poise and buoyancy.

The legs should not be kept too closely together; they are slightly open at the knees to encourage a slightly-inward pointing of the toes. This allows the legs to have an effect upon the water with a minimum of drag following.

As far as possible the movement comes from the hips and spine and not from the knees, which would encourage a raising of the leg above the surface of the water.

The double upward and downward thrash should be thought of as the trailing of the legs in sequence following the submerging and emerging of the head and shoulder girdle. If the arm action is correct it is surprising how many swimmers are able to make a natural adjustment to the leg movement. There is more emphasis on the downward thrust of the slightly parted legs than of the upward surge. The swimmer aims for two leg beats to one completed cycle of the arms. Already experiments are taking place on the number of beats, depth of beats etc. to find out which produces the best results. The initial leg down beat is timed approximately as the hands enter the water to commence the cycle; the second downbeat takes place at the finish of the arm sweep under the water before the arms emerge to start recovery.

FAULTS TO WATCH OUT FOR IN DOLPHIN LEG MOVEMENTS

(1) Asymmetrical leg movements either vertically or hori-

zontally, so that one leg does not match the position of the other. Induces rolling and slows down the stroke. Common among beginners.
(2) Legs too deep in the water, encountering a heavier resistance in the lower strata. Beginners tend to hold the head up too much which depresses the legs.
(3) Kicking at the wrong point of the stroke, which destroys breathing rhythm, balance and poise, as well as retarding propulsion.
(4) Knees bending excessively and bringing the lower legs above the surface, disturbing breathing, balance and progress.
(5) Legs separated too wide, increasing retardation.

BREATHING IN DOLPHIN

This was originally one of the major problems of Butterfly and Dolphin swimming, but research has enabled us to eliminate the difficulty. As the best Dolphin swimmers are usually recruited from the ranks of good Front Crawl swimmers it was natural that one of the methods of breathing favoured was a sideways motion as in the Front Crawl. I find this a retarding move and recommend frontal breathing (as in the Breast Stroke) which is effected when the head rises above the water for inhalation, and the subsequent exhalation is made below the surface.

Research offers different opinion as to *exactly* when the Dolphin swimmer inhales. Some of the top American coaches are encouraging their star pupils to breathe in at the very last second of their arm recovery in an effort to prevent the wastage of physical effort by heaving the shoulder girdle higher above the surface than is absolutely necessary. I conducted several experiments with another English instructor, Dave Luxon, as to the number of Dolphin strokes which could be made on one breath. We found we could perform eight arm cycles on one breath over one 100 ft. bath length, but that few pupils could exceed four and maintain a regular pace. Our findings recommend three *or* two complete arm cycles to one breath.

There are some advocates of explosive breathing for this stroke; however, I believe that most swimmers will find a continuous breathing in and out will be easier and less of a strain. (See fault 3 below.) Nasal exhalation is very often advisable.

FAULTS TO WATCH OUT FOR IN DOLPHIN BREATHING

(1) If side breathing is used there is often a distortion of the balance of the shoulder girdle, which can disqualify a racing swimmer as well as slow him down.
(2) Lack of rhythm in breathing, a beginner's error.
(3) Holding the breath under water. This is a great mental and physical strain in a stroke where there is a continuous movement without any glide.
(4) One breath to one arm cycle, which tends to produce a slowing down effect and a rather jerky, bobbing movement.
(5) Splashing of the face by exaggerated arm movements during recovery.
(6) Neck too stiff and tense, restricting breathing.

POISE IN DOLPHIN

The accepted poise is now much flatter and more horizontal than hitherto. Undulation means that effort is spent in going up and down instead of moving forward. The legs kicks are shallow, and the arm movements are also kept in the higher strata of the water. By using an ellipsoid arm movement instead of a simple circle, poise, buoyancy and breathing rhythm can be easily maintained.

Faults in the poise of Dolphin are best understood by close examination of the arm, leg and breathing movements described in this chapter.

EXERCISES TO LEARN DOLPHIN

(1) The beginner must be able to swim at least 220 metres Front Crawl in good style, and preferably 440 metres without any stop. If this is the case a few simple land-drill movements will suffice to teach the ellipsoid arm movement, which is nothing more than both arms making the Front Crawl arm movement simultaneously instead of alternately.

(2) The same arm movements can be practised in the water, standing.

(3) The leg thrash can be practised while holding on to the side.

(4) The swimmer can then take a float and cross some widths using the leg thrash and breathing once to two leg beats.

(5) The first width without any assistance ... and then continue to build up.

In some ways the Dolphin may be compared to chess; one can learn the movements in one lesson, and spend a very great deal of time afterwards perfecting the game.

Dave Luxon and I have both found it possible to get good Front Crawl swimmers to learn the basic movements in one lesson, swimming at least six widths by the end of that initial lesson.

DOLPHIN START AND TURN

The start is basically the same as that for a Front Crawl or Breast Stroke.

The turn should be effected with both hands touching the side simultaneously, as for the Breast Stroke turn. A double somersault turn is also possible, developed from the Front Crawl front somersault turn, using both hands to establish the initial touch and leading down with both hands presenting their backs to the wall, then a quick head turn, knees curled up into a tuck position against the chest and the feet making contact with the wall. The body makes a slight twist as the feet release the coiled-up spring beginning the return lap, and the twist brings the body into a face-down position. The first arm movement after the turn may need to be slightly deeper than that of the normal rhythm to compensate for adjustment of breathing, until the swimmer is used to the manoeuvre.

Note:

Dave Luxon and I have done a lot of synchronised Dolphin swimming together. The movements must be precisely timed to coincide exactly. It is very impressive at galas etc.

ADVANTAGES OF LESSER-KNOWN STROKES

Owing to their popularity in racing the four main strokes described in detail in this book are too often the sum of knowledge in swimming. But there are many other useful and pleasing strokes.

People who have had difficulty in learning the four main strokes should hesitate no longer and study these other strokes. I once taught an adult who had never succeeded in swimming a stroke in his life how to swim the width of the bath in one single lesson by using the following stroke.

LIFE-SAVER BACK STROKE

(A) Probably no stroke uses so little energy and involves so little movement. It is an ideal stroke for a lazy man or an exhausted swimmer swimming many miles to save his life. Lie on your back in the pool. The legs draw out slightly, bending 45 degrees at the knees, and hanging down *below the surface of the water;* no part of the leg should come above the surface. From this position they sweep together into a straight line coming up to the surface but not above it.

Then the leg movement is repeated slowly and deliberately; recovery is made with limp legs and ankles. What do the arms do? Nothing at all! you can fold them across the chest or simply hold firmly on to your hips; as this is a slow and relaxed stroke there is comparatively no inconvenience from retardation, as happens in the faster movements.

All you have to do is learn the leg kick and keep the body straight from the neck to the hips—if you bend in the middle you will go straight down. The water will come in and out of the ears but the nose and mouth remain fairly high above the water, provided that the swimmer puts his head back bravely into the water. Another swimmer or teacher can help the beginner by walking alongside and holding a friendly hand under the novice's waist giving a feeling of balance and support.

This stroke will help a swimmer save his own life, but a variation is needed when the swimmer is trying to save

another person by towing him through the water.
(B) Firstly, there is no gentle, relaxing glide after the legs come together, but a gentle and unending swirling motion in which both legs make small but regular circular movements in the water. This comes as a natural and instinctive variation to anybody who has mastered the simple version of the stroke, and can be learnt by dint of carrying just a simple float on the chest *with one hand only*. The other hand makes a simple sweeping motion covering about 45 degrees angle and returning to a position flat up against the body with the palm flat against the thigh, thumb uppermost. The palm twists from the wrist, moves out over 45 degrees facing downwards on to the water, and turns as the angle is reached, twists back again to face the thigh and sweeps in. The movement is easy to learn.
(C) A further variation of this stroke is possible, using both hands to effect the sweeping motion. This variation could also be used if a man had to save himself by swimming a very long distance.

OLD ENGLISH BACK STROKE

This is a little-used stroke, but it is one that should be taught more often because it is relaxing, fairly fast, beautiful to see when swum correctly and could be used to make life-saving easier. I often use this stroke at the end of a practice or when I want a change from one of the four main strokes.

The legs make a regular Breast Stroke movement under the water (not emerging above the surface) while the swimmer lies on his back.

The arms are *thrown* simultaneously to the rear of the swimmer, brushing his ears as they pass his head; they are straight and having reached the 12 o'clock position they stay there to complete a glide, during which the swimmer's legs are also straight, pointed toes completing the streamline effect. As the maximum effect of the glide is obtained the arms, palms facing out from the body, complete a wide sweep of 180 degrees, with the hands just below the surface, about eight inches down (20 cm.), at the same time as the legs make their slow kick described above. In this position the swimmer then glides again. This is the only stroke which gives the swimmer two glides for the price of one effort; it is economical of energy.

HAWAIIAN BACKSTROKE

This is almost identical to the stroke described above, but for two variations—

The legs perform a continual Back Crawl thrashing during the stroke and there is only one glide, when the arms are stretched out behind the head. Here again there is no reason why a double glide should not be introduced.

I cannot vouchsafe for the stroke ever having come from Hawaii, but it is the name I know for it.

OVERARM STROKE

Most swimmers who try this swim with their left side lying down in the water, cheek against the surface—just as if they were getting ready to sleep in bed. It depends whether you are right-handed or left-handed. This description is for right-handed people. One ear and one eye lie in the water, the nose and the mouth are approximately on the surface. The right arm skims gracefully across the surface, not rising high up, as this forces the body too deep below the waterline. The hand is slightly bent at the wrist, and from the elbow pointing downward the arm makes a movement like a spear as it enters the water about 16 inches (40 cm.) in front of the nose (say from elbow to fingertips), angle of entry is about 45 degrees (never with a flat hand). The moving arm sweeps downwards keeping the elbow slightly bent. While the upper arm action is pulling back to the swimmer's rear the other arm, which remains submerged, bends back to the chest (between deltoid and upper pectoral muscles), then shoots forward straight and stiff. While the upper arm is recovering and returning forward the lower arm relaxes and drifts back to the first position.

Breathing-in is effected during the sweep of the upper arm while the body is turning fully on the side so that the mouth and nose are exposed to the air. Breathing-out is done during the recovery of the upper arm while the head is more submerged. The leg action is very much like that used in climbing stairs. The knees move in towards the waistline while the arms are recovering, and then shoot back together (remember to keep the right leg over the left leg) making a powerful sweep with pointed toes. Owing to the difference of water resistance at different levels the right leg's movements will not stay parallel to those of the left.

There are some variations with swimmers using the crawl leg kick, and even an out-of-balance Breast Stroke kick.

SIDESTROKE

This stroke is still used for racing in some countries on the European mainland, so there is a marked antipathy to allowing variations in leg kick. Only the kick already described in the section on Overarm, and known as the 'scissors' kick, is permitted. It is one of the strokes which has a long history behind it, and holds a fascination for many enthusiastic swimmers, particularly those of middle age who no longer wish to swim only the popular four main strokes. It is a very attractive stroke and one which attracts a lot of attention when swum well.

The swimmer is lying on his left side; the left arm is pointed beyond the head, while the right arm rests in a relaxed condition beside the right thigh. The swimmer's face is turned upward and sideways from the water so that he can look back along the streamlined, gliding body. The right arm is then moved through the water from its relaxed position, the hand slightly twisted at the wrist to face outward, away from the swimmer. *It does not come out of the water.* As it reaches a position equal to the opposite shoulder, with the hand just slightly in front of the face, palm outwards, it moves down, maintaining a flexed elbow in order to keep the motion through the water near to the body and not dissipate the energy employed, returning to the relaxed position beside the thigh. At the same time the left arm glides upward and forward, there is a short pause and glide, and then the left arm shoots forward under the water then recoils to the left shoulder, not completing a sweep as does the right arm because such a movement would be deeper and slow the swimmer down. Breathe in while the left arm is working and the right relaxing. Breathe out while the glide is operating.

TRUDGEN

Although this stroke bears the name of the energetic and enthusiastic Englishman who brought it to fame, it is believed he copied the idea from some primitive tribe and refined it, codifying the movements etc.

It differs from the Front Crawl in that the head remains on the surface all the time during the stroke. While I would not recommend the Overarm or Sidestroke for a man who has a long distance to swim to save his life, there are occasions when the Trudgen might be useful. I was swimming once in the Black Sea, when I noticed that the current had taken me further out from the shore than I anticipated. The waves were quite high from crest to trough, and I found it most advisable to swim Trudgen to keep my direction. The swimmer lies completely flat on the water as if for the Breast Stroke, and moves the arms as for the Front Crawl, but without any movement of the body or shoulder girdle. The legs can perform the scissors kick which will twist the lower body slightly, or perform the Front Crawl kick if the scissors kick is not known.

Performed with its correct single swirling scissors kick for each completed arm cycle it is a relaxing stroke.

In practice the theoretical flat position gives way to a roll from one side to the other, and the breathing in and out can be decided upon either according to Front Crawl technique or Breast Stroke technique, whichever is most comfortable for one individual swimmer.

Although this a stroke which has been sadly neglected since the introduction of the Front Crawl, we must always remember that *the object of swimming is not primarily racing but saving life;* many instructors would find a quicker response from their pupils if they taught Trudgen first and Front Crawl second.

OLD ENGLISH BREAST STROKE

This is basically the same as the Breast Stroke described fully in this book, but the oldest manuals of swimming in England describe the stroke as bringing the arms concurrently right round 180 degrees sweeping through the water to the thighs.

This is *a more relaxing form of Breast Stroke*, suitable for the older swimmer who has not done any swimming in his youth. It entails a longer period of submerging the head under the water, and demands good breath control. The recovery is also slower, but the stroke can give much pleasure to those who are not in a hurry but want to keep fit.

*   *   *

Some other strokes exist but they are not suitable for practical swimming, e.g. The Corkscrew Crawl, met with in some gala events as a curiosity.

RACING TIPS AND TRAINING SCHEDULES

Racing can bring out the best in a man—or the worst. If you find racing brings out the worst in you give it up or keep away from it until you can make it bring out the best in you. There is no race so disgusting as the 'rat race'.

Basically there is one thing which the racing swimmer must keep in mind. *Speed is an illusion*. What is needed is perfection of movements, with no waste of energy or direction. Attempts to use brute strength to gain speed defeat themselves.

Be completely positive about your approach to racing. If you want to race be prepared to pay the price for it. If your coach says you must not smoke, should give up drink, and so on, then take his advice. Maybe you know some other swimmer whom you know is allowed all the things your coach tells you not to do. That does not mean you can succeed without taking your coach's advice; it may mean that you haven't a chance unless you do. I can speak from personal experience. Pupils come to me; they love swimming; they want to race. But they are nowhere near the standard of fitness they ought to be; sometimes they are older than the usual age groups from which the majority of successful swimmers come. What should I do? Should I deny them the chance of some success? No, I don't do it. I look around to see all of the *wrinkles* I can make use of to screw the utmost power and speed from them; check their starts, turns, polish up their style and crack down upon everything that can hinder their strokes. By this method I have got remarkable success for swimmers who often have not been of the first rank. In big competitions the novice is often up against highly-specialised swimmers who work two to three hours a day for their sport, and rule their diet in accordance with the demands of the sport.

The watch, with its little second hand is the ultimate judge of a swimmer's success.

The biggest 'room' in the world is the room for improvement. My mother (God bless her) always used to say:

*'Good, better, best, never let it rest
until your good is better, and your better—best.'*

The racing swimmer must be prepared to work very hard with a kicking-board or float (or inflated rugger ball bladder). The champions work very hard indeed to perfect the smallest details.

The choice of which distance the racing swimmer should tackle is the deciding factor in whether he wins or loses. The choice should be made with a good club coach, and the swimmer who is not satisfied with his success in racing should not hesitate to seek a second opinion. The second hand of the time-keeper's watch is the best guide, and the racing swimmer should compare his times with those of the champions of the year and work accordingly.

Compare your times for different strokes, ascertain in which stroke and over which distance you give your best performances.

Racing is a dedication. It demands a great deal of *guts*, discipline and ability to take criticism.

The longer the distance raced the more need to use expert starts and faultless turns, especially when such minor details may provide a psychological boost for the morale, insomuch as that, especially towards the final laps of a race, the sudden emergence of one swimmer with more apparent energy and strength can hardly be said to encourage the others.

Every effort must be made to avoid monotony in training. This depends greatly upon the coach. Most swimming clubs are full of jovial, laughing and good-natured companions.

It is not enough to race. Make sure you know the exact description of the stroke, and make certain that whatever modifications you apply are still covered by the rules drawn up by the governing body of the race.

Many swimmers make their fame with minor successes in short sprints for a local club, and work their way from one success to another.

Never be downhearted if somebody beats you! The champion learns more from defeat than from success. Analyse, with the help of your friends, your own stroke, tactics and those of the winner. If you keep losing, take up one of the other aspects of swimming—Life-saving, sub-aqua work, etc., etc.

Sprints. The racer should be in top gear from the moment of emerging from the starting dive because the distance of up to and including 110 yds. (100 metres) is just not enough for the use of tactics such as slow start, warm-up and final burst. The sprinter should always maintain a constant speed, putting every ounce of energy and effort into the whole swim, using his intelligence to remember that within just a minute and a quarter at the outside the 110 yds. will be ended!

Longer races require a certain amount of tactical planning which no book could plan in advance. These are the details that must be planned with a coach according to conditions, and capacities of the other known competitors in the race.

A valuable *secret* is to overtrain—practise over 220 yds. if you are going to swim 110 yds. This makes your goal seem much easier to achieve, although you know how it is done.

Take care not to get stale when training for a big race. Do allow sufficient time for non-swimming activities.

Do not eat or drink anything except lemon juice and glucose or lemon and pure honey for at least one hour before the race.

Women will have to make racing arrangements to suit the needs of the menstrual period. Both sexes are usually advised to leave 24 hours free from copulation before a big race, but this depends upon the coaching advice, as individual capacities and needs differ too widely for a hard and fast rule.

If you cannot lose as gracefully as you win *don't race*. Bad tempers spoil everybody's fun and still don't make you win.

The bigger the event you anticipate taking part in the longer you must train in advance. For the top events this may mean from 18 to 24 months' training! Such schedules always contain 'laying off' periods, so the aspirant need not recoil in horror.

For major events try to train in a 50-metre pool, but do not be lured into heroics if it is an outdoor pool and there is a heated smaller pool which can be used during the winter.

A schedule kept too rigorously may destroy the enthusiasm of the young racing swimmer. Never let the system become monotonous. An old exercise book will be useful for the trainer to note down full details of performances of each individual trainee after specific training schedules etc.

I was one of the first swimmers in Europe (1955) to adopt the Australian technique of shaving every hair off before a race. Scientists have proved beyond doubt that a perfectly smooth skin presents *measurably* less resistance to movement through the water. Men and boys who really want to make the big time in racing should be prepared to accept shaving off every body hair as a small price for fame and victory. Get used to this during the week before the race and get shaved 24 hours before the major event.

In the last week before a major event add at least one hour's sleep to the normal average sleeping time; do everything possible to avoid waste of energy. The biggest help to you now will be a sound nervous system free from stress and worry. In the last three days before the race deliberately refrain from swimming 'full blast', keep something back. The reaction will be like an unlocked spring uncoiling explosively at the race.

The coach, instructor or trainer must never let a promising swimmer swim himself into a state of nervous or physical exhaustion. A good coach knows and understands his trainees so well that he can diagnose their moods, capacity and their breaking strain. The coach must never under-rate the terrible strain of mental activity upon the nervous system.

No swimmer should be encouraged to make any experiments in new style techniques in the final month before a major event. St. Francis de Sales one remarked: *'Sometimes a man may quit that which is good in search of something better, lose the one and fail to find the other.'* I need not say more.

SPECIAL ADVICE FOR FRONT CRAWL RACING

A popular development in Front Crawl technique is to allow the fingers to open during the arm pull. While not objectionable for long distance races it is not advisable for sprints. Would you paddle a canoe with a fork? Do you eat soup with a fork? Only if the racer has weak arms is this advisable.

Girls prefer a bent arm propulsion if their shoulder muscles lack power. Arm and shoulder muscles can easily be developed by exercises.

Racers should never forget that leg kicking affects balance and streamlining, and cuts down speed.

Racing in Front Crawl can be speeded up by reducing the depth of the leg thrash, and keeping the legs close together. When this has been achieved the racer should be encouraged to 'forget' his legs, and put as much power and energy as possible into the arm movements.

P. G. Wodehouse's *Jeeves* once told his master that what was sartorially permitted to the Prince of Wales was not permitted to ordinary mortals. This may excuse the fact that some of the fastest Front Crawl swimmers have actually been seen to *roll* while making the stroke. Basically, the breathing is the key to rolling while moving at high speed. The more the racer can breathe through a twisted mouth in the trough of a bow wave created by the forward-surging head the less rolling is needed. The mass and power of the shoulders and arms play an undeniable role here. Weissmueller had enormously powerful arms, shoulders etc, and he was able to gain fantastic effects by virtue of his muscles and agility.

Do *not* lift your arms into the recovery—*throw them*! Psychologically and physiologically throwing is easier and faster.

Try to see films of great champions swimming. Front Crawl. Try the style most similar to your own physique, size and age.

On the shorter sprints get yourself timed over your distance on experiments in breathing. If, as an advanced swimmer, you can swim your 50 or 100 yards on less breathing and by remaining submerged without surfacing for breath, try it. If it saves you one second it is worth it—provided you can do it regularly.

All experimentation must be judged by the stop-watch.

SPECIAL ADVICE FOR BREAST STROKE RACING

Head-position and breathing account for many victories in this stroke. If you can breathe regularly without in any way disturbing the poise, buoyancy and speed of propulsion you *must* increase your speed and get a better time.

The Dutch swimmers introduced a new theory of Breast Stroke by keeping the pulling arms in a much narrower confine than previously was the case, using the arms in a slightly more downward pull, avoiding movement which went beyond the shoulders (roughly speaking) in an outward direction.

Some Breast Stroke racers find they can make a faster recovery with the backs of the hands coming up to the surface (the backs are convex while the flat palms are concave and have more drag). This means a lightning speed twist of the wrists at the last moment of the downward pull as you go into the recovery 'glide'.

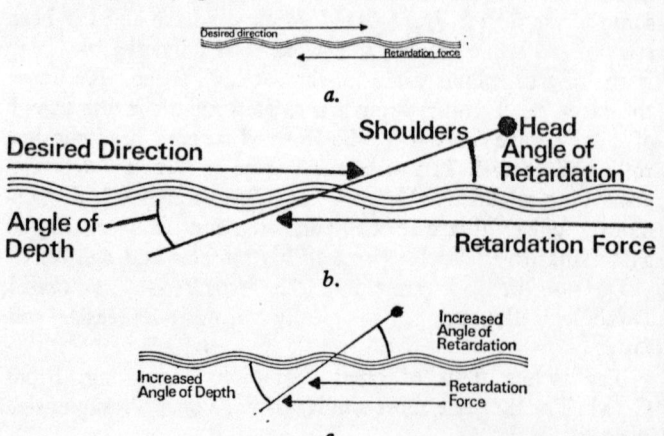

a.

b.

c.

By strengthening the neck muscles it is possible to train them to hold the head fairly high and to maintain the shoulders low in the water. Obviously the shoulder girdle is big enough to tilt the entire surface of the thorax upwards at *an angle opposed to propulsion* and the lower the shoulders the less the angle against the direction.

There has been much debate as to whether more assistance is gained by putting the force of the legs into the closing squeeze as the legs come together or into the kick with feet at right angles which precedes this. In the words of Sir Roger de Coverley: *'Much might be said for both sides'*. The answer depends upon the physique of the individual swimmer.

The amount of pull, width and depth of pull with the arms depends likewise upon the personal capacity of the individual swimmer.

By keeping the leg kick narrower and deeper a certain streamlining is possible, but this does not suit every racer in this stroke.

Control all experiments with a stop-watch, not just once but regularly; note down the results and compare them.

SPECIAL ADVICE FOR BACK CRAWL RACING

Basically, the amount of speed to be obtained by variation of the points of entry (assuming the area behind the head to be like the face of a clock) is relative to the physique of the swimmer. The centre line points to 12 o'clock. Some of the most successful swimmers have used this, but they have had the muscular equipment to make this an easy task.

The actual height and angle of the head may be adjusted according to the swimmer's build.

The degree of rolling permitted in the racing form of the stroke is related to the speed of the arm movement and the depth to which the working hand and arm move down into the water. It is quite a problem for a racing novice to discover at which depth he is getting maximum propulsion with minimum drag.

Strict control of the knees is essential; above the surface of the water they retard progress. Knee action can do nothing but distort direction and retard if the surface is broken.

The racing swimmer must be warned against beginning to pull before the entire hand is below the surface. This weakens the effectiveness of the pull. It is unwise for a swimmer to let the wrist bend during the pull, although the force of the water will facilitate movement of the wrist.

Back Crawl is not a stroke which can be swum badly. It is swum well or not at all (one sinks), so mastery of the details given under the section on the Back Crawl will produce a good racing stroke.

SPECIAL ADVICE FOR DOLPHIN RACING

The undulation of the legs has lost favour with racing swimmers because it has been estimated that the up and down movement produces more drag than progression.

The less violent the movement of the hips the higher the legs stay in the water.

The fingers should spear into the water. The hands may open the fingers under water if the arms are unable to exert full power because of weaker muscles (girls especially).

Dolphin demands a powerfully concentrated mental attitude as well as physical staying power.

The arms should be thrown, not lifted, during the recovery.

Aim for two leg beats to one arm cycle—a slower rhythm produces a jerky, retarded stroke.

The racing swimmer should aim for two complete arm cycles to one breath: more for a short sprint race.

Eliminate all glide from the racing stroke.

Aim for a wholly horizontal poise in the water throughout the stroke.

Concentrate on cultivating a positive and powerful arm action, and do not be leg-conscious.

THE COACHS' RULES FOR RACING TRAINING

Test and check each entrant to discover his first and second best stroke. Swimmers join racing clubs to race; make sure they get lots of racing; do not neglect handicap races.

Test and check entrant for his best distance and times.

Make sure that training takes place under conditions as

near to the actual gala or competition atmosphere as possible —especially in conditions of cheering and noise which can be confusing to a novice.

Make certain that every trainee warms up before swimming, with some physical exercise.

Keep records of every swimmer's performance and diet and stamina under various conditions, weather etc.

Work to build up a team spirit among your trainees. Encourage them to urge each other on to work.

Teach the racers to analyse each other's strokes so that they can guide and help each other when the coach may be busy with other groups.

All stages of starts and turns should be broken down into their elements (as described in this book) and mastered one at a time.

Much of the scientific gobbledygook which is used by some swimming coaches is more valuable for the psychological effect it has upon the less-informed swimmers than for its scientific truth. The fact is incontrovertible that if a swimmer is in any way not making full use of the laws of propulsion and avoiding every form of retardation he cannot give his best. Too many swimmers come to coaches with deeply-ingrained faults and many of the devices now popular are substitutes for the most unwelcome technique of re-teaching the stroke perfectly.

The best judge of performance is the second hand of the timekeeper's watch but we cannot lose sight of the fact that in recent times the best speeds have been clocked up by swimmers between 15 and 18 years of age. In Germany and some other countries it is usual to grade swimmers and athletes according to age groups. In this way many swimmers and sportsmen can continue competitive sport much longer.

Racing swimmers should be reminded that sea-swimming often hinders the development of technique. The waves break rhythm and poise.

Swimmers with good buoyancy usually do best in long and middle distance races. Swimmers with mediocre buoyancy are best at short sprints.

Weight and build fade in comparision with the psychological factors. The ideal racer has an intense will to win, almost a 'killer' instinct, and is possessed of increasing self-confidence and resilience.

The shy type with potential can be greatly helped by winning races in which he is matched against less-talented swimmers. It is almost alarming what response a series of small victories can evoke.

Experts in hypnosis confirm that hypnotic techniques cannot bring out what never existed mentally or physically in a sportsman. Don't bother with hypnosis. (It should be left to experts in any case.)

A relay team should be encouraged to share some social life together.

When a class of young hopefuls despairs and gets tense it is usually because their training programme is too monotonous. Vary it.

Teams in very hard training (four hours or more daily) should have about two days complete rest from training schedule in each week.

SUGGESTED RACING SCHEDULE

1. Warm up with some physical exercise, such as those indicated on page 106.
2. A warm up in the water, of which 220 yds must be in the swimmer's racing stroke.
3. Special stylistic exercises on legs, arms, poise, or some other point to be corrected. Carried out over 220 yds. Supervision of the individual swimmer is essential.
4. A trial race over the distance to be competed in later.
5. Discussion of points gained and lost by individual racers.
6. Some short sprints, either of one or two bath lengths each. The racers can swim up the length, climb out and walk slowly back.
7. Discussion of performances between racers and coach.
8. Starts, turns, take-overs, across the width or one length swim.
9. A warm-down of seven to fourteen bath lengths (220 to 440 yds).
10. Hot showers, drying off. Especial care of ears, feet, hair, etc.

% of the world is water you can explore it by boat

Rowing will take you to the best fishing spots

The start must be well balanced

The air resists speed less than water do

The swallow position

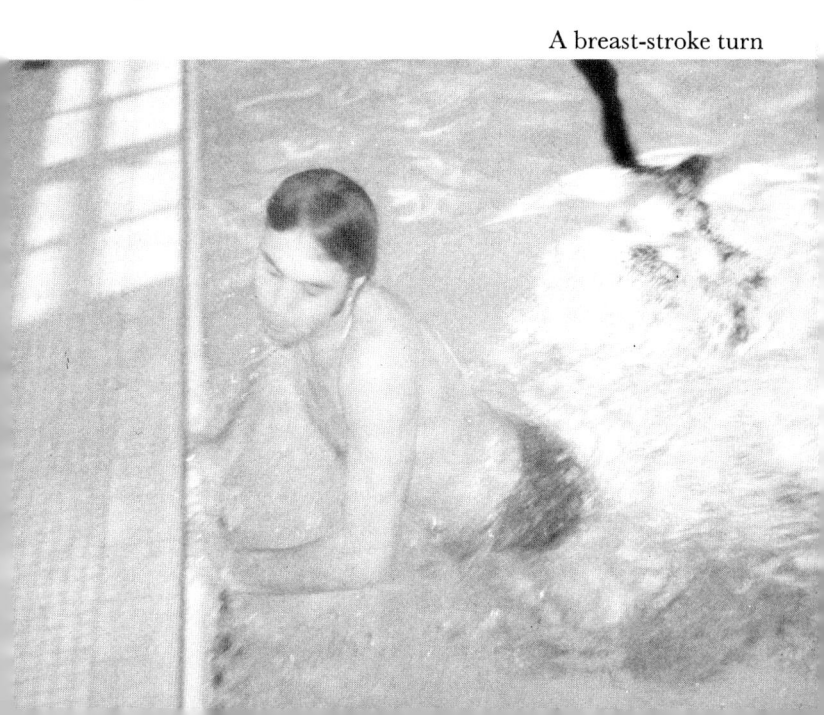

A breast-stroke turn

Ideal for canoe beginners

Such waters teem with fish

11. A social get-together between racers and coach for social chat rather than swimming inquests. This is advisable especially where a relay team is concerned.

The schedule will, of course, be varied for more sprint racing or more long-distance swimming according to the needs of club members.

Many coaches insist upon more frequent sprints throughout a session.

In sunny climes there is a tendency to force the pace much more violently than in Europe, especially in the hours put into training. Australians and some Californians are encouraged to train up to four hours a day. Whether this is beneficial is not proven. I think that more general exercise, weight-training, running and general fitness should be cultivated; this will be psychologically better for the swimmer. I am against the idea of producing swimmers of exceptional ability who will swim for one or two years and then retire from the sport mentally and physically alienated from the severe training.

A CLUB SCHEDULE FOR YOUNG ADULTS

1. Physical exercise warm up.
2. Quarter of a mile swim.
3. Legs only for 220–440 yds.
4. Arms or breathing or poise exercises for 220 yds.
5. Racing distances (relays should usually be included).
6. Sprints. One length, two lengths, or 100 yds. each. Suitable intervals between sprint.
7. Practise for starts, turns and take-overs.
8. A communal swim for 220 yds. Own choice of stroke.
9. Showers, drying. Special attention to ears, feet, hair etc.
10. Hot Bovril or cocoa session in winter or soft drinks and chat after club session.

FURTHER SCHEDULES (SUITABLE FOR SPRINT SWIMMERS)

1. Warm up exercises on the side.
2. 440 yds warm up—any stroke.
3. Five repeats of 220 yds. in the racing stroke. One minute intervals.

4. 100 yds. Legs only with kicking board or float.
5. Three repeats of 100 yds. Two minute intervals or less.
6. Three sprints over racing distance.
7. Slow warm-down swim of 220 yds.

* * *

1. Warm-up exercises on the side.
2. 220 yds. Warm-up swim in racing stroke.
3. Twelve repeats of 100 yds. From three to one minute intervals.
4. 100 yds. Arms only. Using float or kicker board.
5. 100 yds. Legs only.
6. 440 yds. Warm-down swim.

* * *

1. Warm-up exercises of a light nature on the side.
2. One mile swim in two length stints with one minute intervals. Try to keep within the following *maximum* times:
The first ten = maximum of 40 seconds for the two.
The rest = maximum of 45 seconds for the two.
The second ten = maximum of 50 seconds for the two.
3. Warm-down exercises on the side.

* * *

1. Warm-up exercises on the side.
2. Alternate swims of racing distance, the first being flat-out speed, and the second being a recovery swim at 25 per cent effort only.

* * *

Schedules can include such familiar methods of counting the strokes used over the required distance and time used for different stroke counts. It helps create a uniform effect and stroking control over speed of arms etc.

I believe that in the future a great deal more emphasis must be placed upon sheer perfection of techniques and psychological factors. A good club swimmer should be able to take not less than five repeat swims of 100 yds, with one minute rests. The higher up the scale in perfection you go *the less tired you get.*

Notes must be kept of times for each swimmer's times for each of the repeat swims, and details of stroking count etc. entered and compared. The object being to increase *consistency* of speed.

IDEAS FOR SCHEDULES FOR ADVANCED RACING TRAINING

1. Warm-up exercise on the side . . . five minutes.
2. Technique perfection swimming. Careful checking of arms, legs, breathing, poise, starts and turns. The swimmer is advised not to put more than 75 per cent of total effort into these lengths, speed is not required, only technique.
3. Alternating fast and slow swims over the swimmer's racing distance using 75 per cent effort and then 25 per cent for a slow warm-down swim.
4. Different distances of swimming either in racing stroke or others. 880 yds, 50 per cent effort. Two repeats of 440 yards with up to five minutes' interval according to age, condition and ability of swimmer: or Four repeats of 220 yds etc.: or, Eight repeats of 110 yds etc. Adjust the schedule to agree with the needs of individual swimmer and length of training session, especially with regard to the degree of fitness of the individual.
5. Speed work using the racing stroke and/or racing distance. Employ the stop watch for these. Speed is of the essence, in these we are not going to think too much about style . . . this is an attempt to reproduce the conditions of competition.

Always close a long session with a light exercise session on the side of the bath. Stride jumping, stretching and bending exercises are very useful here.

Rest. Top swimmers can often perform repeat swims with as little as 15 seconds intervals. Poor technique means you get tired easily—that is the ultimate criterion for a fit man.

Season. From the end of September until Easter work hard

at the perfection of technique and the building up of water-fitness with plenty of distance swims. From Easter to the start of the racing season work on the shorter distances and speeds especially. During the racing season it is wise to arrange training schedules based upon items 3, 4 and 5 above.

I have often learnt a lot from pupils I have taught, and I believe that a coach who cannot learn from those he is teaching is losing a lot from life.

Medley. Conscientious tests must be undertaken to ascertain that the right man is put down for his best stroke. Medley swimming is a refreshing break during training and can be used instead of handicap swimming if the champions in one stroke are deliberatey made to swim another.

DETAILS OF COACHING HYGIENE

The greatest care must be taken to see that an enthusiast does not wear himself out. A youngster who is very keen and inadequately guided will *run himself into the ground*. This must be prevented. Check his diet, sleeping time and other activities (including sex life) and do everything possible to correct deficiencies or superfluities. In such cases there is invariably a lack of mineral salts, and vitamins—especially B, C and E.

Unexplained *stale condition* is often related to an inadequate social life outside swimming, and invariably related to inability to relax. Increased sleep is essential.

A watch should be kept in the emotional responses of people undergoing intense training. The happy swimmer is unlikely to experience any mental stress. Continued unhappiness or behaviour which is 'out of character' is often symptomatic of severe stress—the first rule is *more sleep*. It is the one form of therapy that many young people are not quick to accept.

Beware of the swimmer whose only *life* is swimming. For a state of good mental balance there should be one other activity of interest which is not related to swimming, e.g. films, chess etc., preferably an interest which does not demand physical effort.

Complaints of peculiar aches at the joints are sometimes related to deficiencies of calcium, phosphorous and/or silica.

Correct diet will restore the swimmer to good health.

Watch any loss of weight which exceeds two pounds and continues for more than a week. A change in training technique, even a short lay-off, and attention to diet and more sleep are all required.

I have often recommended swimmers to do some running—either in the park or round the houses if no track is available. It is *very relaxing*. The aim is to trot for 10, 20 minutes or longer, not to achieve maximum speed—except perhaps for a short burst at the end if this is pleasing to the runner.

Strain in swimmers under training is basically related to mental aspects. A treatise on psycho-somatic medicine is out of place here but the works of Dr. Flanders Dunbar might be consulted.

Whether we can positively assert that the cutting off of a tenth of a second from a World Championship time is only attainable after very long hours of monotonous training is by no means fully proven. Earlier champions did not put such very long hours into the swimming, but were not so very much slower. I believe the answer lies in the *power of concentration* put into the swimming while it is being done. Compare the following times:

Freestyle 110 yds. = 100 metres.

Weissmueller	58.6 seconds, Amsterdam, 1928
Ris	57.3 seconds, London, 1948
Henricks	55.4 seconds, Melbourne, 1956

1 Mile = 1,500 metres.

Borg	19 mins. 51.8 seconds, Amsterdam, 1928.
McLane	19 mins. 18.5 seconds, London, 1948
Rose	17 mins. 58.9 seconds, Melbourne, 1956

(Rose was one of the first swimmers to be subjected to a very rigid dietetic control. Special bread was even flown to him every day! Diet was definitely a factor in the success of this swimmer.)

The fact that in 28 years there was such a small change in the times taken for the events *should* cause coaches to look into their methods. The fact that it is now common at top rank swimming level to check the pulse and the haemoglobin counts of racing stars indicates that they are now being taken to the utmost limits of their physical strength—*to know this evokes emotional strain* and accounts for some of the less glamorous failures. A racing swimmer must feel in his mind that he can beat a certain time. If there is no mental concept there his body is unlikely to strive after it.

One the actual day of an important race it is well for the swimmer to do some warming-up physical exercises and to have a slow swim of either to 220 yds or 440 yds. *Provided that he can rest after it* and does not have to spend the day working in office, shop or factory. A few short sprints and some starts and turns can be made. *It is very advisable for a racing swimmer to have swum before the event in the pool in which the event is to take place.*

If you watch racehorses at the tape before a race you will sense, if not perceive, their nervousness. It is the same for most racing swimmers. It is *not* a bad sign.

All racing swimmers should have their bodies warm before starting to race. Chilled muscles take longer to give their maximum performance. I do not approve of swimmers standing in a draughty bath with a towel round their shoulders. A track suit is essential, they can be zipped off in seconds and provide warmth.

Don't encourage any swimmer to copy another's style unless he has the same physical build!

The coach who cannot laugh and joke with his pupils needs a good holiday—quick.

GALAS

For a top-line gala many officials and helpers are needed. The ordinary club event can clearly make do with fewer officials, sharing the various tasks. Usually there are plenty of enthusiasts who will do some small task, taking up only part of the time. Try not to use up the whole time of people so that they can't see any of the swimming—which is what they (like the spectators) are really interested in.

OFFICIALS YOU CAN HAVE AND THEIR WORK

Commissionaire(s)—To welcome competitors, direct them to their changing room, and tell them where to find other officials.

Programme-Sellers—To sell programmes and collect tickets and tear them (unless there is a lucky ticket for a raffle etc.).

Vestibule Steward—To run and contact other officials in case any emergency arises (ideal for young brothers or sisters).

Competitors' Stewards—One for each sex in the respective changing rooms, to check the name of each competitor on arrival, and see that they present themselves at the bath side *before* the events in announced, reporting to the Whips.

Whips—One for each changing room. To take the competitors for each event to the checker.

Checker—To see that each competitor stands in the right lane or takes the right order in handicap races, and to check each competitor for each event against his list. He should stand at the side of the bath and in front of the competitors. He should avoid them clustering round him while checking; this is confusing.

Starter—He satisfies himself first of all that the Judges, Referee and Timekeeper(s) are ready and in position before giving the starting signal by firing a blank cartridge, blowing a whistle, using a clapperboard (which can be constructed to produce a sound like a shot and is very cheap), or just by shouting 'Go' after a preliminary 'Take your marks'. The starter is warned *not* to start an event before the audience have hushed. It is unfair to expect swimmers to race during a loud babble from the spectators. The starter has the right to disqualify anybody who starts out of order or breaks the rules under starters' orders. The starter stands to the side and usually two yards up the side in front of the competitors.

Judges—Their number varies from two up to two judges for each of the first three places (in very important contests). Many clubs and schools use one judge for each of the first, second and third positions. Generally speaking the rule is for judges to record their decisions individually. If there is disagreement the decision is sent to the Referee. The position of the judges is open to variation, being at the head of the lane in a sprint or at the side of the bath, depending upon the type of event.

Referee—To solve disagreements, if any, recorded by the judges. He also has the task of supervising the swimmers during the race to guarantee that none is fouled by another or interfered with and that all swimmers swim straight in their correct lane.

Recorder—To write the results in a neatly-ruled book, in which the names (Club/School/Swimmer) and event have been *clearly* written *before* the gala starts. In many galas it is customary for a judge to carry a series of coloured markers so that one colour, Blue, is given to the first, Yellow to the second, and Red to the third. These are given, after recording, to the Recorder's runner.

Recorder's Runner—Many galas depend upon the runner who takes urgent communications to the officials, handles inquiries to and from the recorder, and returns the winners' coloured markers to the judges.

Timekeepers—In major events two or three timekeepers are kept busy synchronising their watches, and doing their best to start them simultaneously with the starter's signal. If there is any difference in the time recorded by the timekeepers each speed is added to the other a; division then gives the average time taken.

Turn Judges—Where the swimming of a race involves one or more turns it is common to appoint a person to each swimmer at each end of the baths to check that all turns made conform with regulations. In relay races these are the officials who supervise that take-overs are effected correctly.

Bath Captain—He is in charge of the decks, and supervises that the officials arrive in time to do their office, keeps ends of the bath from getting cluttered up with congratulating relatives, and keeps the officials at the bathside under his eye. He arranges that the chairs, tables, notebooks, programmes for officials, pens, timekeepers' watches and all necessities are in place. He will also check well before the start that the chairs, tables, spray covers at the judges' end and lane ropes are in place.

Nearly all galas have some electrical sound reproduction. An announcer who can speak distinctly into the microphone is very important. Don't have somebody who bellows or whispers. If there is any delay or hitch (it happens in the best of clubs) a sheet of paper with some respectable jokes and/or a tape-recorder with some music could be handy at the announcer's table—usually next to the recorder's table—occasionally at the starter's end.

Usher—To show spectators into their places and check ticket numbers if tickets are numbered.

Refreshment Steward—In control of organising all refreshments.

Prize Steward—To organise all prizes, and check that they do not exceed the limits laid down by the A.S.A. etc.

Press Officer—To inform press, radio, television, chat to reporters and prevent them from cluttering up the bath side or disturbing swimmers while racing by flashlight photographs etc. A novice may be seriously disturbed by a flashbulb going off during a race.

First Aiders—If it is a big event get some help from the Red Cross and St. John Ambulance Brigade to deal with possible accidents. It is a useful idea to have one or two fully qualified lifesavers on hand—just in case a spectator or non-swimmer gets pushed in.

Treasurer—To handle all the money matters and co-ordinate income and expenditure, to keep and record bills, ticket sales, prizes, honoraria and gratuities.

If there is any diving it is customary to have two trained diving judges who can award points corrrectly.

Pity the Club Secretary—He has to book the bath—often months before the event, possibly pay a deposit, arrange for the seating, broadcasting or Tannoy system, arrange printing of programmes, arrange for starting blocks, ropes for lanes, spray covers, prizes, contact important personages to present prizes, remember to mention every single last helper in his speech at the end of the gala, make sure trophies and medals are ordered, arrange for their correct engraving with the winner's names after the event, appoint officials without offending other members, check heating of the bath, make sure that club committees do their job, endeavour to get all the spectators out of the bath after the gala so that tired and overworked bath attendants can shut the baths up and go home. They have to work longer than the officials at the gala (and a gratuity is a small price to pay them for their courtesy and help—especially if you expect to hold another gala there next year). The secretary and/or his committees should check with each swimmer and/or other club secretaries which events are being swum and who is swimming in them *before printing the programmes*. Never ask why club secretaries look harassed, and never fail to give them a hearty cheer when they appear on the bathside!

Towels—Swimmer's don't usually forget their towels, but an extra supply should always be handy just in case something goes wrong.

First Aid—If there aren't any first-aiders present have a well-equipped first aid box available—just in case.

Plan—Do plan the programme so that competitors who are appearing in elimination races can have a breather between events. Don't put the finals immediately after the semi-finals. It is usual to put diving events, sub-aqua show, synchronised swimming or life-saving displays in the middle of a programme. I do not recommend including water polo matches—other than one with a strictly controlled time limit—in a swimming gala, otherwise time may run out, and spectators leave to catch trains and buses before other events have taken place. Some water polo matches do seem to stretch out into eternity.

One of the great attractions of any gala is the appearance of a famous diving star, but they are in continual demand and may not be easy to book. Do not hesitate to include a comedy turn or two during the gala. During a gala some years ago that great coach Jimmy Essex once dressed up as an attendant, climbed the high board, proceeded seemingly to sweep it, made an effective comic dive five metres down and showed every indication of drowning (he was almost unsinkable). While some adult life-savers argued near a microphone which of them was senior and had the right to rescue him, four of the most junior members of the club slipped into the water, towed him out, and applied artificial respiration. Jim was always a great sport and the comic turn revealed a good moral—don't hesitate when life is at stake.

If you have some spectacle do make sure it is in the centre of the pool if possible, so that all spectators can see it.

If you have a broadcasting system of any kind do prevent it from booming or squeaking; test it before using, and tell people how to use it.

A good gala moves fast and smoothly and keeps to a timetable. A noisy audience spoils announcements, disturbs the swimmers, and may ruin a gala. Tell people why you would like them to keep quiet during races, and *especially during diving*.

TIMEKEEPING AT THE GALA

Since fame, if not fortune, may depend on the accuracy of the timekeeper's watch I think it may be useful to mention a few simple points for the beginner.

Always make sure the watch is wound up and working before the race. If I had just swum my very best and was told that the timekeeper's watch had not been working, both timekeeper and watch would have been flung into the water. Be warned!

Make sure the watch stands at 0 before you press the starter.

Find out how the starter mechanism works before you time any event. Many makes of watch have different mechanisms. Test it!

If it is an important event make sure you get some practice in synchronising the starter's signal (gunshot, whistle, a shout, the bang of a clapper-board etc.) with your starting of the watch.

Don't talk to anybody while you are waiting for the start.

Keep your eyes on the swimmer you are timing.

Stop the watch calmly and decisively, using your index finger (the one you point with).

The time is read off the watch and written down as follows: Minutes followed by a colon, then the seconds, followed by a full stop, after which the tenths of seconds are written.

5:03.1 = Five minutes, three seconds and one tenth.

Very important events are checked with three watches.

BALANCE AND FLOATING

The actual position of balance of the swimmer's body is effected by an even distribution of his weight over a surface of the water which is commensurate to the weight which must be distributed.

To explain this simply let us think of an 18-foot canoe

gliding swiftly along a turbulent river. Many people watching it will marvel that anything so slim and fragile can carry such a heavy load as a 12-stone man. It is all a matter of the weight carried being distributed evenly over a sufficient area of water. Putting this in a more precise way we may say that maximum buoyancy of the swimmer's body is effected when the load is evenly distributed.

Take one of the rescue poles which are kept on the side of any public baths (having gained permission first) and place it vertically in the water. Let it go, and you will see that the water forces it into a horizontal position. Most forms of life move horizontally in the water. Even creatures such as the octopus and the sea-horse, in spite of their seemingly vertical position in photographs, actually move horizontally.

Now, in most forms of swimming the arms move above the actual surface during some part of the stroke, particularly during what we call the recovery period (that will be explained later). But the weight of any limb above the surface increases the pressure of the body downward into the water, particularly on the side opposite the limb that has been lifted. This distorts the swimmer's balance, which in turn makes his breathing irregular. And when a beginnner's breathing becomes irregular he can easily panic.

To understand how one limb above the surface can distort balance persuade someone who can swim well to stand up suddenly in a boat—the resulting upset shows how balance can be distorted.

We can describe swimming as floating with added progressive movements made possible by intelligently-applied breathing techniques—which will be described later.

Archimedes of Syracuse was a famous mathematician born in 287 B.C. He made some really exceptional discoveries, among which was the *Archimedean Principle* showing that a body immersed in water loses as much of its weight as equals the weight of the water displaced by the body. The story is that *Archimedes* discoverd this one day while seated in his bath. Elated, he jumped up and ran through the streets crying *'Eureka'* (I have found the answer). Unfortunately, like many inventors, he was absent-minded and had forgotten that he was unclothed!

This principle applied to a swimmer means that the volume of liquid displaced by the body equals the uplifting power of the water in which the swimmer moves. This also shows that although there seems to be greater safety in trying to learn swimming in very shallow 'learner' pools of half a metre or two foot six inches depth, there really is insufficient support for the beginner, because the actual volume of water is not enough to produce the buoyancy or uplift which is the key to real success.

SUCCESSFUL FLOATING LEADS TO SPEED IN LEARNING

The most useful secret of professional teachers is to get the pupil to hold on to the rail round the bath, or to hold on to the steps. Hold on with both hands, arms extended and let the legs come up to the surface—they will float up; *the water forces everything into a horizontal position*—everything that contains oxygen. The beginner soon realises that he is quite safe with the body stretched out on the surface. When confidence is gained and there is no fear when he lets his legs float up the beginner can be held firmly by the wrists (not the fingers, they can slip) and pulled across the width of the pool by an experienced swimmer or teacher, walking backwards. During this exercise the novice will often begin a slight movement of the legs resembling the Crawl leg thrash described later, and one of the most natural movements to make in the water.

About 96 per cent of all human beings can float naturally without any support, lying on their backs, after training and when sufficient confidence has been gained. The beginner should not try this when alone for obvious reasons, but it is important that he should know to what extent his body sinks below the actual surface when he is floating. When he realises that he can float without sinking to the bottom a great deal of his fear will vanish.

To demonstrate how much easier movement is on the surface compared with movement in depth, one can use a pole and move it across an area of water horizontally about a foot below the surface—the movement is extremely easy.

Repeat the movement, holding the pole as deep as possible in the water; the increased resistance of deep water is very impressive.

After this experiment I have found many children make powerful efforts to keep their leg movements on a higher plane in the water. Let us look at another fact. The faster fish swim in higher strata of water than do slow and heavy fish, which are usually found in the great depths of the sea.

Now, if there is hindrance caused by letting the limbs sink too deep in the water, and disturbance of balance by raising them too high above the surface, we see that there is only a certain area below the surface in which movement of any sort can produce useful functions.

Nothing slows down the learning of swimming so much as trying to make progress too quickly: if basic principles are not understood and applied, success will be delayed.

In shipbuilding of any sort there are two basic problems which the constructor of small boats knows all too well— the conflict between streamlined speed and the problem of stability. A kayak is capable of remarkable speed, but in the hands of any but an expert it is far from stable. A racing swimmer moving at speed in the Front Crawl stroke relies on his speed to give his poise to enable him to breath comfortably. A beginner applying Breast Stroke principles correctly has great stability but little speed. Many children and adults are suited by temperament and build for quick, accurate movements. Others are suited for slow movements and need a much greater degree of stability to maintain confidence. *This is the secret governing which stroke we should teach beginners first.*

I refer to boats because it is easier to see in the outlines of a hull the number of different planes or surfaces the boat presents to the water; we watch one of the old Thames sailing barges that the stories of W. W. Jacobs made so famous, we compare it's shape and performance with that of a swift light catamaran, originally developed on the Coromandel Coast of India (around Madras). The wider the prow the greater the resistance offered by the water: the narrower and more streamlined the prow the less is the initial resistance. When we apply this to the swimmer we see that the wider the planes created by sideways movements of the arms (as in the earliest forms of breast stroke) the slower progress will be (this applies to widely-splayed legs as well); particularly in the case of a beginner a great deal of energy will be expanded without proportional progress.

Generally speaking, arm and leg movements should not move outside the width of the shoulders by more than a few inches.

Currently popular, the inflatable armbands available for beginners are a powerful psychological aid to increasing floatability. An inflatable band around the waist will still float if the pupil turns upside down, but inflatable bands on the arms prevent him from turning head down under water. I first encountered them at the National School of Swimming with Reg Brickett, who pioneered their use. We found that the artificial floatability induced usually cut down the time taken to teach swimming. The amount of inflation could be surreptitiously reduced, so that the child would often fail to notice that the movement made was coming increasingly from his or her own balanced poise on the water and unconscious stepping-up of personal effort. Complete withdrawal of the armbands was occasionally countered with a psychological barrier, but after one or two lessons the visible progress of other pupils without their armbands usually overcame this minor problem.

Many facets of swimming are interdependent, and floating and breathing are closely connected. The general tendency is to teach beginners in a small pool which is much warmer than the usual public bath. The disadvantage is that it is much harder to float in warm water than in cold water, which has a greater density. Against this there is a tendency for colder water to increase the need for respiration and create enhanced nervous tension. Of course, since salt water has a much more suitable density it is well suited for teaching swimming, but there is no need to rush off to the Dead Sea, where the salt content is so great that practically nobody can put a limb down more than a foot (30 centimetres) deep.

A great deal of publicity has been given to teachers who

produce infant prodigies who succeed in swimming at only a few months old! Without detracting from the hard work and enthusiasm of the highly-efficient teachers who do this, I must admit that it is easier in one respect than is generally realised. Man spends his first 12 months in a horizontal position; his first attempts to move are in a purely horizontal plane. The younger the pupil the easier it is for him to revert to horizontal movement. The adult has become *conditioned to movement in a vertical positio*n; the older the learner is the harder it is to overcome his mental conviction that he must have the feet pointed downwards. The novice expends much energy in fighting the water, trying to keep his feet down on the bottom or near the bottom. I have often explained to children that the whole object of swimming is to move through the water where the 'floor' is too deep for their toes to touch. I think it is wise when learning (or teaching) swimming to recall that most humans require 12 to 18 months to learn how to walk, but in most cases an intelligent being can learn how to swim within six weeks. I have on a few occasions got children to swim a width of the bath at their first lesson (in each case a child of between six and ten years, *well disciplined at home*, and in each case visiting the bath for the very first time).

The secret we should tell the child is that: *The more of the body that is in the water the more buoyant the body becomes*. Even the head is a heavy part of the body, particularly so when it is fully raised and stretched above the water level. This is why careful instruction is given in another chapter about the techniques of breathing which make it possible to breathe very comfortably with the head partly submerged (we breathe out under water so that it is only necessary for lips and nose to rise above the water to breathe air in).

Persons with poor co-ordination of mind and muscle put a good deal of psychologically-based fear into their efforts, which are often too half-hearted (particularly in floating) to succeed. If the efforts to breathe are not controlled by concentrated will power the learner cannot benefit by the increase buoyancy that increased respiration brings about. *The chief fault of the learner is inability to believe the teacher.*

This is markedly observed when the pupil destroys buoyancy and balance by stopping to take a long deep breath in Front Crawl practice each time the arm is swung (too slowly) over the surface of the water. I cured some boys of this by telling them they could not drive a car by slamming on the brakes every time they breathed, and that the idea of stopping movement every time they wanted to breathe was stopping their swimming and making it harder. The ethics of the suggestion are dubious, but I have found many boys eager to adopt an idea if they think it is a lazier way round their task!

USEFUL FLOATING TECHNIQUES

(1) The pupil should hold on to the rail round the side of the bath with one arm, bring the feet up against the side at a level higher than the bottom, so that with the knees bent the body constitutes a natural spring. The free arm is pointed outward across the pool—preferably towards a teacher or more experienced swimmer who is waiting to receive the gliding novice. On the command 'Go' the pupil kicks hard releasing the spring in the bent knees, and straight as an arrow glides towards the waiting helper, bringing the arm which held on in a straight line with the other pointing arm. With practice at least half the width of a bath can be traversed by such a glide; practised swimmers can easily cross a whole bath width with one such glide.

(2) The technique outlined in paragraph one above is repeated but two arms are used to hold on to the rail, and then rapidly swung forward upon the command Go.

(3) The same as in paragraph 2 above but this is performed while lying on the back, and the entire glide is on the back with the arms swinging over from the hold, in which the pupil is facing the rail, with the knees bent up almost meeting the chin, and upon the command 'Go' flinging the arms over behind the head until they make contact with the water, and holding them in a straight and stiff manner to form one *arrow-*

(4) The relaxed, motionless float on the surface. The beginner had best start by being held in position by a helper and gradually released as the floating posture is reached. Generally speaking, *the essential secret of floating is the ability to relax on the water,* to allow the water's specific gravity to take over and carry the pupil. The more tense the muscles are the more easily will the water allow the body to sink. When trying this advanced floating position the pupil *must breath in deeply and hold each breath a little longer than he normally does*. The teacher will soon spot the correct fulcrum and help the pupil to relax the knees or the waist slightly or place the feet or wrists at right angles so that the toes or fingers stick up somewhat stiffly from the water (all four variations change the weight of parts of the body and so alter the fulcrum of the floating body).

(5) If we think of the outrigger boats (used originally in the South Sea islands) which had a framework of light timber attached to a float or floats on one or both sides we see that these floats could be likened to the function of our arms when stretched out across the surface of the water to increase floating ability. Some pupils find they can float more easily in the position of an X or a star, with arms and legs widely outstretched.

(6) The Mushroom float demands more advanced breath control, and should never be attempted until the pupil can hold his breath under the water without any difficulty. Although it is common to say that the pupil *holds* his breath this is not wholly accurate, because he should be encouraged to breathe out continually at a much slower rate than is normal, so that a small stream of bubbles appear on the surface. The pupil clasps the knees tightly with both arms and pulls them up to his chin; the back is rounded, the face is placed calmly down in the water; the position is then held

for a few seconds with only the back protruding above the surface (like the dome of a mushroom) while the legs point downward like the stem.

(7) Floating enables the pupil to understand the entire theory and practice of buoyancy which is particularly important in the most essential technique of life preservation (that is how one saves one's own life rather than saves the life of another). By extending the arms out sideways in line with the shoulders, and letting the legs descend vertically, the pupil can quite quickly learn to move the legs either in and out sideways or backward and forward as in walking; the motion will enable the pupil to keep the head easily above the surface of the water. An important point about this exercise is that it demonstrates that *little movement is necessary to maintain buoyancy*. Better buoyancy is effected by slow, deliberate and positive movements than by sudden, quick and panicky ones.

THE FULCRUM

I am sure many readers have done at school the trick of balancing an india-rubber and a pen on different ends of a ruler and moving the ruler along an outstretched finger until a point of balance was obtained. A further experiment was to use the ruler as a lever, using the fixed point held in one hand as a point providing energy to transmit some small object through the air. The actual point in both these cases is the *Fulcrum*. Clearly, if the fulcrum remains fixed the transmission of energy from one place to another is easier. Another word which we must use in describing certain motions in swimming is *Lever*, which is a rigid rod (or limb) moving about a fixed point. There are three kinds of levers.

(1) Place a rescue pole on the bath side, then pick up the lower end below the middle and raise it to its full height. What actually happens is that you have applied the most common-met type of leverage to do this simple task.

R = *resistance*.

P = *power applied*.

F = *fulcrum*.

```
                              P
R─────────────────────────────────────────────F
```

Lever 1

The fulcrum is kept against your own feet and the pole is raised towards you, with the resistance farthest away from you.

The actual movement is quite quick but not very strong. This type of leverage is very frequently encountered. The reason why certain movements are banned as faulty and retarding by swimming coaches is because they exert bad leverage, and tire the swimmer without producing adequate progress.

(2) If you have ever tried to use a knife to force open a tightly-closed lid of a tin of paint you have unwittingly employed a second type of lever, a much stronger lever.

```
                  R
P─────────────────────────────────────────────F
```

Lever 2

This can also be used in swimming strokes.

(3) The remaining lever is not quite so frequently met with.

```
                      F
P─────────────────────────────────────────────R
```

Lever 3

But its relationship to balance is clearly shown, and in this way it is useful to recognise it.

Before we leave the subject of the fulcrum let us examine the action of the ball of the foot every time we put it forward and down on the floor when we walk. Clearly, here is the use of a natural fulcrum in everyday life, but the floor stays still when we put the foot on it.

The beginner may suffer from a slight psychological shock when he discovers that the water does not stay still but keeps up a fluid movement.

If the movements in any stroke are made in a hesitant or slovenly fashion the swimmer cannot gain from them a fair movement but will lose energy, breath and balance because there has not been full exploitation of the limited resistance of the water.

GENERAL NOTES

As a fair average the specific gravity of the human body is about 0.986.

The more muscular the body the greater the specific gravity.

The fatter the body and the more oxygen in it the easier horizontal floating becomes.

Even people who cannot float horizontally can usually master the simple *treading water* described on page 144 which is a technique which can save their lives.

The more stable the fulcrum the easier it is to effect leverage; by keeping the thorax and abdomen comparatively rigid the leverage made by the swimmer's arm movements can be made more effective. Although this is a highly advanced technique if we can succeed in teaching it as early as possible there will be correspondingly less time wasted. Many pupils complain that they are often taught one technique, master it to the best of their ability, only to have it modified, further modified, and eventually completely replaced. More teachers and coaches should ask themselves whether this is the best use of their own time or the the pupils' lesson periods.

By going more slowly in the beginning we may often save time later on during the instruction. The beginner must be discouraged from exerting unnecessary force and violence in his arm movements, which will increase the pressure of the water on his lungs as well as destroying his balance and buoyancy and constricting his breathing.

CORRECTING FAULTS IN FLOATING
Horizontal Floating
(1) The pupil must not panic if, especially in the initial learning stage, his face submerges slightly; a good deal of calm thinking is needed. (a) Help is near. (b) As long as the head pops up again to breathe the pupil is safe.
(2) The body is nearly always too tense at first; *tense muscles are nowhere nearly as buoyant as relaxed muscles*.
(3) If the head temporarily submerges the pupil often brings the hands and arms above the water level; this is fatal; it always thrusts the body down deeper into the water.
(4) Nervous people try to sit in the water instead of trying to lie down on it (just as if you are going to bed); sitting produces sinking.
(5) The head is too far forward (looking at the toes is wrong). Learn to breathe out through the nose, this keeps water out.

Vertical Floating
(1) Nearly anybody who finds horizontal floating difficult can float in a vertical position, hanging down in the water like a giant clock pendulum. If the legs do not hang *down* sinking will be experienced.
(2) The back is often left limp; it must be arched in a clearly-seen crescent moon position.
(3) The head must be pushed back; if it is allowed to drop forward sinking is experienced (if you're floating you don't have to see where you're going—floaters don't go anywhere).
(4) The muscles are often too tense; the only tension required is the arching of the back and the pressing back of the head.

BREATHING IN THE WATER

Whether one is a beginner or already a swimmer there is one thing that nobody can neglect when in the water—breathing. Successful swimming is related to balance, floating and relaxation, none of which can be achieved if you are concentrating solely upon how you are going to gulp down the next breath of air.

Theoretically, human beings ought to be able to absorb oxygen from water, so scientists assure us, but for the fact that lungs are too slow in sorting the oxygen out from the liquid; in practice we cannot, so we have to understand what breathing is, and how to learn methods of *breathing comfortably in the water*.

Breathing as a regular, automatic action which we notice only if we get into difficulties, get short of breath, catch cold etc.

The beginner in the swimming pool has to get into the habit of thinking about breathing, and learn to control body movements so that regular, controlled, effortless breathing may take place while in the water.

There is one aspect of breathing while swimming that not many coaches seem to know, it is too obvious! Swimming mostly occurs in a state of near nudity; the entire skin surface is open to the oxygen in the water—yes, the water does contain oxygen which plays upon the surface of our skin, and the pores of the skin, being fairly dutiful servants, respond quickly to the stimulus. They absorb oxygen as best they can from the water, and with those parts of the body above the surface still more oxygen is absorbed. *An unclothed body tends to absorb more oxygen than a clothed one*. The result of this is that the body is getting more oxygen than when you are walking about normally clothed.

This oxygen undergoes the exchange in the lungs I describe later in this chapter, and carbon dioxide begins to accumulate. The body feels the very intense desire to get rid of the noxious, stale gas, and this must be got rid of. The swimmer has to learn how to breathe out harder than he breathes in!

The main problem is how to expel unwanted air—not how to inhale fresh supplies. The presence of carbon dioxide in the body makes for extreme tiredness, and leads to a panic desire to breathe in fresh oxygen through the oral-nasal respiratory mechanisms.

All beginners make the mistake of not breathing out hard enough (under water for Breast Stroke, Crawl, Dolphin).

A good, practised swimmer takes in comparatively little air each time he opens his mouth to breathe in (don't try to breathe in through your nose while swimming), and blows out hard under water (except in Back Crawl). While still on the bath side take as deep a breath of air as you can into your mouth, hold it and then try to breathe in again—it can't be done without getting rid of the first lot of air! Yet this is precisely the mistake novices make in swimming; they try to get a second lot of air without blowing out the first. Small wonder that many of them make a very easy lesson hard going. Since the water presses more powerfully against the body than does the air a slightly more conscious and stronger effort is needed at first to inhale air; one of India's leading Yogis said that for this reason swimming was extremely important and constituted a valuable breathing and spiritual exercise. The fact that one is in a horizontal position makes the effort seem strange from a purely psychological viewpoint. The beginner must take plenty of time to become familiar with the water and the ways of breathing comfortably in it. *Don't fight the water—you'll never win!* Work with it, and you will succeed beyond your wildest dreams.

Learn to build a good foundation for your efforts in swimming by mastering the technique of breathing; do not try to run before you can walk. When I was at Heidelberg University, many years ago I was taught a proverb which ran something like this: '*Nobody just fell down from Heaven knowing it all*', so never get angry at yourself if you find the elementary things take a bit longer to master than you originally thought they would. In mountaineering you may have to climb for hours before you get on to the base of the peak you really want to ascend.

The very nervous beginner who is frightened of the water (do realise that there is simply no shame in being frightened of a new medium) tends to tense the muscles in general and the neck muscles especially. When you are out of the water if you deliberately tense all your neck muscles you will find it is hard enough to breathe. It is more so when you are in it. The neck muscles must be relaxed to make breathing easy. All beginners try to move their arms and legs too quickly; this increases the need for more oxygen and makes their plight desperate. Try to look at some goldfish, or visit an aquarium before going for the first swimming lesson; observe how calmly and slowly the fish move their fins . . . but how very precise and positive every motion is. *If you make slow positive movement you will use up less oxygen and make more progress through the water.*

Remember that if you have a good balance in the floating positions you will be in a favourable place for breathing. Any movement which destroys the equilibrium of the body makes breathing more difficult.

If you watch racing during the early stages of learning swimming you may acquire an entirely misleading picture, insomuch as that the racing swimmers sometimes appear not to breathe at all. For a beginner to imitate this is psychologically disastrous—apart from almost a physical impossibility.

A beginner said to me: 'But it all looks so easy from the side'. While I would not agree that the 'art is to conceal the art', I think that to the untrained eye there are many small refinements which are not noticed simply because the newcomer does not know what to look for.

Some writers encourage swimmers to hold their breath under water, but while this technique has been adopted by some highly-advanced racing swimmers with a moderate degree of success, it should never be used with beginners. Breathing in and out is quite difficult enough to master in the early stages.

WHAT AIR DOES TO YOU

Oxygenation of the blood is essential for life and health. The lessening of the air supply leads to a reduction of the oxygen in the alveolar system of the lungs. This allows a build-up of carbon dioxide in the blood, bringing an overstrong stimulus of some of the cells in the brain. This triggers off an emergency switch in the brain which makes respiration increase in depth and force. If this gets a little out of hand difficulty in breathing may occur, and a far worse condition can rapidly follow that—asphyxia caused by paralysis of the respiratory nerves. The teacher must be experienced enough to recognised a beginner's initial efforts and the desperate plight of a struggler whose respiration has got out of control. In a few cases it is not too easy to distinguish the two extremes, some beginners make such heavy work of what is a relatively simple exercise.

If the learner is in poor physical condition the muscular exertions of contracting the abdominal muscles which hold the diaphragm in position may account for many stops, which to the advanced swimmer or teacher who has forgotten his own early struggles appear unnecessary. Learning to control the movement of the diaphragm (even without realising what they are doing) can exhaust young children when they are working arms and legs as well.

There is a *secret* here: *Teach the pupil not to stop the water with their lips but by closing the muscles at the back of the throat* (posterior cricoarytenoid muscles). This is what experienced swimmers do, and they seldom swallow a single drop of water; as soon as the water flows into the mouth they blow it out again hard.

When a swimmer plunges into a swimming pool which *seems* cold to the skin there is a lightning stimulation of the respiratory nerves, and the entire metabolic system begins to generate heat to offset the sudden cold atmosphere in which the body finds itself. If the cold is more imagined than real (with children this is commonly encountered) the metabolism slows down to normal; if the cold is real the metabolism works at maximum output, generating heat (and losing heat and potential energy). I believe that the former mania for taking cold baths and showers for long periods prior to swimming has died out; it was once thought that this was a manly imitation of the ancient Spartans.

I was elected a Fellow of the Classical Institute many years ago, and one of the things my researches in the field of the Classics revealed is that Sparta lies on latitude 37.7 N, roughly equal to Gibraltar, and on the same level as the luxurious Portuguese Algarve where there is barely three months winter, where spring begins in early February—the

Spartans weren't punishing themselves by taking cold baths in that kind of climate, and the number who did it all the year round wasn't greater than the small number of men who go for a swim on an icy Christmas day in London.

From studies in psychology we knew that emotionally disturbed people tend to increase the production of carbon dioxide. The actual content of the air we breathe is as follows—Oxygen 20.56 per cent; Nitrogen 79.40 per cent; Carbon Dioxide 0.04 per cent (needed to stimulate the respiratory nerves). Note how it differs from the air breathed out—Oxygen 16.50 per cent; Nitrogen 79.40 per cent; Carbon Dioxide 4.10 per cent. The increased tissue activity has consumed the retained oxygen—4.06 per cent—which has been converted into 4.06 per cent carbon dioxide, after the heat and the energy have been liberated by the interchange of gases in the lungs. There is another valuable *secret* which will cheer the beginner and all nervous swimmers: *Even when we have breathed out hard a reservoir of residual air is left in the lungs*. The average person takes in approximately 500 cubic centimetres every time he or she inhales, and exhales roughly the same amount, and accepting the usual rate of breathing as 12 times to the minute *on land* that is about 6000 c.c. per minute, this is six litres of air, equivalent to 10½ pints per minute). If we breathe out very powerfully we can get rid of about 1,500 c.c., but this by no means clears the lungs out of air; scientists have shown that about one litre of *residual air* is left in the lungs from which the body can continue to benefit, even if temporarily cut off from fresh supplies; quite long enough in fact for help to come to a pupil in difficulties.

Pearl divers in various parts of the world have mastered techniques of breath control that enables them to stay alive under water for several minutes, five being about the maximum, although I strongly advise against children or adults not brought up in such a community practising something like this without supervision. May I add that some English humorist convinced some naïve Dutchmen that the people of our islands could stay under water for 72 hours (without submarines!) but that was about 200 years ago! All air passes through the glottis on its way to the lungs, and this opening from the pharynx to larynx is very sensitive to emotions. Fear tenses it, narrowing the opening, and lessening the supply of air. During quiet breathing the glottis is wide open and lots of air can pass in quite freely. Even trying to shout loud for 'help' tends to tense and close the glottis, so the swimmer has to learn how to take care of himself by methods outlined elsewhere in this book.

There are one or two other problems concerned with air—

(a) Humidity or aridity of the air breathed in. It is a proven point that some persons are usually affected more than others by the dryness or the wetness of the climate, by the quality of the air they breathe—a fact experienced by many at the Mexico City Olympics. To those used to humid air a drier air may at first seem a little enervating, and to people used to dry air inhaling damp air may prove depressing. Such changes can affect the performance of a racing swimmer unless he has been given time to become acclimatised. Coaches first had their attention drawn to this point during the 1960 Olympics at Rome.

(b) Self Control in missed rhythm. Even advanced swimmers occasionally take in a gulp of water, or, to avoid doing so, miss the rhythm of breathing. Some clear thinking is needed, but it is not very difficult to recover by calmly breathing out, waiting for the next moment in the cycle, and then breathing in—a slightly larger inhalation will compensate the swimmer.

Generally speaking, the breathing for the Front Crawl is the most difficult technique to learn, taking more time to master than any other. The extraordinarily short time which a full Dolphin stroke allows the swimmer to breathe is actually rather illusory; the author has swum one mile Dolphin non-stop in front of witnesses.

If any swimmer comes out of the water after half a mile, or even a one mile swim, showing symptoms of breathlessness there is something wrong with his breathing technique.

The special techniques recommended for each specific stroke are given under the heading of the stroke.

CLASS MANAGEMENT

'Old racing swimmers never die—they turn instructors' it is said. Let me hasten to add that the fact that a person has been a successful racing-swimmer does not guarantee that he or she will be a brilliant teacher of swimming.

Class teaching is economical use of the instructor's time and knowledge, and if the pupils are paying for advanced instruction it is of course cheaper for them. In the case of a large class, learning elementary and intermediate swimming, class teaching is the usual and most practical method for any pupil who is not in a hurry to learn (then private tuition is essential).

With children and beginners 30 is the absolute maximum that one instructor can reasonably teach at one time; two dozen is the average number of children in any school class. It is essential to grade any class into those who are, shall we say euphemistically 'Good', 'Better', 'Best'? Less politely we can call it sorting the chaff from the wheat. This sorting-out method makes it fairer for the pupils, some of whom are either already better than their fellows or who simply learn more efficiently at a quicker rate.

In the initial stages it is strongly advisable for the teacher either to demonstrate the stroke himself or arrange for an extremely good swimmer to do so. If the instructor enters the water he must make sure that a qualified life saver is available on the side. It is impossible to watch the safety of a whole class from the water level. If the pupils see their teacher swimming they should be able to feel pride, confidence and respect for his ability. I believe that there are some teachers who have for various reasons given up swimming, which makes their task of teaching harder.

The smaller the group the quicker the pupils will learn, because it is easier to enforce concentration. (How the teacher enforces concentration will be discussed further in this chapter).

And the more frequent the lessons the better.

Don't go in for teaching unless you have a lively sense of humour, ability, self-respect, understanding of human nature and firmly believe that you can make a contribution to the welfare and happiness of those you teach.

A teacher who can joke with the class but still retain the respect of the pupils and their attention will go far. All teachers make mistakes in human relations from time to time, but the class will forgive you provided that you show clear attempts to be just. That wily old Empress of Russia, Catherine the Great, said: 'Praise loudly, blame softly'—excellent advice for a teacher.

Never give long lectures to a class longing to get into the water and swim—or try to. Make all instruction short, clear and demonstrate the action carefully. The younger pupils, especially nowadays, tend to find one point at a time as much as they can absorb and put into practice.

Teaching must be enjoyable and not dull; the pupil must go away from each lesson eagerly anticipating the next. I once took a class in a district of London. Two years later I happened to return there for some special shopping. To my amazement two boys who I could barely recognise rushed up to me, grasped my hands and exclaimed: 'Sir, are you coming back to teach us? We would like you back again'—after an absence of 104 weeks! I felt deeply moved that my efforts had met with such unexpected response. Even if they do not demonstrate it visibly your class likes you, so never forget it.

In a small class the aim is to bring as many as possible of the class up to a comparable standard. Where this is not possible a subsquad may develop, and whatever the feelings of the instructor he must devote more time to the 'lost sheep' than to the more progressive swimmers—a variable factor which depends upon whether the instructor has any assistance, and whether that help is capable of helping the beginners sufficiently. The problem of the subsquad can be eliminated sometimes by increasing the bad swimmers' visits to the pool.

Discipline in any swimming pool is a matter of life and death.

The teacher who does not insist upon a disciplined class is risking the lives of the pupils. A drowning child does not cry aloud to heaven for aid; his mouth is half full of water anyway; all that emerges is a choking 'glub, glub, ugh . . .' If there is a noisy riot going on at one end of the pool the imminent demise of 'sad little Sam' in three foot of water may pass unnoticed.

The teacher is responsible for the safety of his pupils. An undisciplined class learns less and puts on the instructor an intolerable responsibility under unnecessarily difficult conditions. Most classes react very well if you explain two things to them—the safety factor just mentioned above and the undeniable factor that nobody can swim and talk at the same time because to talk ruins the breathing rhythm, and if there is no rhythm the breathing technique is wholly wrong.

A swimming pool is not a wrestling ring and no horseplay can be allowed on the bathside. Virile members of the class who feel that combat is essential can either fight in the pool (at their own risk) or get outside.

The instructor who allows pupils to push one another in the pool will one day get pushed in by the 'run wild, run free' rebels. Bones can be broken by the silliest of slip-ups on the floor of a bath. Nobody should ever be allowed to dive haphazardly into a pool without looking first to ascertain that the water is empty of other swimmers (and not about to be entered by a diver from the high board overhead).

Any breach of hygiene is selfish and anti-social and the teacher can never condone things like spitting, blowing the nose in the water or urinating in it. Chlorine does destroy urine but the pupil must nevertheless be checked for his own sake as well.

Many pupils suffer from an inferiority complex and the instructor will only succeed with these if he can encourage them to achieve—nothing succeeds like success.

How do we get the class to listen? This is no easy problem to solve in a large echo-sounding chamber like a bath. The beginner in teaching can too easily suffer from laryngitis and pharyngitis. Shouting is not the answer; the reverberations only increase and the teacher's voice becomes indistinct. Talk quietly and avoid monotone, slow down when you come to some very important point, or else raise your voice slightly. Repeat the important point several times. In the case of a small class or small group in a class the instructor can get the pupils to make a semi-circle around him, or if there is a larger group the instructors stands at one end of a lined-up class and gives slow details of the point to be learnt in a well-modulated voice. *Never give instruction to a class until the entire class is silent.*

If no megaphone is available a whistle is essential, and a class should be trained to respond to certain signals.

One loud blast—Quiet, listen to instruction, and watch the teacher.

Two loud blasts—Stop whatever you are doing and come to the bath rail.

Four loud blasts—All swimmers get out and line up.

Most instructors will find various other signals they wish to convey. As long as the class learns them well there is no difficulty.

HOW TO INSTRUCT SEVERAL GROUPS SIMULTANEOUSLY

Instruction of this kind occurs usually in a bath at least 100 ft. long, and provided that the class consists of groups taking different lessons in swimming strokes there is no need to rope off different sections for them (most public baths object to this procedure). Just make sure that Group 'A' is doing Front Crawl practice while Group 'B' does Breast Stroke, and 'C' does Backstroke or Butterfly; the variations are endless, but the importance of this simple system lies in the immediate visual control of teacher over the groups.

One of the practical problems that arises with children is that a child newly-promoted from a lower group to a higher group often has a fear of swimming in deeper water as he is moved up the poolside and into deeper water for training. The answer is not to promote children until they have swum the qualifying distance for their promotion not once but *three* times; this increases their confidence.

To avoid unnecessary milling in a class the instructor is advised to make each section swim either in circles or in ellipsoids—as per illustration.

Never let a group have an uneven number for long—students young or old prefer to pair up with another learner of similar standards.

HOW LONG SHOULD THE LESSON LAST?

For beginners twenty minutes in the water is ample because they will not have the technique to keep up movements sufficiently vigorous to keep warm. Usually until the swimmer reaches advanced stages lessons last 30 minutes.

If a pupil begins to shiver send him out with a recommendation to dry with a brisk towelling. Remind all beginners to dry their hair.

AIDS TO TEACHING

The teacher who keeps a long bamboo pole to hand during his lesson will rarely have to plunge in fully clothed to pull out some panicky or careless pupil.

Plastic or synthetic floats are commonly used to aid beginners, and it is best to have these on the bath side before the lesson begins. The class should be encouraged to put them back in the box at the end of the lesson.

If a whole class is using inflatable armbands the class must blow up their own inflatables—the teacher is not there as a human pump, and it is unhygienic for him.

Notices for a class must be displayed prominently and the class should be asked if they have looked at the notice board or blackboard if these are in use.

When a class is divided into groups and one instructor is moving from one to another it may be found helpful to have an indicator board for each group—as shown in the illustration.

The author is not in favour of flippers being used by junior beginners. These were invented during World War II to enable highly-trained men to swim underwater for long distances on military operations. Juniors using them are inclined to be more than careless about catching the eyes and noses of their little friends as they speed through the water with little effort. Furthermore, *to learn with flippers makes for lazy legwork in any stroke.*

All swimming aids have to be abandoned sooner or later. It is a debatable point when they should be given up. The longer a swimmer uses the aid the more loath he can be to swim without them.

GENERAL

Try to memorise the names of your class members. If you have a bad memory for names they will not mind if you use some nicknames. If the girls have different-coloured hats you can call them 'Raspberry flavour, Lemon, Strawberry, Ginger, Chocolate, Peppermint, Vanilla' or 'Daffodil, Tulip, Bluebell etc'. For the boys something more robust is needed. But never let a nickname be derogatory or derisive. In time most teachers learn the true names of pupils, so be patient with yourself!

Know your lesson and schedule by heart but don't worry if you have to modify them.

Try to end each session with racing or games: it leaves both instructor and pupils feeling good.

PHYSICAL EXERCISE FOR THE SWIMMER

The better the results the swimmer requires the fitter he must be. The considered opinion of many experts is that the racing swimmer should undertake additional exercises and training to obtain results which he wants to surpass those of his fellow club members and competitors.

The object of the exercises is to increase the responsiveness and efficiency of the heart and of the lungs, to strengthen the muscles—particularly the Deltoids, Trapezius, Serratus and Pectorals, while not neglecting the Rectus Abdominals and Obliques.

Generally speaking, the average recruit to racing-swimming is under-developed, but this is easily remedied. A great deal of sheer bulk is not desirable. The author has in recent years had to dissuade several enthusiastic young men from using certain anabolic steroid drugs which do bring about startling increases in muscular girth, but which do not strengthen the ligaments and tendons which have to carry the heavier muscles, and which tend to snap most frequently. These drugs increase the use of nitrogen to bring protein to the muscles, but like most modern drugs they have unexpected and unpleasant side-effects such as liver damage, sterility and, in some cases, cancer.

The swimmer needs agility and efficiency, not bulk. Here are some exercises to bring about the desired conditions.

*   *   *

(1) A slow march one length of the pool, speeded up to quick march down the opposite side.
(2) Quick march, standing on the spot, involving high-stepping, knee-raising. (Sometimes called 'running on the spot').
(3) Feet astride. Arms upwards stretch, bring the arms down to thighs, fling upwards, then down. 10-20 repetitions.
(4) Feet astride. Arms swing together from side to side, the waist twists, arms are held out directly in front of the shoulders.
(5) Feet astride. The body bends down at the trunk, the hands loosely touch the toes and then swing round in a complete circle taking the entire upper body upwards, round and down again. 5 repetitions in each direction.
(6) Facing a partner, feet astride but with one foot balanced in front of the other, hold each other's hands with firmly-bent fingers, begin a rapid sawing or boxing motion, with alternate arms moving backwards and forwards. 30 to 40 repetitions.
(7) Seated on the ground. Legs stretched out in front, toes pointed. Balanced upon the elbows. Legs open and shut horizontally. 10 repetitions.
(8) Lying on the ground. Legs raised and lowered alternately, left-right, left-right.
(9) Lying on the ground. Legs stretched out, toes pointed. Roll back the legs, keeping them straight, until the toes touch the ground behind the head.
(10) Standing, feet astride. Arms swinging like windmills,

inwards-turning to meet in front of the face. Then to repeat in an outward direction.

RUNNING

Every swimmer who wishes to race is strongly recommended to make time for a little road-running or track work to increase the capacity of the lungs and thereby their efficiency.

There is absolutely no need for hurry, but this does not mean dawdling either. A pair of plimsols or running shoes, sweater and shorts or a track suit and the runner is ready to go. A lot of this sort of training is favoured during the winter season, and however cold the weather no harm ensues provided a simple rhythmic lope is entered into. Running during fog is definitely not recommended.

Concentrate carefully on controlling the breathing, keeping the arms bent and loose at the sides. For this type of work a loose hip movement, allowing comfortable swinging of the legs, is best. Although speed is not important there is no reason why, if the runner desires it, the last 25, 50 or 100 yards should not finish with a really fast sprint. Remember to have a quick towelling-down with a dry, rough towel immediately after the run, or to start on some other exercises.

The frequency of the runs depends on the advice of a coach. Unless there is contrary advice from an experienced coach runs on two nights a week will be found helpful and invigorating.

WEIGHT TRAINING

Whereas a swimmer is ill-advised to do weight-lifting at the same time as his swimming training, many have undertaken weight-training with gratifying success.

The ideal situation is that the swimming instructor should also have a qualification in weight-training, because this is a highly-specialised subject.

For the swimmer who is going it alone there is a golden rule: Light weights and many repetitions. How light is a light weight? Well, from 30 to 60 pounds (15-30 kg. approx.). How many repetitions? From 15 to 30 movements in sets of five with a breathing pause between each set. Although some trainees may not need such frequent pauses it is well to start out with the pauses and cut them down if found to be unnecessary.

SUGGESTED SCHEDULE FOR WEIGHT TRAINING

(1) Warm up first with free exercises, stride jumping etc.
(2) Stand with feet slightly apart; bend forwards from the waist; grip the barbell with hands at shoulder distance. Lift the weight up to the shoulders by bending the arms, elbows pointing outward from the sides of the body. Lower by stretching the arms. Breathe in when lifting, breathe out when lowering the weight down to the floor by stretching the arms downwards again.
(3) Lie on back on a bench (put towel under shoulders of lifter). A partner hands the weight to the supine lifter who grips it with hands at shoulder width, lowering it backward behind the head, then returning it to position above the shoulders. The partner should stand ready to take the weight back.
(4) Stand with the feet well-balanced and apart. Place the barbell behind the neck, gripping it firmly with the hands roughly at shoulder distance apart. When well balanced bend the knees raising the heels slightly from the floor, breathe in on going down, and then breathe out coming up. Start with six repetitions, continue through 10 repetitions up to 20.
(5) Stand with the feet balanced. Bend the knees. Grip the barbell with the hands about eight inches apart (20 cm.). Lift the weight upward, bending the elbows outward, lift right up to the nose, then lower it again. 10-20 repetitions.
(6) Stand with the feet balanced. Hold the barbell down by the thighs, bend arms using biceps mainly to lift weight up to shoulders slowly; lower, then raise again. 10 repetitions.
(7) Lie supine on the floor. Support a light weight behind the back of the neck, holding with hands slightly outside shoulder width. Raise trunk by bending at the waist, then lower to the floor again.

(8) Stand with feet apart and well balanced. Weight suspended behind the neck, held with a grip slightly wider than the shoulders. Twist the waist to fullest turning power without moving feet from one side to another and without bending the body at all.

(9) Stand with feet wide apart and well balanced. Weight held behind the neck, gripped slightly wider than shoulder width. Bend the body down until trunk makes a right angle with the legs, then straighten slowly. Breathe in while coming up from the bend.

Time taken for these exercises indicates your fitness.

We can call the complete set of nine exercises a *lap*. The enthusiast should complete a lap easily within 15 minutes. In strict training two to three laps may be required by a coach during each training session, particularly in winter time. Generally speaking, two sessions per week are advisable. The swimmer is particularly warned not to get impatient if his coach does not allow him to handle bigger weights than those mentioned.

EXPANDER EXERCISES

Steel or rubber expanders are also useful for exercise, providing graded resistances according to how many strands you add to the set. These have the advantage of taking up little or no room at all (unlike weights), and can even be taken away in a suitcase or grip when travelling.

With all expanders on sale a chart is provided showing the exercises which promote activity and growth of certain muscle groups.

The author has used a set for many years in addition to weights and other exercises because they are convenient and portable.

Beginners are warned not to do the exercises with the total resistance until they have learnt to make the exercising movements correctly—this produces the best results.

PULSE TAKING, HEART RATE AND ENDURANCE

Both in Australia and in the United States a great number of experiments have taken place to check the influence of training on the pulse rate of the swimmer as a measure of heart efficiency, health and the endurance of the person tested.

The human heart is a miracle in its own class. The weight of the blood in the human body is about one-thirteenth of the total weight (if you weigh 13 stones your blood weighs one stone). The heart pumps this enormous weight on a complete circular tour of the body in less than half a minute—generally estimated to take 27 heartbeats. The heart is the strongest muscle in the body; it beats about 103,000 times a day, and if we count each lot of blood which passes through it as a separate measurement the total amount of blood the heart shifts in one day is 5,000 gallons.

A great deal of nonsense has been written about weak hearts. A person in bad condition physically has obvious difficulties in keeping the circulatory system healthy. Fitness is complete; one is either healthy or not healthy; if unhealthy all the parts are liable to suffer sooner or later. If you are only partly fit no one part of you is more than partly fit.

The heart, believe it or not, is extremely sensitive to the mental (particularly emotional) life of a person. Continued emotional stress frequently brings chemical changes in the body which induce circulatory troubles. Recent research has indicated that chronic anxiety and acute unhappiness may cause the bloodflow to leap up to double the normal rate. (Refer: Kelly, Royal Waterloo Hospital.)

The more vigorous the exercise the faster beats the pulse, and it is not alarming if after some supreme effort in swimming the pulse rate increases from twice to two and a half times the normal rate, provided that it returns to normal within three to four minutes. One of the techniques which any instructor can apply quite simply is to test the *rate of recovery* from maximum effort. The object of the exercise is to measure the endurance of the swimmer and prevent him swimming beyond limitation levels before he is in sufficient condition to attempt greater effort.

We can take a starting block or a chair etc. The swimmer is then asked to step up and down, using both feet, as fast as he can during one clocked minute, controlled with a stopwatch. Then his pulse is taken immediately at the end of the minute and taken again at 30-second intervals until it returns completely to the average beat which should be tested in the changing-room before the swimmer comes on to the bath side because even coming on to the side may cause some excitement and increase of pulsebeat.

The next step is to get the swimmer to swim a specific distance (50 or 100 yards) and take the pulse, noting down all the variations at 30-second intervals. As soon as the pulse rate registers average again the swimmer repeats the swim over the same distance. The usual procedure is to do this over three swims, and to take the average of the three for working purposes, but it is wise to keep detailed notes for each swimmer.

Clearly, the faster the recovery the better the condition of the swimmer being tested. The indication is that the lower the rate the more efficient the swimmer.

Let us say that the swimmer has registered at the end of a maximum effort swim a figure of 160 beats per minute on finishing the effort. Thirty seconds later that can drop to 140, a minute, later to 120 or 110. One and a half minutes later it can show a further reduction by 30 or 40 beats until normal rate is reached. Since all swimmers and athletes are highly individualised it is not to be expected that these suggested figures are anything but general outlines.

This method is of most value when used with very highly skilled and advanced swimmers.

I consider it unwise to establish any dogmatic pulse rate for all swimmers. The coach must make up his own tables for each swimmer he is testing, and repeat his tests at one month intervals.

The system is very popular with Controlled Interval Method training.

SWIMMING FOR THE PHYSICALLY HANDICAPPED

The greatest difficulty for the person who suffers from any physical handicap, e.g. spastic, paralysitic, spina bifida etc. comes from the trouble they have in achieving balance (as is described in the section on Balance and Buoyancy, page 83). The instructor who is helping them must bear in mind that any progress they can make on the surface, regardless of style, is of tremendous importance to them. It is often the greatest freedom they ever know because the water supports the poor twisted bodies and gives them a delightful feeling of motion without strain and without pain. In a word it is an occasion when the instructor should not be too critical, to relax. These cases need all the praise and encouragement they can get, and as little carping as possible.

The physically-handicapped person is subject to frustrations and exasperations which the normal human being does not fully comprehend. Persons who have had limbs amputated retain in their nervous system the feeling that the missing limb is still linked to them, and it is consequently difficult to feel that limb moving when the stump (particularly without an artificial limb) does not respond; such persons will often tell their instructor 'but I am trying to move my legs like you say.' Too much instruction, like too much physic, may do more harm than good. Swimming is essentially recreational for these people, let it stay that way.

Sufferers from poliomyelitis (infantile paralysis) are acutely aware of the difficulty in controlling the useless limb, which will float near the surface and is so often more hindrance than help. The instructor should tell this type of sufferer about some of the classic Japanese swimmers whose leg movements are almost *imperceptible*, and whose entire propulsion in the Front Crawl comes from their well-developed arms. I had among my friends Kennosuke Koyama, a champion from Tokyo, a gentle, charming and most cultured man, who was in the days when I used to swim with him as fast as greased lightning in the Front Crawl stroke. I can honestly say that he swam with less leg movement than I have ever seen before or since, but the speed and the power of his arms was incredible—it can be done.

Whereas an average swimmer may need one plastic or inflated float, the physically-handicapped person may need two or even four. Let the novice have as many as he thinks are necessary to establish buoyancy. The use of inflated armbands will depend upon the mental reaction of the individual learner. Two yards swum alone opens up a new vista of enjoyment and physical achievement to the handicapped person, and once the first width has been swum there is usually no holding them back. Their need and enthusiasm is such that I have personally found them much quicker at absorbing instruction that the average person who has other outlets for his physical energy.

In the case of a person with only one arm explain the way in which the paddlers of the Red Indian birchbark canoes could steer their craft by paddling *on one side only*, by using a stroke like a J (put the arm in, pull, then curl it round in a motion like the curling of the capital J); it is appropriate to their own steering problem. I do not favour the idea of one teacher to every handicapped pupil; this does not allow him to hide his embarrassment; the handicapped learner doesn't want to feel a fool, and still less look like one. Would you enjoy being watched all the time you were practising something simple and continually getting it wrong?

Never show off in front of the physically-handicapped learner, however well you can swim. Your own brilliance (if you teach you *ought* to be good) may make them wistful and lessen their own achievement; if you demonstrate, do it gently, *modestly* and well. The phyisically-handcapped person who has stumpy limbs will often work out some extremely unorthodox movements which are mechanically sound for the propulsion and directional guidance of his body. Never correct such attempts until you are quite sure that they don't work efficiently.

In the case of handicapped children special sports events and galas are arranged by their schools which enable them to compete within their own class; there are very inspiring and some very remarkable results are forthcoming every year.

SWIMMING FOR THE DEAF AND DUMB

Most deaf people learn to lip read, and provided you speak in a normally-pitched voice but move your lips slowly they will understand you. I specifically learned the Deaf and Dumb finger alphabet to facilitate teaching.

One boy, Tony, achieved a one-and-a-half forward somersault from the five metre divingboard before he was 11. He was able to interpret my fingered instructions while on the board, whereas owing to the usual noise of the swimming pool a child with hearing would never have heard last-minute instructions shouted! The boy was an exceptionally good swimmer in Dolphin and Front Crawl. Remember that the deaf and dumb are by no means mentally deficient; far from it; they are often unusually sharp, and love swimming. The Royal Association for the Deaf and Dumb issues a number of very good booklets which help us communicate with these pupils.

Some of the children within this category have an understandable complex about their ears, and may show fear when they first go into the water and find it entering their ears. The gratitude of these children is frequently disconcerting, but try to give them the affection they need; they cannot hear kind words, they miss soft tones of the voice, they only feel affection and give it by clutching your hands, or hugging you; putting your arm round their wet shoulders will congratulate them better than all the spoken praise in the world.

The usual techniques of entering the water, armbands and floats can be employed; initial progress is fairly good, many learning faster than unhandicapped pupils.

TEACHING THE BLIND TO SWIM
Jim Essex of the Islington S.C. was the most successful teacher of the blind I ever met, and I pay tribute to his talent, his patience and his genius. He got blind persons not only to swim but to race, and coached several into passing the higher awards of the Royal Life Saving Society. Jim, and all like him, open up a new and wonderful world for people without sight.

Since the sight is not there avoid the words 'you see' when training them; do not describe the movements in abstraction —you must go into the water and show them patiently by touch, by guided movements and by frequent repetitions. When they are swimming train them to move to the left if the teacher blows the whistle once, and to the right if the whistle is blown twice—they are very quick to modify their direction, and can be trained to race with sighted persons (and sometimes win!). Try to avoid the blind pupil being in a position where he or she can crash into the steps or the bath rail.

The balance and poise of blind swimmers usually leaves something to be desired: the blind do not like to immerse their ears in the water because their main link with all communications is through their hearing—concentrate with them on the Breast Stroke, primarily at any rate.

SWIMMING FOR THE EDUCATIONALLY SUBNORMAL (ESN)

I wrote a paper on '*The Development of the Educationally Subnormal Child*', and have some valuable experience in teaching swimming to E.S.N. children. Swimming is physically recreative and psychologically therapeutical for the educationally subnormal. Although their intelligence often is low these children can be charming and affectionate. It is essential to remember their names just as an actor learns his lines: his own name is the most sacred possession of any child. I can remember several hundred names, and the trick is to use the name (and get accustomed to that name with the face of its owner) as much as possible when you first meet. I have coached E.S.N. children through the A.S.A. survival tests—and trained some to swim half a mile or more (without stopping) which has contributed in no small way to their development; several graduated to normal schools.

The *secret* is that nothing succeeds like success, and the E.S.N. child is in more desperate need of success than almost any other child of similar age. Such children have for many years been treated by exasperated parents, teachers and acquaintances as ninnies and noodles: the discovery that they can actually learn to do something and get it right is the first and most significant step on a slow road to normalisation. The reader who is familiar with my writings on psychology will know that I maintain that Mind can overcome Matter, therefore no mental aberration is incapable of improvement. The E.S.N. child has usually considerable ability as a mimic, and all the movements of the stroke which is being taught should be made slowly and very distinctly, and taught with as much humour as the teacher is capable of. I advise the teacher to make the entire lesson as much like a game as possible.

Do not try to teach the E.S.N. unless you have abnormal patience, they can be excessively slow to learn and unusually quick to forget. Never get angry with an E.S.N. child; he doesn't usually know why you are angry; and even if the event is only a few minutes old the ability to concentrate on one subject is often so low that by the time you get him out of the water he may have only a vague recollection of what he has done. On one awful occasion I discovered an E.S.N. boy *holding another of his class under water, hands tightly clasped round his victim's throat*. I reached him with a safety pole, tapped him on the shoulder, he let go and came out, slowly enough. He at once denied what he had been doing (perhaps he will grow up to be a politician?) in spite of all who had seen it. Very gently I pushed him on to his knees, placed my hands round his throat as gently as I could. 'N . . .' I said, 'If you ever do this to a boy or girl and hold them under water, I will never let you come swimming again'. A sudden look of understanding came into the boy's eyes. He smiled, 'O.K., Sir,' he agreed, 'I won't,'—and to give him his due he never did. This brings two more points for consideration.

(i) The E.S.N. child may sometimes learn with rapidity. When this happens *praise the*m as if they were fresh from the Olympics with laurel wreathes in their hands; they are so used to being blamed and scolded that a little praise goes a long way to encouraging them and the others. (ii) Concentration for the E.S.N. is a terrible strain, so never make any theme in the lesson a long one; if you would normally ask a child to practise some skill over six widths of a bath, you may find that two or four are as much as the E.S.N. can accomplish in the first year without forgetting what it is all about. Never make instructions complicated; do not give them a long chat about any point; keep all instructions simple, and short—as if you were writing an expensive telegram!

If an E.S.N. child wants to work with one or more particular friends let him, because then if he is naughty you have an effective weapon to encourage him to be good, and together the friends will usually have more confidence. As regards class management, it is usually assumed that one

E.S.N. child is as much work as four average children. If a child is known to have epileptic seizures try to prevent any undue excitement, and if possible keep him near the bathside, or at least swimming near an older and responsible child. I know of few children who can sense your inner feelings and mood so much from the slightest inflection of your voice (which in itself is an indication that the Gall and Spurzhem statement that nobody is ever *wholly* unbalanced is true).

Try to ensure that the E.S.N. child finds the bath a friendly place but understands the dangers of deep water. At first the E.S.N. pupil may show (a) excessive fear of the water (b) complete lack of fear and foresight. One little boy on beholding the water fell so much in love with it that he spent every moment trying to jump in—before he could swim a stroke. Whatever the danger the instructor must keep a calm voice and speak sharply only when there is actual danger.

The E.S.N. child is often a terrible show-off in success, and the instructor is advised usually to let the successful ones gratify this wish (however dubious the ethic). *Success is quite infectious.* The reaction is so often: 'If he can do that so can I' springing from jealousy as often as from a wholesome desire to emulate, and the efforts which are made are often rewarding. I once had two boys who fought in the changing rooms and fought on the pool side at every lesson; by directing their rivalry and energies into racing I was able to make both of them very good swimmers, and into very firm friends. Both of these boys later graduated to normal schools but not before winning several events at special swimming galas for E.S.N. children.

Remember: It's all done by kindness—my motto.

Don't teach E.S.N. children unless your love and patience exceed your sense of discipline and desire for success. Some E.S.N. children show excessive precocity and lack of all inhibition in sexual display. Tact is needed to avoid offending members of the public who may be at the bath, and also avoiding disgracing the child.

Some 'mongol' children are so intense in their affectionate regard for the teacher they do not listen to his instructions well. All E.S.N. children have to be chivvied a bit when they are supposed to be drying, and care must be taken to ensure that they dress properly and remember to put on *all* their clothing; most baths get littered with articles of clothing that children (even some normal children forget) have failed to remember to put on . . . One boy even forgot his trousers, I will never know how he got home. It is not really the instructor's job to supervise dressing . . . thank heavens!

Always insist that every E.S.N. child goes to urinate before entering a swimming pool, many of them have inadequate bladder control.

In my writings on 'Nutrition of the Brain and Nervous System', 'Diet as a Factor in Improved Cerebral Functioning' etc. I have dealt with the dietetic and botanic-medical help which can be given to sufferers. Other papers of mine include 'Treatment of Diseases of the Nervous System' and 'Mind and Brain in Hypnotherapeutics' which is concerned more with the psychological angle.

The pleasure of knowing that one has helped an E.S.N. child to attain normality or near-normality is ample reward for all the efforts involved.

SWIMMING AS A FORM OF THERAPEUTICS

One of the basic problems of massage is to provide exercise and an invigorating blood supply to damaged limbs and internal organs without placing undue strain upon them. The use of the water as a more gentle medium in which to effect this was known to the Ancient Greek physicians, and has in recent years been explored and used for this purpose by that genius of the swimming world—Reg Brickett.

When I was studying at the National School of Swimming we had patients sent by Harley Street specialists for remedial exercises. The help which Reg's methods brought them was increasingly visible as the weeks went by. In a short time the victims of accidents etc. gained in strength; many recovered complete use of their limbs and perfect health without any discomfort at all—the water is so gentle.

Many years ago I broke an ankle as the result of an accident in an acrobatic trick. I was in plaster for several months following two operations. When the doctor removed the plaster, I asked him: 'When can I go swimming?' He shook his head sadly, 'Ask me again in two months,' he said. I didn't, the weather was hot, it was summer. With the aid of two very good friends Karlheinz Wettengel (German) and Matti Piekkari (Finnish) three days later I got down to the baths on crutches and was gently lowered into the water with their help and the aid of a bath attendant—I could swim! I could still swim! The psychological stimulus was more valuable than the gentle physical exercise. Within seven days I could swim 400 metres; a month later I swam a whole mile without halt. I asked the doctor whether I could go swimming. He said he would think about it. My leg was mending fast. I still needed a stick to walk with, but I could swim. The foot healed up very well.

As regards the use of swimming in this field I must emphasise that it is highly specialised work, and must not be lightly undertaken as a form of therapeutics without the advice of a doctor. In my own case, with a famous masseur for a father, I had professional advice; I had been a swimmer for years, and was quite prepared to risk anything to get back into the water.

Usually, moderate exercise is very good for recuperating the human body.

With regard to ailments such as indigestion, constipation, poor circulation, nervous headaches and a host of similar ills, swimming is extremely therapeutic, but following bone breakages and operations care should be taken not to strain the physical or mental capacity of the patient.

Never encourage an invalid beyond the bounds of his endurance, and make sure you *know* what that means for the individual. The more anatomy and physiology you know the better if you intend going in for this aspect of swimming teaching.

HYGIENE: SPEEDY-REFERENCE SECTION

(1) Be responsible and socially conscious, be clean and free from infection before you go into a public bath.
(2) A good shower in warm or hot water should be taken by everybody before they enter a swimming pool.

Where possible, soap should be used, and the suds ought to be washed off before swim trunks or costume is put on.

(3) Never neglect to clean and dry your feet—precautions against athlete's foot and verruca, and treatment for these conditions.

(4) Remember to take care of your eyes. Don't rush to complain about the chlorine; it is usually properly controlled and kept at standardised levels—check your own health first.

(5) Dry your hair first—not last.

(6) A few physical jerks at the end of the swim.

(7) Towels and how to use them.

(8) General notes.

HYGIENE—START BY PLAYING FAIR

Some people are quick to notice the hygiene of others in the swimming bath, but a little less conscious of their own. Let us remember that no matter how we cover our feet with shoes and socks the dust of the streets penetrates them and our feet can easily become coated with a thin, almost invisible film of dirt—which has no place in a swimming pool.

This is why every swim hall has a special foot bath and why every visitor to the baths should use it to scrub the feet —not just stroll through it like an absent-minded duck on her way to the river.

Every user of the baths should use the toilets *before* the shower and not afterwards. Children frequently find that the cold water stimulates the bladder to action. The slightest motion by a child's hand which indicates it wants to get out and go to the toilet should be dealt with at once to avoid involuntary micturation in the water of the bath. The chlorine content of the bath destroys urine, but nevertheless this loss of control can be avoided by intelligent forethought.

Some baths in England do not provide big enough shower baths and consequently prohibit the use of soap in case the soapsuds overflow and get into the swimming pool itself. In Germany and Switzerland, on the contrary, a proper shower with soap is insisted upon, but in both countries the showers are large enough to permit rinsing off.

E

To ensure complete hygiene of the body all showers should be taken before the costume is put on—privacy permitting. Costumes should be rinsed out after each swim—in clean water (not in the foot bath). Some materials need soap or detergent and others need only water. As soon as possible the costume should be hung up to dry in fresh air. Regular swimmers are advised to have two or three costumes, to ensure that their costumes can dry out before being used again—continual use without proper drying wears out a costume very quickly.

Yes, a word about the choice of costume. For men the side of the costume from waist downwards at the thigh should not be longer than four inches (ten centimetres); this ensures free and easy movement of the legs—if it is *fashionable* rather than practical you can hinder your leg movements, because some manufacturers (clearly not swimmers themselves) often make what professionals call *play* costumes, the wearing of which marks one out immediately as not being a *real swimmer*. This is the chief consideration in the buying of any swimming costume for men, women or children—it must be *functional*. A well known international champion may wear something eyecatching (but will rarely practise in it).

If you wear glasses never, never wear them in the water. I have seen two accidents happen because the rule was not followed. Extracting glass from a cut eye is a job for a surgeon.

FEET

My father, T. J. H. N. Law, established an unrivalled reputation as masseur and chiropodist. I am indebted to him for the following details about the care of the feet.

When a foot is kept for a long time in water it loses, at least temporarily, its natural quality of waterproofing (inherent in everybody's skin) and it also becomes more sensitive to the heat-absorbing properties of water, so that beginners especially may get *cold feet* in the physical sense as well, perhaps, as in the psychological.

Frequent or prolonged swimming tends to wear away the

protective body product called *Keratin*, a nitrogenous compound. If this is noticed attention must be given to diet. When we speak of people being in the water a long time, well, for how long is long? Racing swimmers are often in the water for two to four hours a day, having training sessions of about an hour each spread out over the whole day. But these champions and aspirants are often so well-guided on diet that they suffer less than the novice who has no guidance. One golden rule about the human body is that you cannot take out of it in fuel what you don't feed it. A German farmer once put it to me this way: 'You don't get milk out of a cow unless you give it fodder.'

The first rule is *take care to dry between the toes* every time you swim, and as soon as each foot is dry stand it upon a towel until you put on socks and shoes.

If you notice that the flesh between the toes is getting soggy and broken you are advised to wash them with *Eau de Cologne* and then sprinkle some antiseptic powder between them. Most chemists stock such powders especially for this purpose. The reason why you must act on the appearance of this symptom is that when the skin is broken germs may get in causing pain and serious infections. Broken skin makes the contagion of verruca and of mycotic diseases, such as athlete's foot, much easier to contract. The first sympton of athlete's foot is a persistent itching which seems to defy all the efforts of soap and water; it should be dealt with quickly by the application of special cream and powder manufactured by various pharmaceutical companies for this purpose. Never wear any pair of socks without changing them frequently, and should athlete's foot develop remember to dust every pair of socks with the powder before you put them on. To prevent the contagion spreading please stay away from the bath until it is cured and your skin is healed—this should not take long, and if you should be re-infected whilst you were there you would be irritated by it maybe for weeks instead of days.

Verruca is, of course, more serious. A verruca is a wart, but whereas some warts grow visibly outwards the verruca tends to grow inwards, and the symptoms first noticed are sheer discomfort when the part of the foot affected has weight placed upon it, and a sensation as if a needle had been pushed into the flesh. The verruca is contagious and must be attended to. Many neglected warts may turn into malignant growths in old age if not dealt with properly.

As a general rule the verruca develops only in people whose health is in a slightly run-down condition. The first thing to do when you notice a verruca is to get yourself a tonic. It is common for young swimmers to work very hard at their sport but to neglect their diet, so that they are putting out more and more energy but simply not taking in enough mineral salts, protein and vitamins to re-stoke the 'fires' from which their energy comes.

There are a large number of substances such as caustic potash, nitric acid, or carbon dioxide 'snow' which cauterise warts, but I have found that some of the herbal wart-removing substances (which have been used for centuries) are the speediest and most effective. I especially remember L . . . a really brilliant girl, the hope and pride of her racing team, coming to me one day and saying: 'Oh, Mr. Law, I've got a verruca, I'll not be able to race next month.' Although not on an international scale, the race meant a lot to her and to the club. I recommended her to try a herbal preparation made by a friend of mine in the London Elephant and Castle district. Within a week L's wart had completely gone, healed as clean as a new pin. She swam in the big race, and won her event. Verrucas, like all warts, should be kept away from moist conditions; and should be kept covered up before and during treatment. If you have a verruca remember to disinfect all shoes and socks or stockings to prevent re-infecting yourself after it is cured. Under no circumstances be selfish enough to visit the pool until your condition is cured.

Somewhat more rare is the condition known as moluscum contagionum, which produces watery-looking warts. Tonics, attention to diet, and intense care of towels and personal hygiene is needed, an anti-mycotic ointment usually clears the condition.

If at any time you see a person in the baths with a recognisable skin ailment ask the attendant on duty to investigate— or call the baths Manager.

If you wear sandals or some form of bath shoes do remember to use some antiseptic power to dust them out at regular intervals.

EYES

A lot of beginners complain of the chlorine content of the water of a swimming pool. The reaction is invariably a personal one because the rules of chlorination are standardised, and the chemical content of the water is regularly checked, usually more than once a day!

The cause is the irritation of the protective film over the surface of the eye. Due to being in contact with a hitherto unaccustomed substance it is liable to irritation, more or less depending upon the health of the person involved.

Occasionally, at some seaside resorts the chlorine is put into salt water instead of fresh (because the local authority finds it cheaper to use sea water), and the effects of this are often much more intense than those of chlorine in fresh water. No irritation of the eye should ever be neglected under any circumstances whatever. The slightest itch, the slightest soreness, means that you should stop everything to wash the eye. I recommend to all people the use of a small eyebath, a cup kept for the eyes alone (on sale at most chemists for a few pence). Every morning and every night bathe both eyes with a separate filling of water, preferably just plain water, and try not to wipe your eyes with a cloth towel—it can easily contain more irritants than you have just wiped out of your eyes!

If the eyes turn red and stay red for more than an hour after a swim your health is not quite up to scratch (however hearty you may feel); increase your Vitamin A and D intake with halibut or cod liver oil capsules, and rest the eyes from swimming for a few days. If you work under bad lighting you may have, unawares, a poor occular health which the swimming accentuates. The condition known as conjuctivitis (inflammation of the modified epidermis (skin) covering the cornea) is closely linked to catarrh.

Personally, I look askance on some of the high-faluting preparations which are available to help professional swimmers. I prefer to recommend application of a little castor oil to the surfaces of the eye before entering the water (don't wash it out in the shower) and in the event of conjunctivitis developing some of the simple herbal preparations such as Eyebright (*Euphrasia Officinalis*) and Golden Seal (*Hydrastis Canadensis*) mixed together are as safe and good an eye lotion (for external application) as you can find. Once in an emergency, when suffering badly after a demonstration of swimming in a bath using chlorine and sea water I used the oil from a crushed halibut liver oil capsule; it brought speedy relief, but I do not recommend it as standard procedure.

Never rub the eyes with your fingers. If the itching in the eye irritates you excessively *close the eye first*, then place the palm of your hand over the closed eye and massage in a gently circular motion once or twice. As soon as possible wash the eye with water using an eyebath. Alcohol consumption increases eye sensitivity to chlorine.

Racing swimmers cannot wear goggles, but those exploring under the water usually do. Some baths object to their use.

As a matter of hygiene never lend your goggles to somebody else unless you wash them thoroughly afterwards, and remember to dry the water off them—a suitable pair of goggles is fairly expensive, and of little use if the rubber is allowed to perish by neglect. When dry keep in a polythene bag to prevent dust accumulating on them; the dust gets in your eyes and may become so thick that a cursory swill round under a tap may not remove it all, thus also obscuring your vision.

EARS

Comparatively few people experience any discomfort in the ear from swimming, but for those who do a number of earplugs are on the market. I usually recommend lamb's wool or cotton wool with some grease on it.

NOSE

If you get water up your nose you are breathing wrongly. See the section of this book dealing with breathing.

HAIR

I have written a complete book on the care of the hair; it is entitled '*How to Keep Your Hair On*' and the reader will clearly not expect that I can do more than briefly mention some of the most useful tips which apply to swimmers.

Firstly, always wash the chlorine out of your hair, always. If you do not take this simple precaution you will find that your hair will suffer for it.

Secondly, almost all diseases of the scalp, and loss of hair, have their origin not in one simple thing but in a general rundown of health. Hair grows inside the body, not just on top of it—what we actually see is hair which has grown so long that it has pushed right up through the skin's ducts and emerged.

Thirdly, do not plaster your hair down all the time with this or that messy, greasy lotion (however good the adverts look). Too much grease may choke your hair cells to death. Fourthly, try to dry your hair first, and not after you have used the towel to dry your feet. Sorry to say that, but I have seen so many boys and young men do just that, absent-mindedly while they are busy swapping yarns with their pals.

Fifthly, if you hair loses its natural sheen, it is in need of attention, and the changes are that the cause lies in your diet. Many budding swimmers who should have reached at least a club championship ruined their opportunity by eating white bread sandwiches when they should have been eating cheese, apples, figs, dates, nuts and honey (since these are the real nutritional foods you actually need to eat less of them than you do of foods which contain little or no real nutritional elements, so it is *not* more expensive).

EXERCISE

In another section of this book, page ooo, I have listed some recommended exercises. If you have time to do a short round of physical jerks before you dry yourself, I recommend you to do it. I usually spend about three minutes in some simple and rapid exercises before I go to dry myself.

TOWELS

In modern baths the towels are nearly always rigorously cleaned, subject to officially approved hygiene laws, and it is better to have a clean and sterilised towel or two than to use one every day of the week when you swim (or however often you swim during the week). A towel is safest when used once only for drying your body after a swim. Use it more to massage your limbs than to soak off the wet drops adhering to your skin, which moisture you should flick off with your hands!

GENERAL RULES OF CONDUCT IN A SWIMMING POOL

1. Do nothing to spoil the enjoyment of others enjoying their swim.
2. Make allowance for the inexperienced and beginners; do not get in their way, they may not be able to save themselves!
3. Never jump into the water without ascertaining that it is clear.
4. Never indulge in horseplay or wrestling on the side of the pool; pools have stone floors; these are hard and dangerous if you fall; the water on them makes them slippery.
5. Don't run on the pool side; you may knock somebody over and seriously injure them.
6. If you talk to the attendants stand at one side to avoid blocking their view of the pool they have to watch.
7. In the event of an accident do not crowd round unless you know you have the skill to help.
8. Don't go in the water to save somebody who is in danger of drowning unless you have been properly taught how to save life and how to give artificial respiration.
9. Keep well clear of the diving boards when somebody is diving. If they dive on you both parties will be seriously injured—and maybe killed.
10. Do not wear a watch while you are swimming; even if it is waterproof, it could catch somebody in the eye and seriously injure them.
11. Never wear glasses when swimming.

12　If you want to use a ball, flippers, snorkel or any similar apparatus, ask the attendant first. *The pool attendants are there every day. They not only know the conditions of the pool, they know the swimmers present, and they know whether any harm could come of the use of some equipment.* Usually they will say 'yes' but remember they will never say 'no' without good reason. I know several pools where the attendants address about 75 per cent of the visitors by name (often on first name terms too). The pool attendant is there to be your friend—treat him like one.

13　Never wear outdoor shoes on the side of the pool; you could bring infection on to the pool side. All baths personnel change their shoes for the poolside.

14　Never expectorate or blow your nose in the water; well, I know my readers wouldn't, but just see that the children don't.

15　Never carry a glass or bottle on to the pool side. Broken glass can cause terrible accidents—it is invisible if it gets into the water.

16　If you use a training float, do not leave it on the side for somebody to fall over, and do not let it drift unattended on the pool. Never throw a float; you can easily knock a swimmer out if you hit him with it.

17　Do not swallow under water, it may upset your ears.

18　*If you use ear plugs* (simple cotton wool or lambs wool is best) do not leave them floating in the pool.

19　Never eat or drink one hour before going into a pool.

20　Ladies should carefully remove all make-up before entering the water, in the interests of hygiene.

21　A swimming pool is a very happy place, keep it that way.

DIETETIC ADVICE FOR THE SWIMMER

It must be understood that good health is the result of a number of factors and not of one single magic cause. Nevertheless, the human body's efficiency is in direct ratio to the quantity of the *fuel* with which it is provided. Quantity of food is never a substitute for quality and even quality is of little value unless the right quantity for the individual is provided, although you will get better results from small quantities of properly balanced foods than from large amounts of poor quality fodder.

The food required by the body varies in accordance with the amount of exercise (expenditure of energy) which is undertaken. If any athlete continues to eat exactly the same quantity of food when he is not in training (or has given it up) as he does when working hard at his sport he will find that he tends to put on weight and get fat.

Feeding does not guarantee that the eater absorbs and makes use of the food consumed. A high protein diet needs an increase in the Vitamin C consumed; a high carbohydrate diet needs correspondingly more Vitamin B; but if there is a Calcium deficiency the Vitamin C will not be fully absorbed, and if there is a heavy consumption of alcohol the Vitamin B will be negated.

The first rule for the swimmer is to avoid as many patent pills and tablets as possible, to absorb as many as possible of his vitamins and mineral salts from simple, natural and healthy foods.

Many books have been written on dietetic theory and practice; this chapter sets out to simplify the general rules as much as possible for quick reference, consequently the scientific reasons for many of the suggestions must be omitted. Foods are divided into Proteins, Carbohydrates, Fats, Mineral Salts etc. I shall start by describing briefly what these mean.

Proteins

These are essential to build healthy, effective muscles, repair and service blood, glands and most bodily tissues. Some 22 amino-acids are found in nearly all forms of protein food; of these, eight are vital to the maintenance of human life. The body seldom has excess of protein, for it can convert unwanted protein into carbohydrates by a series of wonderful chemical changes. Any athlete in daily training needs at least 100 grams of protein food a day. When protein food is eaten it is broken down into components which can be converted into enzymes, hormones, tissues and almost anything the body needs.

Meat, fish and eggs are the best protein foods.

Nuts, soyabeans (and flour) and wheatgerm are excellent vegetable proteins.

Protein needs a good acid medium to facilitate absorption. If any protein is subjected to high degrees of heat it loses much of its natural nutritional value. Avoid roasted, baked and fried proteins as much as is practical.

Cheese, corned beef, soya-flour, peanuts, fish, beef, mutton, eggs and milk have very good content of protein in grams per ounce.

I mentioned amino-acids; some years ago a scientist coined the phrase VITal-AMINo-acids, this wording was far too long for ordinary use and it was shortened to Vitamins.

Here is a brief list of the principal vitamins with details of their working, and explaining what use they can be to the swimmer.

A   This vitamin is needed for the healthy structure of bones, for youthful elasticity, health of the eyes, for efficiency of digestive, excretory and respiratory systems (and because of this for the health of the skin).

    Scientists indicate that accident-prone subjects may be suffering from acute deficiency of Vit. A because lack of this substance slows down our reactions.

    It is found in halibut liver oil, cod liver oil, ox liver and in watercress, apricots (dried), carrots and butter.

B   This is not one simple vitamin but a whole complex of related vitamins. The efficiency of the nervous system, intestinal tract, blood-formation, defective vision (Vit. B^{12}), carbohydrate mechanism, insomnia, chronic constipation, diabetes, hair falling, weakness, throat troubles and so on are all linked with the sufficiency or deficiency of the Vit. B complex. Many heart conditions are linked with Vit. B deficiency. Brewer's yeast, yoghurt, black molasses, wheat-germ, liver and skimmed milk are rich sources of the B complex.

C   This is essential for the health of our connective tissues, for health of gums, teeth, glandular organs and muscles.

The body does not store this vitamin so that an intake is needed fresh every day; up to 400 mg. is advisable for swimmers in training for racing or other strenuous forms of sport.

Cigarette and industrial smoke consumes Vitamin from our body at an alarming rate. The more protein you eat the more C you need. The vitamin is found in citrus fruit, watercress, tomatoes, blackcurrants, rose-hips, paprika etc.

D   For the proper use of the essential mineral salts calcium and phosphorous an adequate supply of Vit. D is required. A deficiency of it causes unhealthy heart action and nervous instability, and leads to pronounced muscular weakness. No swimmer can afford to be without Vit. D.

When you are at the seaside do not hurry to get brown (never use skin dyes either) which means that your skin cannot absorb more natural Vitamin D from the rays of the sun. It is found in eggs, butter, milk, most fish livers, especially halibut liver oil.

E   This valuable vitamin enables us to keep our blood pressure healthy, maintain heart, lungs, liver and muscles in good working condition. Lack of Vit. E threatens our natural fertility, and robs the body of efficient oxygenation processes. Nobody should take large doses of this vitamin suddenly, but should begin by taking small amounts. Research has shown that Vit. E is most helpful for the combating of asthma, diabetes, thrombosis and many other illnesses.

It is found in wheatgerm and wheatgerm oil, sunflower seeds, eggs, lettuce and many other forms of salad food.

The above is a list of the most essential vitamins: there are others, but they are more complicated.

Carbohydrates

These are the main sources of energy, they can be converted into fats, and stored as such, but they cannot substitute for proteins. The Carbohydrates consist of Sugars, Starches and Fats.

Sugars. These are pleasant tasting, soluble in liquids and in the form of white sugar, vastly over-used. Swimmers should take their sweetness from brown sugar, only this contains any real nutritional value, otherwise pure honey or black molasses should be used. What manufacturers often refer to as 'refining' may mean that every nutritional element has been *refined* out of a product (and then sold back to you in pills). Avoid white sugar and cakes and biscuits and sweets containing it.

Starches. Heavy preponderance of starches in the diet leads to indigestion, constipation, various skin troubles and many inflammations. The starches are often the cheapest forms of food available, and while, especially after muscular effort plenty of starch is needed *it should be eaten alone, never eaten at the same time as protein foods because this lessens the nutrition your body can get from either type of food*.

Unripe fruit contains more starch than does ripe fruit. For long-distance swimming (across the Channel etc.) a fairly-high carbohydrate diet is essential, and a somewhat fatter development of the physique is most likely to result.

Fats

Fat is the most compact form of carbohydrate and has a very high concentrated fuel power for providing energy. As against this it is less easily digested, and a diet rich in fats may increase the tendency to cardiac and digestive complaints. There are two kinds of fats—the *Unsaturated Fatty Acids* which are safe, and the dangerous Saturated Fatty Acids which destroy many of the vitamins in our bodies. Olive oil, wheatgerm oil, corn oil, cottonseed oil, sunflower oil and linseed oil are the best sources of UFAs. Lack of UFAs impoverishes the nervous system. Halibut liver oil is also a safe source. Frying destroys most of the virtues of UFAs and many vitamins. Frying, particularly in aluminium ware is very dangerous; see, 'Aluminium, a menace to health' by M. Clement.

Many cases of duodenal ulcer own their origin to deficiency of UFAs.

White Bread and white flour are particularly nutrition-poor foods; most of their natural virtues, vitamins etc. having been extracted or damaged by chemical processes of bleaching etc. In *'How to Keep Your Hair On'* I have shown that the use of white bread is in many cases harmful to health. Bread is naturally brown or a dull, stone colour; I always eat bread as rough as possible, and the darker it is the more I like it. Racing swimmers should stick to brown bread and if they can get full-corn wholemeal they will feel better for it. The following foods are rich in Carbohydrates: sugar, bread, oatmeal, jam, raisins, dates, bananas, potatoes, baked beans, most root vegetables (beetroots, carrots, parsnips etc.).

Mineral Salts

This is one of the most interesting elements of nutrition; without a proper supply of salts our entire body chemistry can grind to a halt and produce shocking results.

Something in the number of 40 different mineral salts are traceable in the chemical constitution of the human body. Some of them such as cobalt, chromium, gallium, germanium and nickel are present in microscopic quantities, but if this almost insignficant presence is deficient serious results follow, and the health declines. Many of the mineral salts are found in one of the other groups of classified foods (cobalt is found in Vit. B^{12}), but because they are of such interest I am listing some here so that the swimmer can check against the list any weakness or symptoms of poor performance and alter his diet accordingly.

Calcium. Speeds up recovery from injury and illnesses; essential for the health of the bones (especially teeth); promotes healthy heart action. Tetanus seems to occur most in persons with very low calcium level in the blood.

Chocolate destroys calcium. Swimmers should either give up chocolate (and foods containing it) or cut down their intake to the lowest possible level. Records indicate that the generations born in the last 30 years appear to have less calcium than earlier generations.

Calcium foods lose about 25 per cent of their mineral salt if they are cooked.

Almonds, cauliflower, cheese, eggs, figs, milk, oranges and yoghurt are very rich in calcium. So are many herbs.

Sleeplessness is often due to calcium deficiency so do not take pills or tablets, if due to excitement and exhaustion you cannot sleep—take a large spoonful of honey in warm (but not boiled) milk; these foods are rich in calcium.

Iodine. This mineral salt is not to be confused with the brown medicinal substance you buy in bottles from the chemist. This is a natural mineral salt which has irreplacable value as a regulator in glandular efficiency. The blood cells that destroy and eat up tiny organisms which invade our bodies need iodine to function efficiently. Iodine is very valuable as a factor which stimulates the natural tranquillisation of the body. Obesity is often due to lack of iodine.

Artichokes, asparagus, bananas, cabbage, carrots, lettuce, melons, mushrooms, onions, oysters, rhubarb and watercress all contain iodine.

Iron. Without iron the blood simply does not transport oxygen properly, and the nerves and the muscles are the first to suffer. Coldness in fingers and toes, flabby skin, bad muscle tone, muscular weakness and poor performance are symptomatic of iron deficiency.

Never take iron by tablet form if you can get it from natural food sources which are more easily absorbed and will not induce constipation as some tablets do.

Barley, brown rice, dates, eggs, figs (dried), lentils, molasses, oats, olives, prunes, rye and wheatgerm contain iron.

There is plenty of iron in meat, but for some reason the body does not seem to absorb this as quickly as it does the iron in fruits and vegetables etc.

Phosphorous. Without phosphorous, brain, lung and nerve tissue degenerates and this is the quick way to lose performance. Without regular supplies of phosphorous the life and correct structure of the body cells is damaged.

Phosphorous makes for speedy repairs of body tissues and muscular growth.

This extremely valuable food element is found in the following: almonds, brown rice, cheese, eggs, fish, fruit, kidneys, lentils, liver, milk, peanuts, radishes, salmon, shrimps, watercress and wheatgerm.

Potassium. For flexible muscles which respond to nerve impulses and carry out the instruction with lightning speed you must have plenty of potassium.

Catarrh and constipation, two enemies of swimmers, are symptomatic of potassium deficiency.

From 50 to 70 per cent potassium is lost when potassium-containing foods are cooked.

Bacon, blackberries, carrots, coconuts, cod, figs, fruit of most kinds, lentils, peas, pumpkins, tomatoes and turnips are among the best sources of potassium.

Silica. It is one of the most important of substances, a natural antiseptic. Without it, exhaustion and nervous inefficiency can easily set in.

Some forms of baldness (see '*How to Keep Your Hair On*') and skin diseases, arteriosclerosis and many forms of rheumatism are connected with serious silica deficiencies.

Some of the foods which are rich in silica are asparagus, barley, cabbage, celery, cucumber, figs, leeks, lettuce, milk, oats, radishes, spinach, sunflower seeds, strawberries, tomatoes and turnips.

Sulphur. It is a powerful cleansing substance but it consumes oxygen. It resists most forms of bacteria and is useful in speeding up protein metabolism which is important for the swimmer.

Cabbage, carrots, cauliflower, cheese, coconuts, cucumber, egg-yolk, figs, garlic, horseradish, molasses, oranges, potatoes, pineapple, radishes, red currants and many herbs contain sulphur.

Zinc. Efficient muscular control is related to the level of zinc in the body. It facilitates respiration of the tissues.

It is found in beans, egg-yolk, greenleaf vegetables, legumes, nuts, peas and seeds. If you take wheatgerm you will get an adequate supply of zinc.

Health is conditioned considerably by nutrition. What we eat determines the rates of recovery, repair and the production of energy. I counsel swimmers to consider the actual content of foods rather than actual number of *calories* consumed. Many people spend an inordinate time working out how many calories they eat at any one meal during any one day. When we consider that white bread, white sugar, chocolate, and many other foods whose nutritional value is slight can be counted on to provide calories, the counting of calories is rather for the expert and its value has been severely criticised over recent years (for the reasons given here).

It has been estimated that leisurely swimming needs 10 calories per minute (600 per hour), but this does not take into account the temperature of the water, the temperature of the bathside air, the stroke being swum and the efficiency of the swimmer (Dolphin takes up far more energy than does breast stroke or a quiet side stroke), so while it is academically interesting to learn that per square 39 in. (metre) of body surface you need about 40 calories hourly to keep alive this becomes gobbledygook (or science making a fool of itself) when we are told that one calory is the amount of heat required to raise one kilogram of ordinary water (not chlorinated) one degree centigrade. There are some dieticians who like to blind their readers with science—I don't. I'll give you a golden rule: *Eat as much as instinct prompts you from the foods listed* and here is a silver rule to go with it: weigh yourself regularly, check your weight against the tables given below, and give or take a pound or two cut down your intake of fats and carbohydrates accordingly (you can often eat things you like by cutting thinner slices!). The Red Indians of the woods and plains particularly were (before they began to eat the carbohydrate-rich diet of the European settlers) recorded as being extremely thin and muscular; their diet was principally meat, fruit and vegetables.

The vegetarian should remember that nuts contain oil, and as such may prove fattening. That famous champion Murray Rose, of Australia (three gold medals in one Olympic, and a gold, silver and bronze in another) was a vegetarian.

Extremely good and appetising meals can be prepared consisting solely of seeds, nuts, honey, cereals (millet, oats etc.) but these often take much more time than the average mum has to spare unless the entire household is vegetarian. Myself? I eat meat but always with plenty of salad and never with mixed carbohydrates; I eat cheese with honey or with fruit, occasionally with crisp bread but not with soft bread; I eat protein with fats—with olive oil, butter etc. A Chinese friend of mine always ate pineapple with roast chicken; you should try it!

If you are a racing swimmer don't become a food faddist, you may develop a psychological complex about food; just use these notes as a general guide, use common sense and swim hard, you'll do better that way, and enjoy your swimming more. I have told thousands of pupils that there is no sense in becoming a champion in anything if it completely ruins your life to do it. Aristotle said that a gentleman should play the flute but not too expertly: this is what he meant; remain the master of your sport or hobby, do not let it master you.

Many years ago when coaching the *Swallows* sports club I told them that they should regard the race as a *test* of their fitness, and not regard the race as the sole end of the training. *Train because training is good for you.*

Generally speaking, do not eat for 90 minutes before a race, or 60 minutes before an ordinary swim or work-out. Few foods upset the stomach so much as do our emotions. If you have a problem on your mind before you go swimming, spend longer in the shower (hot shower) making those muscles warms and relax yourself mentally and physically. Never take the shower so hot that it drains your energy away; just keep it a comfortable heat.

Never hurry your meals, even if you do fear you will be late for practice, a hurried meal is not so easily absorbed; food costs money, don't waste it. If the emergency is so desperate, go without the meal, drink some fruit juice (not out of a can) instead—keep your hunger till later.

If you are cutting down on some things do not bother to cut milk and sugar out of your cup of tea—they are the only nutritional elements in it apart from the slightly tranquilising herbal properties; use less milk if you must, and use brown sugar, you'll need less of that anyway, the same may be said of coffee.

Frequent and small meals are healthier than huge repasts. I have often wondered whether the politicians of the world intoxicate themselves with their frequent banquets. The human stomach was never designed to be a dustbin for mountains of food.

FOODS YOU SHOULD SEEK TO AVOID

(i) *Permitted artificial sweeteners*. Many a bottle of refreshing drink contains this strange sentence. What does it mean? The most common artificial agents used are called cyclamates; these are one fifth of the price of sugar and 30 times sweeter; they are a great saving for the manufacturers who foist them upon the unsuspecting public. German scientists have been investigating the long-term effects of cyclamates on the human body, and in 1968 a report in *Der Spiegel* reported cases of damage to the heart, blood circulation and to the liver; the report compared the effects of eating or drinking cyclamates to the disaster of Thalidomide. Another report from the British Sugar Bureau refers to the cyclamates as potential carcinogens—causes of cancer. In my boyhood days the custom was to squeeze out a few lemons or oranges, add brown sugar and water, keep the full jug in a cool place, and serve as needed. This method is cheaper than buying fancy bottles with pretty labels and heavy advertising costs included in the price—it was also healthier.

(ii) Fluoridation of water is another matter the enthusiastic swimmer had better know something about. The claim is that fluorine can prevent dental decay. The proposal being adopted, after too little examination, in Britain, is the compulsory addition of sodium fluoride (made from the waste products of aluminium factories) to the drinking supplies of the entire country. Apart from the wholly undemocratic procedure of forcing all the people to swallow medicines whether they want to or not, there is the fact that in many countries with a *better educated* medical profession than our own, adding fluoride to water supplies is forbidden by law. In cases where it is felt that fluorine is essential for the health of the teeth it can easily be supplied in special sweets given to the children concerned.

By a calcium-enriched diet, balanced supplies of phosphorous, and by dropping the habit of popping sugary sweets into a child's mouth almost every time the child finds life less than a bed of roses the entire need for any additives to water or anything else can be avoided.

An excess of fluorine can lead to irreparable damage to the spinal cord.

Finally, while it is known that fluorine is a suitable mineral salt, the difference between this and fluor*ide* which is made from a toxic substance such as aluminum and has been, in one form, associated with making atomic bombs) is considerable.

Check up whether your water supplies are fluoridated!

(iii) Salt is essential for the healthy functioning of the muscles and mucous membranes. Do not buy a cheap salt; that is mere sodium chloride. Buy only a biochemically-balanced salt or a sea salt; these are more expensive but infinitely more 'salt' in taste; you use less and they are therefore more economical. I first tried this experimentally some years ago and felt so much fitter and healthier that I have always avoided ordinary so-called 'Table Salt' and the like ever since.

THE SWIMMER'S HANDY GUIDE TO WEIGHT
Men

Height Ft. ins.	Age 18-25 Wt. in lbs.	26-35 Wt. in lbs.	36-45 Wt. in lbs.
5 3	127	133	138
5 4	130	136	141
5 5	134	140	145
5 6	138	144	149
5 7	142	148	152

5	8	148	154	154
5	9	153	159	165
5	10	158	164	171
5	11	164	170	178
6	0	171	176	184
6	3	189	195	204

Men who are over the age of 45 can expect to add between two and four pounds weight to those given in the 36-45 age groups; adding more than four pounds should be immediately suspect.

Women

Height Ft. ins.	Age 18-25 Wt. in lbs.	Wt. in lbs. 26-35	36-45 Wt. in lbs.
5 0	115	119	128
5 1	117	121	130
5 2	119	126	133
5 3	123	129	136
5 4	126	133	140
5 5	131	137	144
5 6	135	141	149
5 7	140	145	153
5 8	144	149	157
5 9	148	153	161
5 10	152	157	165
5 11	156	161	168
6 0	163	166	172

Women who are over the age of 45 can expect to add between two and five pounds weight to those given in the 36-45 age groups; adding more than five pounds should be reason for investigation.

GENERAL NOTE
At any one time a variation of two pounds up or down on the weights given above should not cause any concern at all. Weigh yourself regularly.

SWIM TO SAFETY!

Every swimmer should aim at the following basic *minimum* requirements with which to meet an emergency.

(a) Be able to swim one quarter of a mile comfortably without strain—any stroke.

(b) Be able to swim 50 yards or more in clothing, including shoes.

(c) Be able to jump fully clothed from the three metres diving board into 12 feet of water. (Many ship's decks are actually higher than this above the surface of the water.)

(d) Know how to remove clothing in the water.

(e) Know how to swim at least 10 yards under water. If there is burning oil on the surface at the time of an accident you must be able to swim *beneath* it—never swim through it.

(f) Be capable of diving down into 12 feet of water from the surface of the water. Supposing you had escaped from a car below the surface of a pond but a relative was still trapped there!

(g) Be able to tread water. If there is an accident and a ship sinks you should know how to stay still in the water to wait for a lifeboat to be launched.

When you can do these things you will have a good chance of coming forth unscathed from an accident off the coast. It is clearly advisable to learn to swim a mile or more without any stopping, pausing or holding on to the side of the bath; and having achieved that to repeat it at least once in six months. In the average British bath a mile is 54 lengths. The Amateur Swimming Association has a very good series of Survival examinations and presents medals to successful candidates—their examinations cover nearly all the points outlined above.

When you have to *swim in clothing* it is easiest to swim the Breast Stroke or one of the back strokes. Do not hurry. Front Crawl is unsuitable for swimming in clothes. The general theory is that in an accident the swimmer swims far enough away from the upturned boat or sinking ship so as not to be taken under by the suction produced by its sinking.

When beyond the suction area the swimmer first kicks off his shoes (they weigh most in proportion). Then trousers or skirt are undone and wriggled out of while the arms perform the treading water movement described below. The legs are essential for swimming long distance swims. In tropical waters try to keep a vest, blouse or shirt on if you have a raft or small open boat—to minimise the effects of possible sunburn; in this case rip the sleeves off or roll them up tightly. In normal waters of the Temperate Zones open buttons or pull the rolled up shirt or blouse over the head and abandon. In Arctic water the cold is so intense that a person would freeze in winter within only a few minutes. In summer months there would be no difference to the technique followed in the Temperate Zones. In the tropics, if possible, keep light plimsols or sandals on to protect your feet.

In long distance swims during emergency, such as following a shipwreck, one would only use the Front Crawl in a very smooth sea where the shore or point being swum to was easily and continuously visible by slightly lifting the head. If the shore or direction known is not visible the Breast Stroke is the best stroke to swim. If the swimmer becomes tired a change over to one of the back strokes is advisable. In fact, if it is positively known that over one mile has to be swum the swimmer might find it better to change strokes at some interval he works out for himself during the swim, particularly if he thinks cramp is likely to come on. If *cramp* does appear during a long swim the swimmer can either float or tread water. A very experienced swimmer will have learnt how to relax his muscles and reduce the force behind the stroke and be able to swim in this way without letting the cramp develop.

The accident that befell Senator Edward Kennedy drew attention to the difficulty of *escaping from a car* which has been driven accidentally or otherwise fallen into the water.

(a) Don't panic. Some air will be trapped in the car, usually enough for the travellers to breathe for a bit.

(b) According to how far the windows were open (if at all) water will pour into the car. Close the windows while falling—as fast as possible—if possible.

(c) The heavy pressure of the water outside the car will

stop the people inside from opening the door. Let the water seep in slowly and when it has risen to a certain height (depending on the size and make of the car) the pressure will be equal and the trapped people can take a deep breath, open the door, and kick powerfully until they reach the surface.

If you have to *dive down from the surface* swim calmly until you are ready to descend, take a normal breath (you do not want a lot of air trying to burst out of you) sharply and positively bend the chin downwards, forcing the whole head down where you are going (the movement always fails if done half-heartedly) while the arms sweep down in a definite pulling movement, and the legs are swung up above the surface of the water in a straight line above the body (depressing it downwards quickly). Keep the eyes open (no fish goes around with its eyes shut). When you reach the bottom you can usually use your feet to effect a coiled-up spring position and shoot up to the surface again quite quickly. The Breast Stroke is recommended if you wish to make a dive from the surface. Make sure there is no thick mud, silt or weeds before pushing from the bottom.

Treading water is a very simple method of keeping afloat with practically no effort at all. The object is to keep the head above water so that the swimmer can watch something or someone. The whole motion is *vertical*. The head leans slightly backwards. A breast stroke kick can be used: A cycling motion can be used. Whatever leg action is used remember to keep the legs within the shoulder area, if the legs part widely during this the head will sink. Hands make a sculling action. *If you wave use one hand only: never wave with both hands* you will sink quickly.

If you ever have to abandon ship realise that most ships are provided with excellent lifeboats which are equipped with such things as emergency food rations, torches and rocket signals, water supplies, oars, sails, fishing tackle to catch fish, and first aid equipment. Aircraft which are ditched are invariably equipped with some type of automatically-inflatable boat which, if it lands upside down in the water, can be turned the right way up by one person quite easily. The author has done this himself. If there is an emergency do exactly what a ship's officer tells you; he has been trained to meet such difficulties.

If you jump overboard alone try to wear something *orange*; this colour is easily seen at sea from many miles off.

There may be some sort of accident where no lifeboats are available. If you find that the sea below the ship's deck is full of floating debris and it is dangerous to jump it is advisable to use a rope to descend into the sea. *Don't let it slide through your hands*; this will burn the flesh terribly—you must grip it with your legs as well as your hands and lower yourself quickly one handhold after another. Handburns would smart dreadfully after some hours immersion in salt water.

In the Second World War is was realised that some items of clothing—especially trousers or blouses of cotton—can have tight knots tied in the legs or sleeves and then be *inflated* just like balloons. If they are held with one or two hands at the inflated end they give excellent support. If a lifejacket is available the new British Standards ensure that it has been designed to bring the shipwrecked person quickly to the surface and maintain him at an angle which will minimise the chance of being suffocated by waves if he is a poor swimmer. On a long sea voyage never grumble if you are asked to take part in a mock exercise to test lifebelts and escape equipment—that exercise may save your life.

If you are on a deck which is showing a heavy list to one side it is exremely dangerous to abandon ship on that side. *Try to enter the water as straight as a spear*, toes pointed, legs tightly pressed together, arms close to side—never look down: the impact may spoil your good looks for ever.

Never scorn a humble piece of floating debris. Grasp it if you can; you can swim with it easily enough and it will support you when you get tired; also it makes you *more conspicuous for air-sea rescue*.

If you are capsized in a river or lake do not panic if you find your *limbs trapped in weeds*; manoeuvre slowly, in nearly every case the weeds will part themselves and let you through; violent excited movements tend to tie the weeds in knots. Keep calm. If you have ever swum in a Dutch canal you will know this is quite true. Use a slow breast stroke with a full armpull and maximum glide.

Never waste energy *fighting a strong current*. Swim diagonally across it to reach your objective. This applies to rivers and sea.

If you are swimming in a *heavy sea with waves* the technique is very simple. Turn round and face the big wave you know is following you. Take a reasonably good breath, lower your head and dive through the middle of it. You have little chance of defeating a moving mass of thousands of gallons of seething water six feet high or so! Remember, the sea is not trying to kill you; millions of life-forms live with it and in it; just keep calm and apply scientific knowledge.

If you have been *swept out to sea* while bathing, try to decide whether the tide is coming in or going out. If it is going out from the shore swim diagonally across the tide to a corner of the bay or shore. If the tide is coming in to the shore you should aim for the middle of the bay or the shore because there is often a powerful counter-current at the outermost arms of a bay which can force you out even although the tide is in flood. Never relax on a floating, inflated airbed. Danish experiments showed that these can move out to sea at a rate of four kilometres an hour (2½ miles): that is pretty fast!

If you are in a *river estuary* make for the nearest bank, whether you want that one or not. Help can be obtained to get you back where you want—provided that you are alive. Never scorn the power of a river. In some estuaries where tidal water is known a small counter-current is experienced which could carry you out to the middle of the stream again. Watch out for eddies or any water flowing in circles; try to use this so that you can use the outwards movement to throw you further in the direction you want to go.

If you experience an *upset in a canoe* or similar small boat hold on to the boat; do not try to turn it right side up, because it still contains some *trapped air* without which it wouldn't float. Also in this way you make a conspicuous object and help can find you more easily. If you can save your canoe paddle try to hold it in the same hand as that gripping the canoe, this means you have one arm free to guide the direction of your swimming—the author (like most canoeists) has done this, and it is not as difficult as it sounds.

How long can a man survive at sea? The reader is referred to the remarkable work by Dr. Alain Bombard '*Naufragé Volontaire*' which describes how he simulated shipwreck and lived on plankton and sea foods for 65 days! His research will save many men from unnecessary death.

What to do for cramp when unable to return to shore. Reverse to swim or float on your back. Bend the knee or knees in towards the chest as hard as you can and then release them slowly; repeat the movement several times; this should relieve the cramp. Another method is to lie on the back, stretch the cramped leg so that the toe turns strongly inwards to the body; grip this with the hand and pull vigorously to the body, repeat several times. Variation of these methods may help. At the first sign change stroke, *try to relax the muscles*. Try vertical floating. Keep calm.

Helping a person in difficulties if you are in *a boat* is a totally different technique. It is essential that if it is a rowing-boat you approach the drowning person so that the bow or stern of the boat is nearest to him, otherwise when he grabs for the boat or you lean over it to pull him in, it would capsize and everybody would be in trouble. A rowing boat will not capsize if entered or left at the narrow ends. If it is a canoe, paddle near enough to the person to throw a painter to them (nearly every canoe has at least one line aboard); on no account come near enough to the person you are trying to help to let him make a grab for the canoe; all you can do is haul him along; if the person is fairly insensible you must be careful not to upset the canoe. Never use a canoe paddle to reach out to the man you want to help, otherwise you will have nothing to paddle with, and many canoe paddles are joined in the middle (coming apart easily).

Accidents on the Ice. Should the accident occur within reach of the bank of the lake, pond, canal or river you should throw out a wooden board, tree branch or something that will float. If the water is shallow the unlucky man should simply walk in to the shore, breaking the ice before him as he moves. If it is a skating party attach a skate to some knotted scarves (use a reef knot) if no rope is available to tie it to—then throw the skate out to the person who is to be rescued. If this is not possible those present can form a human chain lying on the ice, extended flat out on their stomachs, each person holding the one in front by the ankles until the unlucky companion is reached. The reason for this technique is that the more evenly the rescuers are distributed over the surface the more likely the ice is to hold. If the ice breaks easily, break it and wade or swim out to the one you want to help. If the ice is very thick but a companion has fallen into a hole do not dive down after him *unless you are roped* because it is easy to lose all sense of direction under ice and even if you find him you may never find the hole by which you entered the water.

If you are alone on the ice (a foolish trick) and it breaks try to throw yourself full length on to the surface and move forward by a sweeping (swimming) movement of the arms. By thus changing the distribution of your weight there is a very good chance that you will reach the bank safely.

On the Continent every canal and lake where people skate has some safety apparatus nearby. Unfortunately this is not so common in Britain. Use this technique also if you fall into *Quicksands*.

Never dive head first into unknown waters. People have an odd habit of chucking old bicycles, bedsteads, barbed wire and farming implements into lakes and rivers. A dive into water which ends with a rust-infected cut may put an end to your swimming—if not your life.

If you are present after a saving of life *Don't forget to pull out the rescuer as well as the person he rescued*. Especially on a steep river bank it is important to recall that the rescuer may be exhausted by his efforts. Relatives and onlookers are always extremely anxious to pull their loved one out, and it is not unknown for them to leave the rescuer gasping on the side when one firm arm would haul him to safey.

Man overboard is a cry which everybody on ship should react to quickly. Somebody must run to get the ship's engines stopped and the vessel reversed, otherwise within 10 minutes the unlucky man may be almost out of sight! Do not dive overboard unless you are an exceptionally powerful swimmer. Every ship has lifebelts and ropes, and this is the emergency they are intended for. When you throw a lifebelt try to estimate wind speed and direction.

You are on the bank of a *fast-moving* river. Out in the middle somebody is drowning. Do not swim straight out to where you see him; swim out to meet him where he will be *downstream* by the time you have reached him, and then bring him in diagonally across the current.

If you are caught in a *whirlpool*, remember that its greatest circumference is on top, and the least is below the surface in a descending and decreasing orbit. If you find you are going down, take as good a breath as you have time for, and swim several yards under water outwards from the whirlpool. Its power will be less below the surface than on top; if it is very powerful you may have to go down several yards under water before you can kick free. Keep calm; you can surface when your breath begins to feel short. Swim a powerful breast stroke under water, bringing the arms right back to the thighs to get the best results. Such whirlpools may often occur during a very high tide, especially around an estuary.

How to find a sunken body. In a fast-moving river make sure that you dive well upstream of the place where the person was last seen. If there are still some oxygen bubbles rising to the surface remember that these will rise *obliquely* with the current, and the drowning person lies further upstream than the bubbles indicate. Such bubbles may rise for a short time off-shore on the coast and the same rules would apply. In anything but a calm sea such bubbles could not be seen. It is easier to see under water with goggles or a sub-aqua mask on.

In the case of *mass drowning*, where a ship is going down, it is possible for a very powerful swimmer to save two other lives by towing the victims by the hair, one with each hand. Do not try to take two panicky individuals; you don't stand a chance! Try to take two fairly calm but exhausted or weak swimmers. It is far better to save two people perfectly than to fail in the task or be drowned by the people you are trying to help. If you are a fairly powerful swimmer and two members of your own family are panicking it is suggested that you use a knock-out blow to quieten them, explain the circumstances to them when you have got them to safety

In *Mass drowning*, if possible get hold of wooden debris or any floating material and swim with it to as many people as you judge can safely hold on to it. The number can be increased if there are some powerful swimmers who can take it in turns to swim while other rest and hold on to the flotsam.

CARRY THEM TO SAFETY

In Britain the Royal Life Saving Society, in Germany the *Deutsche Lebensrettungsgesellschaft* (DLRG) in Holland the *Koninklijke Nederland Bond tot het Redden van Drenkelingen* (KNBRD) have done marvellous service in initiating regular training among swimmers for the saving of life. I earnestly recommend every reader of this book to learn how to save life; societies exist now in every civilised country of the world. Instruction is usually free or provided for a purely token payment.

Many different techniques are described in the handbooks of the life saving societies. Of these I shall describe those which are most easily used by a swimmer whose sense of duty to his fellow-man exceeds his technique in life-saving.

(1) When you *approach a drowning person* panic may induce him to grip you so desperately that he will drown you with him. A drowning person will often try to grip his rescuer round the throat, round the waist, or round the shoulders. If this is the case place your hands at once on his elbows and push him upward while you sink down into the depths of the water. Swim away from him under the water. The one way to escape a drowning man's clutches is to descend—this is the last thing he will do with you, and he will let go. When you are free from the clutch keep out of reach and try to talk calmly to the victim. If you cannot calm him down by talk and do not know how to handle him, just keep far enough away to catch him when he becomes exhausted from his struggles and sinks; he is in no real danger as long as you can get him back to the shore or bank. Tread water while waiting for him (see page 144).

GUIDE TO SWIMMING AND WATER SPORTS 151

(2) The easiest method of *carrying a drowning person* is to swim on your back, using the life-saving Back Stroke (see page 58). The important rule is to ensure that the victim's *mouth and nose remain above water;* there is no point in carrying him back if he drowns on the way! Provided he is not bald the victim can be towed and controlled by the rescuer *holding on to his hair* and maintaining a good rhythmic kick; hold on with your strongest hand.

If you are fairly confident, and if the swimmer is fairly quiet and not panicky, place your hand round his chin (not his throat); you can tow more easily this way.

It is possible to tow a person using a two-handed grip on the chin. *Another method of towing which is very easy* is for the rescuer to swim sidestroke (see page 61) and place one arm over the shoulder or under the shoulder of the victim who is placed in his back, the rescuer's arm stretched across the chest of the drowning person, the fingers gripping round the opposite ribs. This is a very easy method, and is very reassuring for the person being saved. All of these methods were in use in Germany 40 years ago, and have been universally adopted since then because they are so easily applied.

(3) *Landing a saved person* when you are alone is not difficult if you place one of his hands on the side, bank or shore and hold it there while you get out yourself. There is no difficulty if the side is sloping, but if it is steep, necessitating climbing out, you must hold on to that hand all the time while you climb out yourself. As soon as you are ashore transfer the holding hand from the hand to the arm of the person you are saving, haul on this until you can grip the other arm as well. There are two ways in which you can haul him out; either pull both arms directly up or twist the arms in front of your chest by holding left to right and right to left arm so that the victim twists in mid-air while being pulled out—many people say this is easier. If the water is fairly deep you can use momentum to get him

up. Holding firmly let him sink down a little, pull up and allow him to sink more deeply, repeat and the third time the water will help lift him up (very useful with very heavy bodies).

(4) *Fireman's lift.* If you are on a very shallow shore you may have to carry the rescued man a long way to dry land. The easiest method is that described here. Let the body float face down; dive underneath so that as your head come up on the other side of the person you can grip the arm with your right hand and place the left arm through his legs holding one leg firmly; now as you rise up to full height transfer the arm to your left hand, this leaves your own right free, and you can walk very easily carrying a person much heavier than yourself if need be. (The human spinal column is stronger than that of a horse because it is vertical.)

(5) You have got your rescued man to the shore; lay him down on his back and use your fingers to *clear mud or debris from his throat* and nose.

(6) If the person you rescued has stopped breathing you must try to give him *artificial respiration* because the lack of breathing does not mean that a person is dead—although unless help is given speedily death may soon take place. (Read the chapter on Breathing in the water.)

(7) In ancient times it was the custom of mariners to roll a recovered man backward and forward over a barrel. In spite of the crudeness of the method it was quite effective because it flexed the spine, forced the diaphragm to move and forced some air into the lungs. The Silvester method was developed around 1861 and recent experiments indicate that it is still one of the three most useful methods available.

   (a) *Silvester*: The man is laid on his back. Place some rolled up towels or clothing under his shoulders. The man's neck is stretched back. Remember to check the mouth for debris and mud, and then pull the patient's tongue out and forwards to prevent is rolling back and blocking the air passages. Repeat this if the tongue falls in.

The rescuer kneels, preferably on one knee, placing the foot of the other leg against the patient's ear which is nearest to it. The rescuer is now looking down the length of the patient's body. He leans forward and grasps the wrists, folds them across the diaphragm just where the breastbone ends and *gently* presses downward to force some air out of the diaphragm, then the arms are lifted upward and outward until right back behind the patient's shoulders and lying against the thighs of the rescuer but *not forced back on to the ground*. Then return the arms the way they came back on to a crossed wrist position on the patient's diaphragm. *Keep your arms straight while applying the Silvester method* and *on no account apply your bodyweight when pressing down;* if you do you could rupture the patient's breathing apparatus and kill him. *This method is easy to apply aboard a small boat.*

(b) *Holger Nielsen*: A method which has been very popular since the Danish Lieutenant-Colonel invented it in 1932. American research showed that it can induce 60 cubic centimetres more air when applied at a dozen movements per minute than does the Silvester method. It took about 20 years to be popularised throughout Europe. It has a great advantage in that the tongue of the patient cannot fall back inside the mouth because the rescued person is placed face down in the prone position. His arms are folded, and after making a careful check for mud and debris in the mouth the rescuer turns the patient's face to one side and places it carefully on the backs of his hands. (The arms thus form a diamond shape from shoulder to below the head.) The rescuer adopts a kneeling position on one knee only to make a rocking and rolling motion easier. The bent knee is near the patient's head, and the foot is placed parallel to the head, roughly about the patient's ear. The rescuer places the heels of his hands between the shoulder-blades of the patient, letting his fingers splay comfortably. *The rescuer must keep his arms straight and not apply full body weight.* Swinging forward gently the rescuer exerts a *gentle* downward pressure to cause a blowing out of some air, and follows this movement by rocking back towards his own rear, bringing his hands quickly along the outstretched arms of the patient, grasping the arms slightly above the elbows, raises them until a natural resistance of movement is met, pulling them upward and forward. The arms are lowered into place, and the rescuer's hands return to their first position for another gentle push down between the patient's shoulder blades. Roughly 10 to 12 presses per minute should be worked.

How much pressure to apply? For adults, between 30-40 lb. for men, 20-30 lb. for women, and for children press with fingers only using up to an estimated five pounds pressure. If there is suspicion of broken or damaged bones be careful to reduce the pressure applied, but to increase the rate of application. Young children usually need a faster rate of pressure.

(c) *Mouth to mouth* artificial respiration is now recommended widely (often somewhat dogmatically as the *only* method you should employ) but it has one insuperable objection. It implies a very close physical contact which the most humanitarian of us may be selective in making. I asked some teenage students about it once. The reply of one of them was most lucid: 'If I rescue Brigitte Bardot she can have mouth-to-mouth artificial respiration, but if it's some hulking great docker he'll have *Holger Nielsen* or nothing'.

Clearly if the rescued person looks in any way unclean the rescue cannot be obliged to catch an infection.

It is a simple method to learn and it can force more air into the the water-logged lungs than most other methods; furthermore a strong swimmer can apply the method while still swimming with the person rescued. I have done this myself.

(i) Check mouth for mud and debris.

(ii) Patient placed in supine position (lying on back). The head is tilted to stretch the throat and facilitate the passage of air. The rescuer kneels by the side of the patient.

(iii) Place one hand firmly over the nose to close it. Inhale deeply and blow air down through the patient's mouth. Do not blow violently. Don't be half-hearted either.

(iv) The rescuer turns his head away quickly (after the first blow *the patient is often sick,* a point which some instructions fail to mention). If the patient is sick, turn him quickly to one side so that the vomit rolls out and does not choke his windpipe. When the sickness ceases return to supine position and carry on blowing. (Wipe his mouth if you have a cloth available.) Sickness is usually a good sign.

(v) During this mouth-to-mouth resuscitation the rescuer can notice two things: whether the patient's chest is rising and falling as for normal breathing (if not the tubes are still blocked) and, secondly, whether the metallic blueishness of a drowning person is being replaced with the rosy-pink hue of normal flesh.

(vi) Try to keep a rhythm of 12 breaths a minute. This is not difficult—it is the average breathing rate for most of us.

(vii) It is possible to blow into the nose and cover the mouth so that the air must go down into the lungs, instead of blowing into the mouth.

(viii) Use your common sense and reduce the power of your blowing for women and children according to age and frailty. I was taught this method by an American swimming friend from the University of Utah. Within a few months it was being adopted widely.

GENERAL RULES
(1) Don't argue about which method to apply. Use the one you can apply best and most efficiently whichever it is.
(2) Be prepared for at least 10 to 20 minutes' hard work when you take on artificial respiration. One friend of mine worked for nearly half an hour before the person came round, but she saved his life.
(3) Some cases need external cardiac massage; this is quite a difficult technique to apply without training. If you are untrained don't risk it, send for a doctor or somebody who knows.
(4) Never make an attempted rescue a double-tragedy. *Only try to save somebody if you know how to do it.*
(5) Life Saving Societies run classes at nearly every bath, everywhere. Learn how to save life. Join a class!
(6) Use common sense. Don't leap into a fast river after somebody and risk your own life when there is a lifebelt maybe two or three yards away.

HISTORICAL NOTES

The ability to swim was one of the first great conquests made by man. When it happened it was as epoch-making as a voyage in Space, but of more immediate benefit. Speculation has it that the Breast Stroke was developed from observation of tadpoles and frogs, while the Crawl was developed in its earliest stages by watching quadrupeds (dogs etc.) move through the water.

In North Africa there are rock carvings which have been dated over 6,000 years old. One of them seems to indicate that man could swim. Further along the coast lies Egypt, and hieroglyphics of about 3,000 B.C. imply that at that time swimming was fairly widely known and used there, at least among the educated classes. The earliest record of the teaching of swimming is nearly 4,000 years old, dating about 1970 B.C. It too was found in Egypt.

The British Museum contains some relief carvings from Ancient Assyria which show beyond all doubt soldiers swimming some form of Crawl, and others holding on to inflated bladders and paddling across a river. The carvings are *c.* 1,000 B.C.

In Classical Greece swimming was frequently referred to by many writers, the inhabitants of Delos being known as the best swimmers of Greece. Young Spartans were taught swimming as a normal part of their education. Homer's *Odyssey* refers to Ulysses swimming to save his life. Schoolboys who have suffered from *De Bello Gallico* may regret that Julius Caesar once saved his life by swimming and holding his treasured manuscript clear of the water. Surely all of us have heard of the tragic death of Leander who used to swim the Hellespont every night (four miles) to visit his lady love Hero. He was drowned when the guiding light in her window on the opposite shore blew out and he lost his way in the dark. I visited the spot, now called *Canakkale Bogazi*, while in Turkey; the current is very strong.

Biblical references are: Isiaih xxv. 11; Psalms vi. 6; Ezekiel xxxii. 6; and Ezekiel xlvii. 5; and Acts xxvii. 42.

The writings of the Saxons and Vikings are full of references to swimming. It was clearly a popular pastime among them as it was for the American Red Indians and Hawaiians, of which races early explorers imply that they were as much at home in the water as on the land.

During the early Christian era and especially during the Middle Ages some preachers railed against swimming as immoral (one had to take off one's clothes to do it) but nobody took much notice because swimming flourished and increased.

That most athletic and remarkably interesting author George Borrow is reputed to have gone swimming almost every day of his life—well into his seventies, being a familiar figure on Wimbledon common.

As populations multiplied so more people learned to swim, and several ponds and waters became polluted due to laziness and carelessness. This led to a serious falling-off in popularity of the sport, but towards the end of the sixth decade of the nineteenth century the discovery of chlorinated water for swimming pools came about. The fact that men were prepared to undertake scientific investigation in this field shows how popular the sport must have been, and how eagerly pollution's defeat was sought.

It is, of course, a very practical sport; without swimming

there is inevitably an unnecessary loss of life.

The average swimming pool in Britain today is 33⅓ yards long (30 metres) and goes from 3 ft. 6 in. to 12ft. depth. It contains about 156,000 gallons of water which is kept in continuous movement and filtration.

The natural water which is delivered to by the public supply contains various mineral salts and occasionally dissolved matter. Even after a shower and soaping, the human body usually deposits some dirty matter as well as bacteria in the water. In a public bath chlorination and filtration deal effectively with all this, but often in a small, private pool lack of money may lead to some negligence so that conjunctivitis, ear infection and sore throats may ensue. Many small private pools are chlorinated by hand which is not a really satisfactory method. Pools which are emptied only once a week can easily become contaminated. There is no need for small private pools to suffer in this way provided it has regular and continuous attention like all the public pools.

The University of Keele came to the conclusion after its experts had researched the subject that swimming is the top favourite sport in Britain.

All swimmers will be grateful to learn that, thanks to the Institute of Baths Management, continual effort and research is conducted into keeping their sport clean, safe and enjoyable. Behind the scenes of every public bath men and women are working hard to help the swimmer and provide the best facilities available for the enjoyment of the recreative sport—when you visit a bath do give them your unstinted co-operation.

Never think that swimming need be an end in itself; it can always develop into a means to enjoy many other fine water sports and activities such as Canoeing, Channel Swimming, Diving, Sub-aqua exploration, Synchro (water ballet), Water Polo and Yachting.

Canoeing

CANOEING

Canoeing is one of the oldest sports in the world, and an art form linked to Man's survival. It was soon appreciated that, however well he swam, his strength had limits, but the use of arms only means that a man can go on longer than if he has to use all four limbs. He can rely upon the balance of the canoe to keep afloat while he rests his arms.

A canoe is the boat that everybody can afford. It is easy to build for oneself, it costs very little to maintain, and some, such as glass-fibre models require practically no time or attention at all.

It can be stored in a garage, slung to the rafters, in an attic, or under a bungalow; some can even be stored under a bed.

The natural instinct of the human race makes it very easy to swing the arms in the fascinating rhythm of a canoeist's movements. Little physical strength is needed. Less than cycling!

No other boat can move in such shallow water. A canoe can glide through four or five inches of water, (about 10 centimetres). Quiet streams, creeks and brooks are open to the silent canoe which can probe and explore where no other means of progress can be used.

Once I explored some marshland. I found a small island, barely a few inches of land above the water, and camped alone save for a chorus of wildfowl, and was able to enjoy one of the most beautiful sunsets and radiant dawns of my life. Camping comes naturally with canoeing; most canoes can give room to store a tent and camping gear.

If the paddler comes to an awkward patch—weirs, rapids, or waterfalls he can simply lift the canoe out of the water and carry it (we say *portage*).

160 GUIDE TO SWIMMING AND WATER SPORTS

Most young people can learn to handle a canoe in one hour; after that most of the details are common sense which can be worked out with a little calm thinking.

Of course, like most other water sports, one must be able to swim at least 200 metres (220 yards) before one takes to the water ... safety first!

Do not be over-confident in your swimming ability; do use a buoyancy jacket or similar life-saving device if you adventure with a canoe on to a very big lake, the open sea or into very turbulent rapids.

Never take a passenger, however light he or she may be, into a canoe which is built for one person only; it would alter your balance, gravity, fulcrum for paddling and endanger both of you.

Before finalising plans for an expedition it is advisable to check currents, tides and speed of flow. It is important to remember that your initial training will have taken place on comparatively still waters, and any expedition taking one across country will necessitate meeting of varying conditions.

WHICH CANOE DO YOU WANT?

When you are first attracted by the fascination of paddling your own canoe the first consideration is what type of canoe is most suited to you. So a word about the design of canoes is needed.

Let us first look at canoe keels, and we can see that there is a great deal of difference.

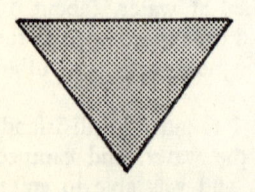

a. (Triangular) very fast. Very unstable

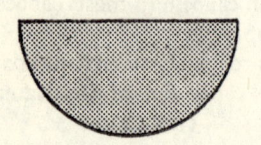

b. Fast, unstable. Popular with racing enthusiasts

To understand the illustrations let me explain that the more the surface of a vessel touches the water the greater the resistance of the water to the progress of the boat. But speed is not our only interest; we must have a canoe which we can rely upon to keep its balance easily in an emergency. Most glass-fibre racing models are made like B, while for general canoeing C or D are most useful, being fairly fast and stable enough for touring, camping expeditions etc. I personally recommend the many-chined D. *Chine* means the angle between one surface of the hull and the next.

Now we must look down from a height upon the lengthways shape of a canoe, because this also affects our choice.

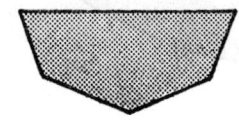

c. Fairly fast, fairly stable

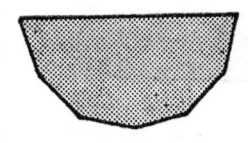

d. Double Chine. Fast, fairly stable. Excellent for touring and fast travel

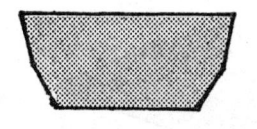

e. Slow, heavy to paddle. Fairly stable

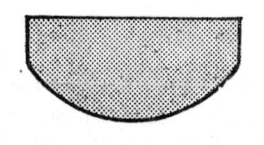

f. Slow, not very stable. Many cheap tourers made this way

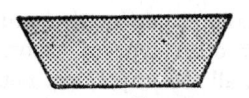

g. Very stable, used only on marshes or mudflats unsuitable for general canoeing

For most purposes c and d are most useful

Canoe hulls

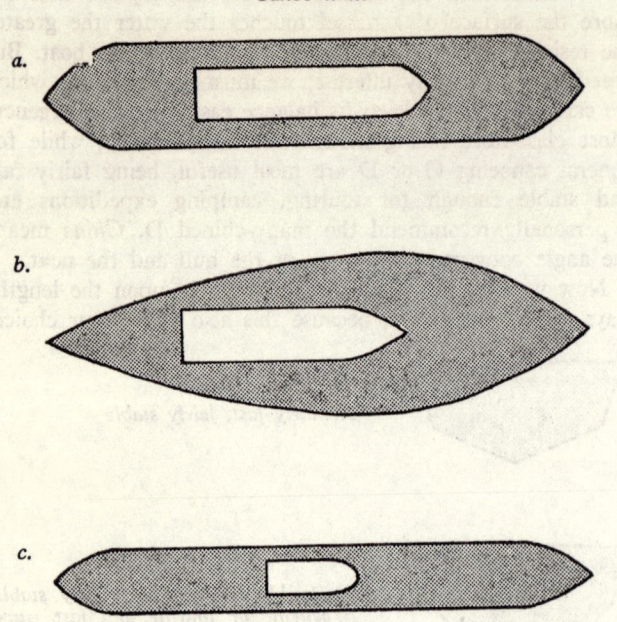

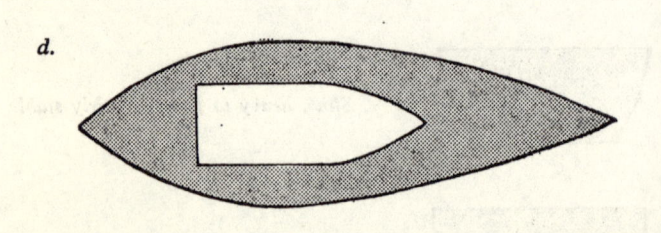

(a) Commonly met with in do-it-yourself kits. Look at the cockpit; the paddler is sitting almost dead-centre. It looks safe but is not. Usually it sits light upon the water ... too light. I have personally experienced more upsets in this type than in any other type of canoe. Notice that it is the same width all the way along, not much different from the shape of a tramp steamer!

GUIDE TO SWIMMING AND WATER SPORTS 163

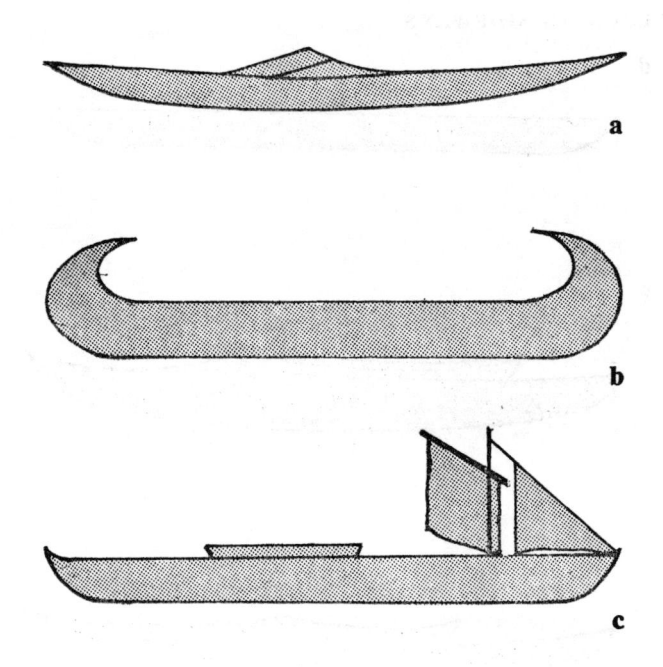

(b) Known widely throughout canoeing circles as the *Fish* shape; most fish bulge more at the front than at their rear ends. It is distinctly faster, but since we rarely (if ever) get anything in this world for nothing, it tends to pay for the speed with less stability. It should never be taken out to sea or into white water (rapids etc.).

(c) Racing canoe, for racing only. No other uses recommended. Usually with keel type B. Usually unstable for slow paddling or rough waters.

(d) This is the incomparable *Swedish* shape. I personally recommend this for general touring and canoe-camping expeditions. It is a canoe you can relax with and love but still get a good turn of speed from. You can steer best by a flick of a paddle, something which is difficult in other canoes. Very stable. Safe at sea and in nearly all conditions. Easy to manoeuvre.

LOOKING SIDEWAYS

d

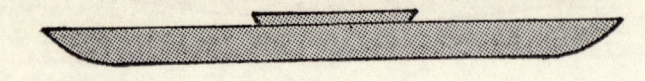

e

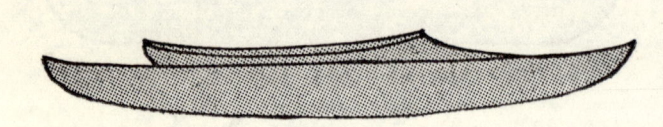

f

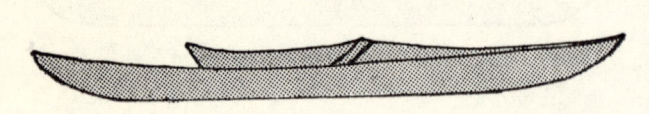

(a) This is the true Kayak of the Eskimos which was popularised after Gino Watkins and Freddie Spencer Chapman, whom I had the pleasure of knowing, brought back this and the exciting technique of the *Eskimo roll* (described later) to Europe. They financed from their own meagre funds a full expedition to Greenland when they were in their early 20s, and although it was *done on a shoestring* it was of historic importance, marred only by the sad death of Gino Watkins on a food-hunting trip. I was privileged to see Spencer Chapman's unique collection of slides of this trip. The true kayak was made of sealskin stretched over polished bone frame. The high front (prow) enables the boat to be paddled up on to an ice floe; this canoe is custom-built for hunting on rough seas. The Eskimo fits an apron-like skin to the cockpit, wriggles in and draws it tight about his short, podgy body. Air is trapped in the canoe by this method, increasing its buoyancy; the canoe rides high on the waves but is very unstable. It is extremely fast, and modifications of the original design are used by canoeists throughout the world. Several original kayaks are on view in the British Museum in London and other museums. This is the only type of canoe suitable for the *Eskimo roll*. If I remember rightly Freddie Spencer Chapman told me that there were 27 basic types of *Eskimo roll* which an expert Eskimo could perform.

(b) This is the American Indian birch-bark canoe, now called the *Canadian* canoe. There is one major difficulty, this was made of birchbark fixed by resins (got from trees) to thin tied sticks. The white men used the design but with much heavier and more solid materials. So much so that now the *Canadian* canoe is little used by the majority of sportsmen. Frank Luzmore, of the Richmond Canoe Club, was a great expert in handling the *Canadian,* and has taken his own canoe down the Thames round the dangerous currents of North Foreland (try them in a canoe!) along the South coast of England. The original Indian canoe was light, fast and less stable than the modern counterpart. This is the only type of canoe which is suitable for use with an outboard motor, and as such the heavier modern version is used upon many wild, lonely rivers of the Canadian North today.

(c) This is the *Rob Roy*, which is shown with the lateen and foresail as used to cross the estuary of the Thames, the Bristol Channel etc. in the 1870s. You are not a true canoeist until you have read J. MacGregor's *A Thousand Miles in a Rob Roy Canoe*. Probably no man did so much in England to make canoeing so famous. The book is republished by the British Canoe Union, London. The Rob Roy canoe was 15 ft. long, built of oak with a deck of cedar—a very heavy construction but its sturdiness was to influence canoe building for half a century or more.

(d) Average racing canoe outlines, but many variations are available.
(e) Average touring canoe. (Two-seater.)
(f) Swedish shape.

PADDLE YOUR OWN CANOE

Few sports teach a person to be so self-confident and self-reliant within such a short time. If you do not exert energy and use intelligence the current will sweep you away. There is absolutely nobody else to blame, and usually nobody to help when only your own courage, hard work and determination are needed to paddle your way out of a difficulty.

With what shall I paddle it? A question you must ask when you see that there are different types of paddle.

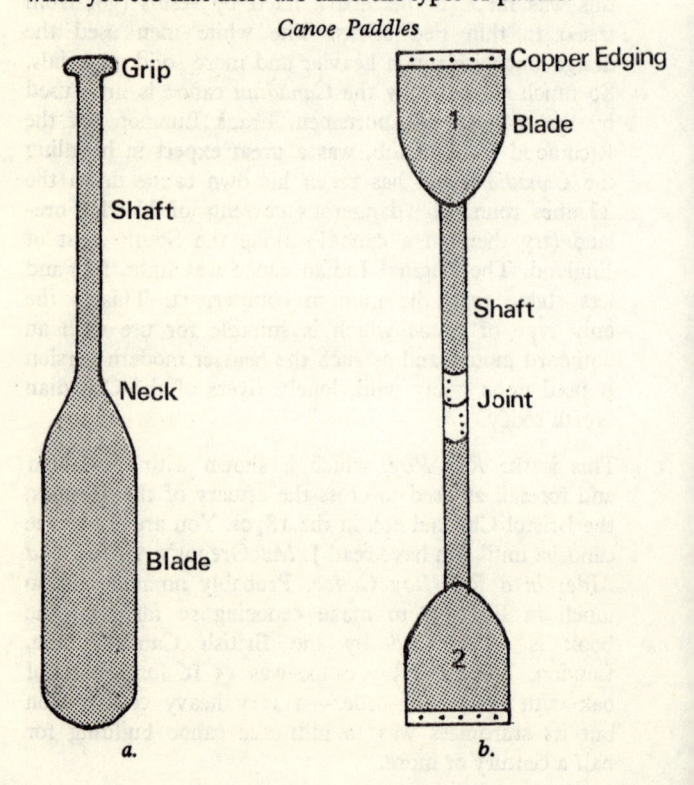

Canoe Paddles

Paddle a: Grip, Shaft, Neck, Blade

Paddle b: Copper Edging, Blade (1), Shaft, Joint, (2)

a.   b.

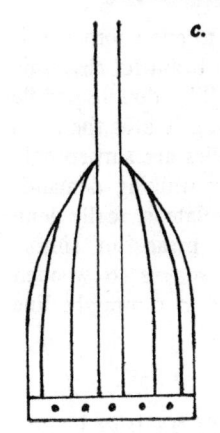

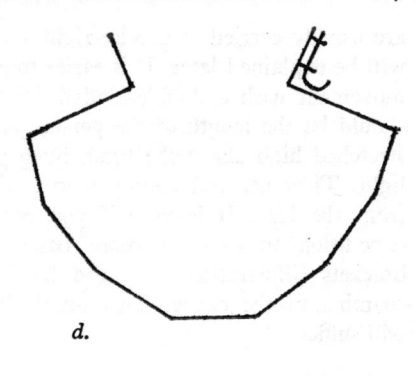

brackets (two) fixed to the cockpit coaming to rest spare paddle

(a) This is the correct paddle for the American Indian or Canadian canoe. Occasionally there are variations in the actual shape of the water-end of the paddle. Usually it is five feet long, and a little longer will not hurt ... do *not* use one which is shorter; it will change the fulcrum of the sweep and make paddling harder work. I was once told that a single Canadian paddle should be the height of the paddler less the width of one hand at the knuckles. Single paddles are best made of hard wood, and some of the best exponents prefer a paddle of one single piece of wood. If you are touring with a Canadian canoe, you may find it better to have a paddle built up to make any repairs easier. The matter is debatable.

(b) Usual paddle for use with kayak and most racing and touring canoes. Copper-tipped edges, joined and held in the middle by metal male and female sockets, easily dismantled into two halves by a pull and a twist. Sometimes rounded at the water-end, mostly square. In (c) the blade is shown to be put together and comprising various strips of wood to lessen the chance of a split destroying a paddle. Not really necessary for general touring.

All paddles should be coated with marine varnish to lessen the likelihood of them becoming soaked with water and so getting heavier. In illustration (4b) the blades 1 and 2 are usually carried at precise right angles to one another, this will be explained later. It is easier to get a beautiful rhythmic movement with a double-bladed paddle. The double-paddle should be the length of the person paddling it plus the arms stretched high above the head. Such paddles are surprisingly light. They use less energy than ordinary walking demands from the legs. It is wise if you contemplate a really long expedition to carry a spare paddle by means of simple brackets (illustration 4*d*) fixed by *brass* screws to wooden coaming of the canoe. Two simple hooks in a straight line will suffice.

FURTHER EQUIPMENT

Spray cover—For use on rough rivers or sea trips to prevent the canoe becoming filled with water from spray or rapids, which would make the canoe heavy, spoil any camping gear or clothing you have on board. I never camp or tour without a spray cover ready to be clipped on.

Painters—No, you do not take a budding Rembrandt or Renoir with you. It is the name you give the rope used for mooring your vessel to quay or river bank. In an emergency one severs a painter (i.e. cuts it); some canoeists talk of a small painter, this in no way refers to Toulouse Lautrec, but means a short rope or cord used in fine (summer) weather. As tides rise and fall it is essential to have a painter at least the same length as the canoe; longer still does not hurt if it is an all-night mooring. Usually I haul my canoe up on the bank beside the tent, upside down against the dew if the weather indicates this would be wise. A painter is essential for lining a canoe down rapids which may be too dangerous to shoot or are under low water so that if you did not line down (i.e. go up on the bank and guide the canoe along with one or two painters) your added weight might damage the canoe and make the passage unwise. Carry a small metal or wooden stake with you.

Drip Rings—Look closely at paddles; they usually have a small rubber ring just where the shaft meets the blade; these rings prevent water dripping down the blade, wetting the hands, weakening the grip and incidentally filling the canoe with a continually growing amount of water. Wet hands may

Thames sailing Barge – (Upnor)

Note the twist of the mouth to facilitate front crawl breathing (*Donald Law swimming*)

et really comfortable at the start of a back-crawl race

The mood of the sea changes. Don't take unnecessary risks

A swimming pool is a happy place – if you can swim

Hoisting sail is ea

blister more easily! These are essential, especially for long tours.

Repair Kit—Either glass-fibre repair outfit, or some patching material of the fabric (e.g. p.v.c. etc.). Some brass screws etc. And a first aid kit for yourself.

Keel Protector—If you have a p.v.c. canoe (or any other fabric) a long trip should be preceded by fixing a strong strip eight to ten inches wide along the keel; this protects the real keel from sharp stones, sea shells, gravel etc. Take the protecting material all the way along.

Sponge—A really bulky absorbent sponge or plastic substitute, tied to a long piece of nylon cord attached to part of the interior woodwork is essential. There is no point in having a bailer, the boat isn't that large; the sponge can be used to clean the canoe as well as bail out any water you ship during a voyage (especially if a wildly-driven motor launch whips across your bows). A loose sponge would get lost or blown overboard too easily.

Lifejackets—Many approved models are on sale for sailors of all kinds. Take one with you if you go out to sea or venture on to white water (rapids etc.). Make sure you never store them wet; dry them thoroughly before putting into some cupboard ashore. Do accept the advice of local authorities. Make sure you have an approved and tested brand—your life may depend upon it.

Safety factors—Many seagoing canoes are now equipped or easily equipable with extra buoyancy provided by polystyrene blocks, air in plastic sealed containers, or air in rubberised inflatable tubes. For serious canoeing some firms make tubes which form the gunwales (*wale* is old English for the upper edge, and in later days, since guns were pointed from them, they became gun-wales—pronounced 'gunnels': Life does get complicated sometimes doesn't it?). With such tubes made up as part of the boat it is virtually impossible to sink it!

TO FOLD OR NOT TO FOLD?
It is possible to have canoes which fold up into parts which are easy to carry and store. These are the pros and cons of folding and rigid canoes. The decision is your own.

Folding
  (i) Easily transportable by train, coach, car etc.
  (ii) Easy to get at any part of the canoe for repairs of any kind.
  (iii) Must never be stored until 100 per cent dry. Otherwise they rot rapidly.
  (iv) Replacing the stretchable skin to cover the woodwork is expensive.
  (v) Usually 50 per cent dearer than a rigid canoe.

Rigid
  (i) More difficult and unwieldy to carry about. Private car almost essential.
  (ii) Cheap to build yourself, replacements cheap.
  (iii) Difficult to get at parts to repair interior.
  (iv) Beware of 'bargains' offered second-hand.
  (v) Glass-fibre canoes are fairly trouble-free.

'I NAME THIS SHIP . . . AND MAY GOD BLESS ALL THOSE WHO PADDLE HER'

I got my girl friend to launch my canoes by emptying some cheap wine over the stern (rear part), after which I would paddle away stylishly, complete a short circular tour of the river, and then dock smartly, dry the boat, put her on the racks, and go off with the girl friend.

Well, it sounds fun. It is, let's examine it step by step.

Your canoe is your boat. Within the bounds of reason you may call her whatever comes to your fancy.

You may go so far as to affix gold letters to her bows . . . do get them in a symmetrical line.

Do *not* slap the stern with a bottle of wine, the bottle may crack the woodwork . . . some girls do not know their own strength. Helen, who launched *Sjøulven* (Sea Wolf) for me drove fast cars, glider planes, controlled hefty horses with one hand, stood barely five feet and looked quite *helpless*! . . . Emptying the wine will do! We used elderberry wine (see my *Concise Encyclopedia of Herbs* for a good recipe).

A MOMENT OF TRUTH

This is what comes to you as you step into your canoe for the first time, to take it away all alone. (Do make sure you

GUIDE TO SWIMMING AND WATER SPORTS 171

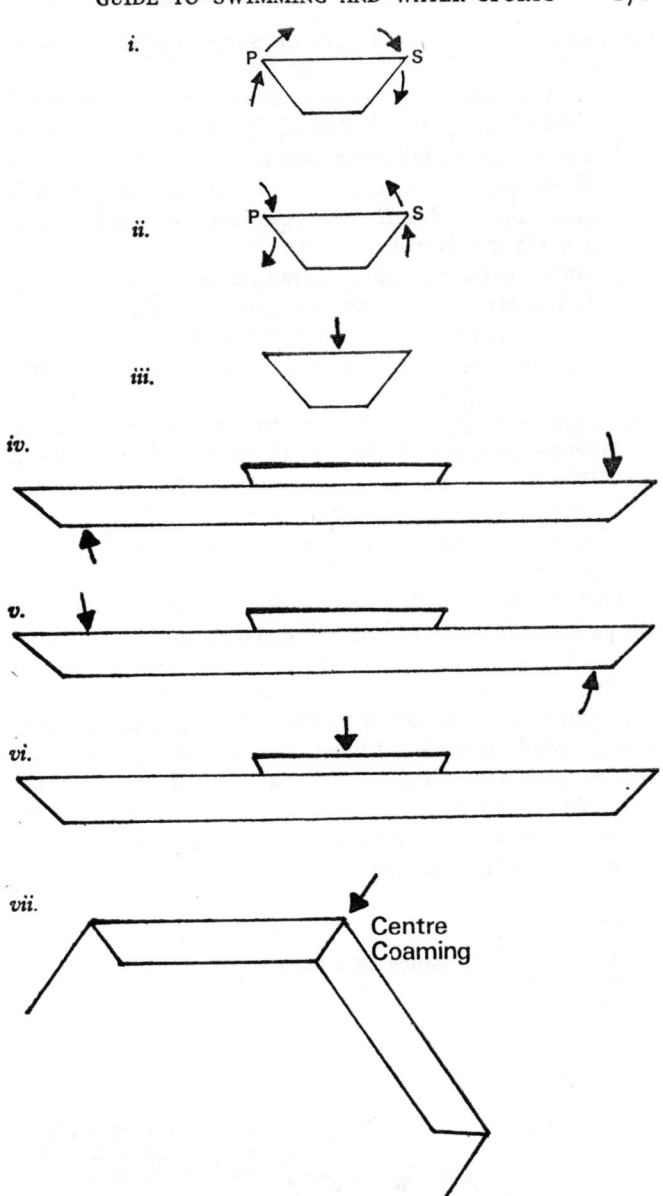

i.

ii.

iii.

iv.

v.

vi.

vii. Centre Coaming

can swim well first). Let us take the simple matter of getting on board!

i If you put your weight down on the starboard (offside) the port side (nearside) will rise up as a reaction . . . you fall in the water.

ii If you put your weight down on the port side, down it goes, the starboard rises up, and you sink down beneath the river etc.

iii Only one place is left . . . dead centre.

iv If you enter at the stern the prow rises up.

v If you enter at the prow the stern rises up.

vi Try to balance the boat by entering as near the centre as the cockpit allows.

vii Bend down parallel to the moored canoe. Take the centre coaming of the cockpit firmly with one hand, lift one foot to the centre, balancing the canoe as you swing the other foot over into the middle. Now sit down calmly without rocking the boat unduly and balance yourself.

There is one essential when entering a canoe—do not leave the paddle behind on the bank when you shove off!

A canoeist must be attentive to the position of his body in the canoe. There are no rowlocks against which oars may pull—only man and a paddle. The seat must be really stable, avoid movable cushions, use a fixed plastic-foam-covered seat if you find it comfortable, or if you are hardy a simple seat (a box can be made underneath this to keep things in, but not more than two or three inches deep). There should always be a backrest.

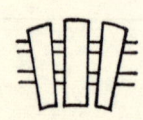

a. design for a backrest

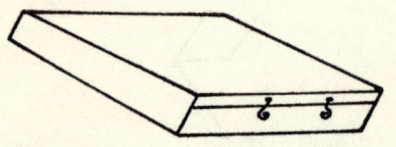

*b. boxseat with hooks
Slightly raised in front, lower at the back*

c. Backrest being used

d. Backrest not in use

e.

f.

Avoid sitting high up. Never sit on a kitbag. The lower you sit in the canoe the better your total stability. Seated inside the canoe one must aim at making a distinct three-point hold. *Seat* firm; *knees* apart and *pushing tight* on either side of the canoe under each of the side decks outwards inclined; *heels* fixed on part of the framework of the canoe's bottom. If there is no proper framework (i.e. as in a glass-fibre boat, fix a crossbar as a footrest).

It will do no harm for you to practise (wearing swimming costume) how you can control the canoe by exerting muscle pressure through knees, feet etc. on the movements of the canoe. The experience may well help you keep the boat upright when some unexpected wave comes at you.

When you are paddling in a leisurely fashion you will lean against the backrest quite naturally. When you are paddling earnestly to hurry along the inclination is to lean forward. See illustrations *c* and *d* page 173.

HOW TO HOLD THE PADDLE

The double paddle—Stretch your arms out just slightly wider than the breadth of your own shoulders; keep the elbows supple and loose; slightly bend them as you grasp the paddle.

N.B. To avoid blisters you are advised to sandpaper the commonly-used marine varnish off the paddle shaft where your hands hold it. See that the drip rings are on the water side of your hands.

For normal paddling the blades of a double paddle are turned at right angles so that whichever blade is going through the air presents the smallest surface possible to the air resistance. Do not underestimate the use of a paddle as a small *sail* in a high wind; in estuaries or marshlands it is positively alarming how fast the wind can drive a canoe using a paddle in this way. See illustration *e* page 173.

Try to keep the centre of the shaft level with your chin; if you let the paddle droop below this level you will alternately put the paddle blade too deep in the water, which will make you lose balance, and skim the water without pulling sufficiently. The deeper the paddle goes the greater the resistance and the less distance covered for the energy expended (See illustration *f*.) Getting the paddle too deep in the water means that the opposite blade rises too high and so can add to loss of balance. If the blade is too shallow (i.e. high up) it will not get sufficient purchase on the water to pull you along. Dip the blade in the water as far ahead as you can comfortably reach; the trunk sways forward following the outstretched arm. The blade is just below the surface, about two or three inches deep where the tip is covered by the copper protective strip. The secret behind this movement is that while one arm is pushing blade number one ahead into the water the other arm is completing a pull with blade number two.

It will be found that by keeping the shaft well up you can more easily start and keep a good rhythm (which is what makes walking so easy a movement). Try not to pause between the strokes because that means your arm muscles are carrying the weight of the paddle (light as it is). Each stroke one each side of the boat must be about the same length as the other one (exceptions explained later). The point of pivot through which the paddle twists must be consciously kept well in front of you, to the centre of your body. *Remember to push as well as pull.* If one arm pulls but the other fails to push it seems like hard work; make it a double movement and it will be much easier. (See *a* below).

a. feathered blades (at right angles)

Pull in towards you ←   **Left wrist up** ↑   **Roll forwards** ↷

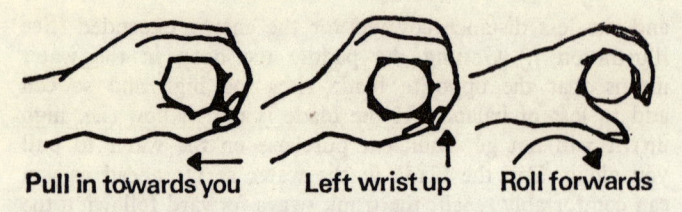

b. fingers and thumb holding paddle shaft

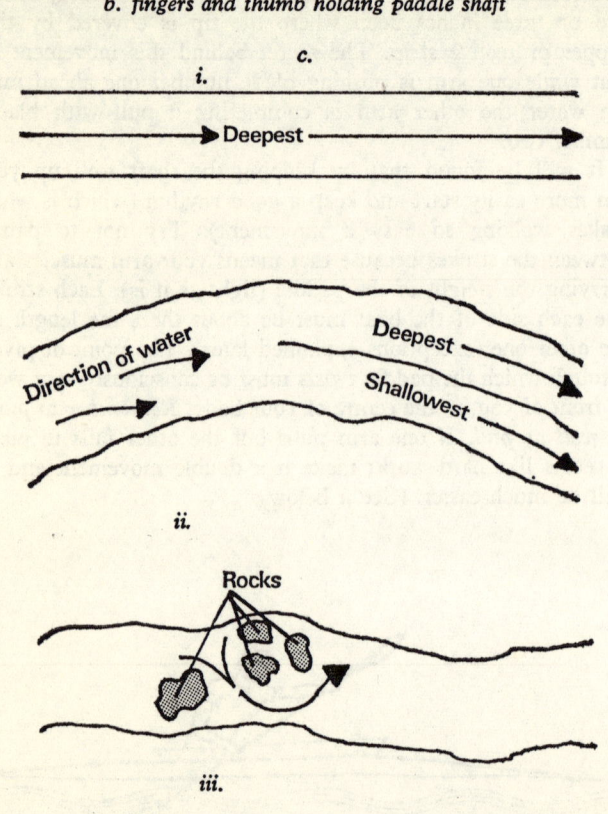

c.

i.

→ Deepest →

Direction of water →   Deepest →
    Shallowest →

ii.

Rocks

iii.

The flick of the wrist is made very simply by creating a *figure of eight* movement in the air with the paddle, it is simpler than it sounds, and is indeed such a natural movement that five minutes is quite sufficient to learn it in.

Your paddle should be as long as you are tall with arms stretched above your head.

You arrange the paddle so that if you are right-handed your first pull on the paddle comes from the right, and remember that when you feather (blades at right angles as illustration page 173 the spoon (concave) side of the blade is twisted uppermost to the air.

Keep the grip comfortably wide.

When learning you can say:

> *Pieces of eight*
> *Or else I'll be late.*

The paddle is not only your means of propulsion, it is your brake, your sail, your quickest means of navigation. You will soon learn that if you break the rhythm, just leaving one blade in the water slightly longer than the other, your canoe will swerve to the side. You can turn a canoe by one single paddle movement when you get more practised.

The Quick Turn
Hold one blade firmly in the water to create and keep resistance. Lean slightly in the direction of the "stop", tilting the canoe a little—this causes the boat to turn

The Slow Turn
Paddle harder one side than the other. You turn towards the side with the least paddle pressure!

CHANGE OF DIRECTION

(i) To start with, paddle faster on one side of the canoe than on the other side.

(ii) Or—paddle fast on one side and back-paddle on the other—this is a simple instinctive movement, and can swing a canoe round quite quickly. Do the back paddle stroke on the side towards which you want the boat to go. A good canoeist can perform this so deftly that there is no visible break in the rhythm of his paddling!

(iii) Place one blade of the paddle quite flat alongside the canoe, then press it outwards 180 degrees all the way until it touches the canoe again; the canoe turns in the direction the stroke follows, two or three such strokes turn you right round.

GALE WINDS ABEAM

A great source of anxiety to the inexperienced canoeist is a powerful wind coming up on one side of the canoe (*abeam*) instead of head on or from behind.

Throughout the section on paddling you have been warned to keep the shaft of your paddle balanced with its centre opposite your centre. This is one occasion when you can break the golden rule. Let us say that the wind is blowing your beautiful canoe towards the left; however hard you paddle the bows drift left with the wind. The answer is simple; you hold the shaft so that the left side is longer than the bit you are dipping to your right—the effect is to keep the canoe head on in the direction you want to go, with minimum effort on your part. A minute's practice will show you exactly how much to lengthen or shorten one end of the paddle—and it is no heavier to manipulate this way.

SHOVE OFF!

Always point a canoe against the current, never with the stream, otherwise when you put the first foot in she will shoot off with the flow of water and you'll get an extra bath free of charge.

HEAVE TO!
Strictly speaking, this term is employed only when you come to a stop with the bows facing the wind. But stopping your canoe with the current or with the wind is usually called *coming alongside*.

Apart from the movements given in the section on changing direction you can simply lay one blade close to the stern, use it as a rudder, and let the current do the rest. If you are very practised in the art you may leap the wavelets, cross diagonally towards the landing stage at a good lick, stop suddenly and drift alongside . . . but do not try that on your first outing, or indeed during your first month of canoeing, you can smash a lot of good canoes if you get it wrong. The secret of coming to land gracefully is to slow the canoe down by using the blade as a brake and a rudder without perceptibly altering the rhythm of the arms paddling. In this fashion one drifts diagonally across the current, and gracefully alongside with little *apparent* effort. If the current is very strong you *must* land with the bows pointing up against the current . . . if you want to get *out* of the canoe and stay dry, that is.

IN REVERSE GEAR
By simply reversing the direction of the figure of eight made with the paddle you will go backwards. If you wish to make a very fast turn to avoid a collision you'll get better results backpaddling on one side than by other methods.

The single paddle—The method of using this in the Canadian-type canoe is quite different from that of the rhythmic double-bladed paddle.

Normally the paddler kneels in the centre of the canoe, inclining slightly backwards against one of the crosspieces (thwarts). One hand (usually the right hand if you paddle on the left-hand side of the canoe) holds the grip at the top of the paddle. The other hand is low down on the shaft. The position allows more versatility of body movement. If you sit in this type of canoe you limit the swing of the paddle.

The general idea is to make a continuous series of *J* movements in the water.

The curl of the *J* movement is essential to prevent the canoe yawing (going to the side); as the stroke comes to the end of its straight sweep the rear (aft) surface of the blade is swerved outwards away from the boat, circled and swung through the air to start the next straight run. Even if two or more canoeists are paddling this procedure must be followed. A few minutes' practice will teach you a lot about the steering of the canoe by using the paddle more to the fore (front) or rear (aft). By not using the *J* stroke the canoe naturally turns away from the side on which paddling takes place.

Rivers are roads that travel, claimed Pascal. The trouble is that they do not always carry us where we would go, and they don't worry at all about leaving us on some isolated sandbank or shoulder-deep lump of useless marsh.

Always try to find out something about the currents, rapids and tides of a river (many rivers have an ebb and flow from their estuary) before you go on them.

As a general rule remember that if the river is straight for a certain length the deepest part of the river will be its centre.

If the river curves round a bend (or a series of bends) the strongest current will be on the outside edge of the bend, page 176.

If there are boulders or some obstructions in the river the river will take the line of least resistance (channel) which is the only safe course for a canoeist to follow. This course is easily recognised from afar by a giant V like the tip of a huge arrow at the head of the channel.

Currents move at their own speed; like Time and Tide they wait for no man, and may hurl you on to boulders, rocks, snags (this originally meant a hidden tree trunk whose branches below the waters could tear the keel of a boat), weirs and much else.

Normally, follow the plan shown on page 176 and let the deep water save your arms some energy. If you get by accident rather than design into a powerful current on an unknown river make for the shallows and slower-moving water which will give you time to think and plan ahead.

Currents are not to be laughed at. Strangely enough, the

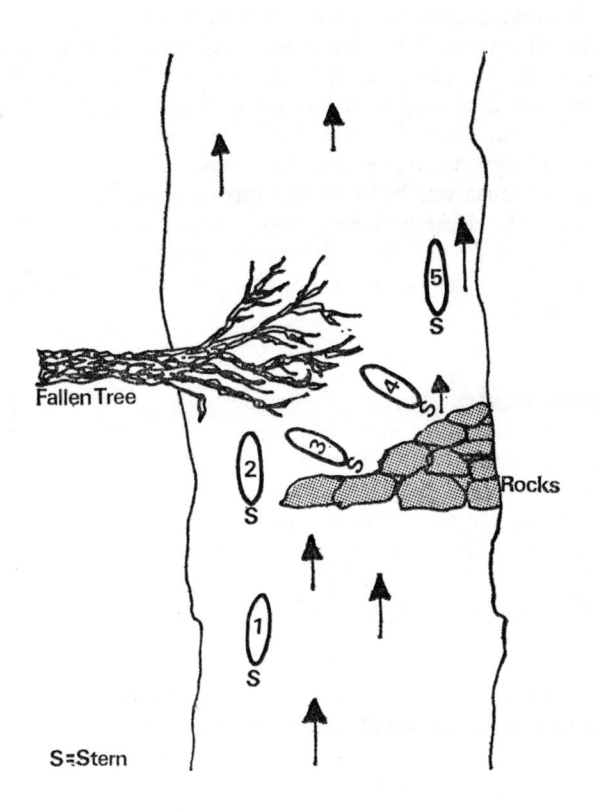

For obstructions use the transverse glide in 3 and 4. Turn your stern the way you want to go!

speed of a current varies in different places on the river. If the river narrows the pull of the current increases (as Leonard Snow discovered in the gorges of the Marañon which he descended on a raft!) If a river has boulders or the iron girders of a bridge there will be an increase of turbulence of water as it impatiently swirls around them. Avoid this where possible.

BLOW YE WINDS HEIGH HO—A ROVING WE WILL GO
In a word, a canoeist does not like wind too much; unlike a sailor they rarely help him. A mere zephyr on a summer day can make the water choppy and demand extra work from your muscles to keep your boat on course. To go off course is called to *yaw*. Wavelets may deceptively cover rocks or snags. Refer to the heading *Gale winds abeam*, above.

If the canoe was badly loaded this can become a source of trouble; the decks go awash, and you may ship water which weighs you down, makes the canoe uneasy to manage—and so on. Fit a spray cover if you expect trouble, and head for the shore!

DON'T PANIC
If a storm catches you on a large lake, keep calm. Cross waves as close to a right angle as you can judge, and be prepared to take a diagonal course home rather than make a beeline for the shore. You'll certainly remember the trip with pleasure (and possibly with pride) afterwards.

You must always use feathered blades in bad weather. If you are blown or swept aground it is essential to clamber out upstream of the canoe, otherwise the boat you treasure so much may swirl against you and knock you for six; if you don't get pushed under you'd certainly have a bruise or two from the encounter—and all unnecessary.

A large lake

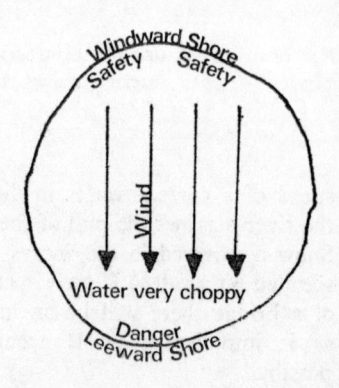

A little poem you should engrave on your memories:

> *From Windward shore the wind is blown,*
> *So leave a lee shore well alone.*

In my book *Young Person's Guide to Nature* I have described in detail how to judge weather signs, and anybody who ventures out to sea or on a big lake needs to be able to read weather well. Do not rely solely upon some meteorologist's report, for the weather may change without his permission within an hour or so. Strange as it may seem, the old-fashioned signs are invariably correct. Naturally a strong wind will tend to blow any boat to a leeward shore, and the man in the canoe must strive with might and main to get to a windward shore where some cliffs or trees might provide protection against the full blast of the gale.

WHITE WATER IS WETTEST

It is surprising how much wetter than wet some rapids can feel, but they are very exciting to traverse. The term *white water* is used because the result of the hidden rocks, uneven beds and boulders is foaming, tossing water, bubbling with trapped and escaping air. Before approaching rapids go ashore and inspect them from a safe distance. Seek out the natural course of deep water (line of least resistance); if in doubt carry your canoe past them, or line it down on the painters (see *Further Equipment* above). In narrow places you must be prepared to lift the paddle high above your head to avoid smashing it. The deeper the water the safer you are, and the higher the waves and spray will be! A heavy, solid canoe has less chance of coming through bad rapids than a light, plastic-covered wooden frame which has more bounce and elasticity. If trapped between rocks, think most carefully what to do—generally stick to your canoe (there is no need to go down with your ship like a romantic captain of olden days, but can you survive without it in this difficulty? Can you swim strongly enough? Maybe help might come; sooner or later the current may diminish enough for you to wriggle free). With a well-fixed spray cover and buoyancy the canoe may well be the safest bet you have.

A LONG FAREWELL TO ALL MY GREATNESS

It was my privilege to know Eric Roberts, one of the actors who was with the famous Sir Frank Benson of Shakespearean tradition. Eric would on occasion recite in costume some of his old parts, such as Cardinal Wolsey's speech from *Henry VIII*. This speech ending *'when he falls he falls like Lucifer, never to hope again'* might be studied by some canoeists who think lightly of waterfalls and weirs.

Weirs hold back vast quanities of water and are deceptive as regards currents, and may even be opened by some unthinking hand just as some adventurer is approaching. The answer is get ashore—portage or line down with painters. At twilight the task of judging depth of water is so difficult as to make it unsafe.

As regards the other hazard:

> *This is the tale of John and Paul*
> *Who took their canoe over a waterfall,*
> *Their map was right, right all along,*
> *They're just as dead as had it been wrong.*

A final word . . . Don't! Noise will warn you of weirs and waterfalls long before you ever get to them.

ALL AT SEA

So all those sea shanties are calling you away . . . *'for the call of the running tide is a strong call and a clear call and may not be denied'* as Masefield put it.

Take a compass with you, and make sure you know how to read it, a chart may help . . . just in case you get blown off course. The sea is not entirely without distinguishing marks because there are lanes of shipping, currents, buoys and lightships. Generally speaking, unless accompanied by another vessel *a canoeist is ill-advised to get out of sight of land*. Try to prevent your canoe ever being caught broadside by the waves.

In a bay there is almost always an *undertow;* expect it. Remember that at the equinoxes the tides will be higher and currents stronger.

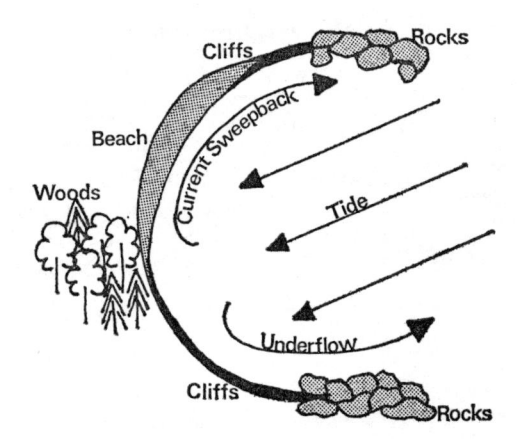

Launch out into waves by standing up to your knees in water; when a wave is receding shove the canoe off, straddle the back deck and wriggle in. Never let go of the canoe in this situation. If you have a good keel you can allow the waves to lift your canoe right high up on to the shore, make certain you travel in on the crest of the wave. Among long-distance canoe trips are complete round-Britain trips, cross-Channel trips, and many lengthy voyages down N. American and S. American rivers. Always ask the locals for advice on tides, winds and local hazards.

In theory steam gives way to sail. In practice many large tugs, tramps and liners can't even see a canoe, and wouldn't stop if they did.

If you think that you are likely to be at sea or in an estuary where there is much traffic you should carry lights and show them.

Most water traffic keeps to the right. So if you pass another boat your portside light (green) will overtake that vessel's starboard light (red). If you approach a vessel coming towards you it is correct to pass green light to green light. Only a very experienced canoeist should risk being abroad in deep waters after dusk has descended over the waves, but the above rule must be kept.

Note hands position!

If in danger of capsizing shoot the paddle quickly in the direction of capsize, slap flat blade down hard on the water and lean on it then to right yourself

Whistle signals—Whether at sea or on other waters it is good for a canoeist to have a whistle with him. Blow loud and clear.

1 blast —Turning to starboard (right hand side).
2 blasts—Turning to portside (left hand side).
3 blasts—Strong wind abaft, avoid me.
4 blasts—Move out of my way I cannot avoid you.

General

An ebb tide is stronger and faster than a flood tide.

There is always turbulent water just outside a harbour-mouth.

Short diagonal runs are necessary to cross a strong tide.

If the wind and the tide are opposite in direction, try to use your paddles as sails, the wind is often the stronger.

Never rely upon other canoeists or water-users knowing the international signals; seek to avoid collisions!

CAMPING WITH A CANOE

The canoe carries your gear! Virtually no extra effort is required to paddle twice the gear you might be tempted to pack on your back! If you have never camped by canoe you have one of the greatest joys to come.

Gliding along beautiful river scenery, across rippling lakes, you reach a quiet place with a wonderful view; you paddle alongside the bank, leap ashore, drag the canoe out of the water with you. Within 10 minutes the tent is up, the cooking gear is set up, your blanket and sleeping bag are lying in front of the tent, your chosen book is there.

Before settling down to a delicious meal you turn the canoe keelside up so that morning dew may not lie in the canoe (always strive to keep the interior dry).

Wild duck wing their way overhead. A couple of swan pass in front of you. Sunset glows over the murmuring current before you, the fragrance of a small fire of pine twigs gives a coil of smoke keeping insects away, warming the evening before you turn into the sleeping bag inside your tent, drop the flap, and drowse into relaxing sleep on the bosom of our mother the Earth.

When you wake in the morning the twittering of the water fowl on the river, the calls of the thrushes and blackbirds from the bushes on the bank alert you to the dew-laden morning air . . . soon to be made even more attractive by the smell of your two rashers and two eggs frying on the stove. (You'll eat more in the open air!)

Take care to load the canoe so that the weight stored fore and the weight stored aft *balance* the canoe. Too much gear stowed forard, too much gear stowed aft make the canoe quite unmanageable.

Suggestions for stowing gear on a canoe camping trip

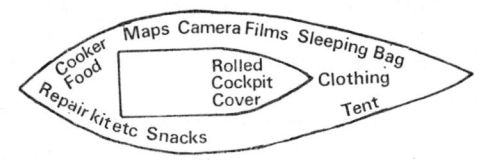

All items should be wrapped in waterproof bags

Too much gear stowed forard

Too much gear stowed aft

Don't forget the matches! Keep one box of spares wrapped in two waterproof layers of plastic.

If you leave the canoe in the water—something I would never do—use a *painter* to tie each end up to the bank; one end may pull loose.

There is the most marvellous sense of freedom, you paddle slowly (or fast if you wish) whither you would go; deserted river banks and lakesides await you; later on when experienced, you may paddle the seashore along: the world is your *oyster* waiting for you to open it—you travel as Ulysses of old, the first man (so it seems) ever to travel into unknown waters! As soon as you have mastered the simple techniques outlined here do try the excitement and joy of canoe camping.

Sailing

SAILING—A SENSE OF FREEDOM
Freedom can be enjoyed only by those who are disciplined and responsible. No water sport can be as dangerous as sailing if certain essential obligations are neglected. Sailing must be taught by a proper, qualified teacher, and it must be practised patiently (and it takes time to learn), and its rewards are then enormous.

It would be presumptuous for me to pretend that the section of this book about sailing is more than a guide to explain to the beginner what sailing entails. Men far more expert than myself at sailing have written about the subject, and in the long run a few hours spent with a good teacher in a boat will teach you more than hours of reading. Consequently I confine my activities to speeding up the process as best I can. In this chapter there is an illustrated mainsail, naming all the parts—these must be learnt; men have learnt them for over a thousand years; we should not be less capable of learning these words than our ancestors were. It is useless to talk of a *rope*; in an emergency you must know whether it is a sheet or a halyard—(a halyard hauls a sail up or down the mast; a sheet trims the sail's position). Emergencies happen at sea, and when they do they are more terrible than those on land, insomuch as just one mistake may well be your last on this planet! Even on a river or in a seemingly-safe estuary a storm may rush up with little or no warning, and the wind may cut across the pull of a powerful tide rip; what was a jolly, comfortable little craft becomes unmanageable; even with orange (safety colour) sails you may not be seen—ever again.

Learning seemingly-useless words means that you can obey a command by an experienced sailor and save your boat (and yourselves) from a watery grave.

A number of diagrams are given to explain the behaviour of the sails vis-a-vis the wind and the directional thrust of the keel. A young person could experiment with a model yacht on a small pond to observe how the wind *slots through* the sails and thrusts the boat along.

The beginner should make sure the boat is pointing into the wind while putting the sail up, otherwise you may find yourself moving somewhere you do not wish to go. It is usual to put up the mainsail first and then the jibsail.

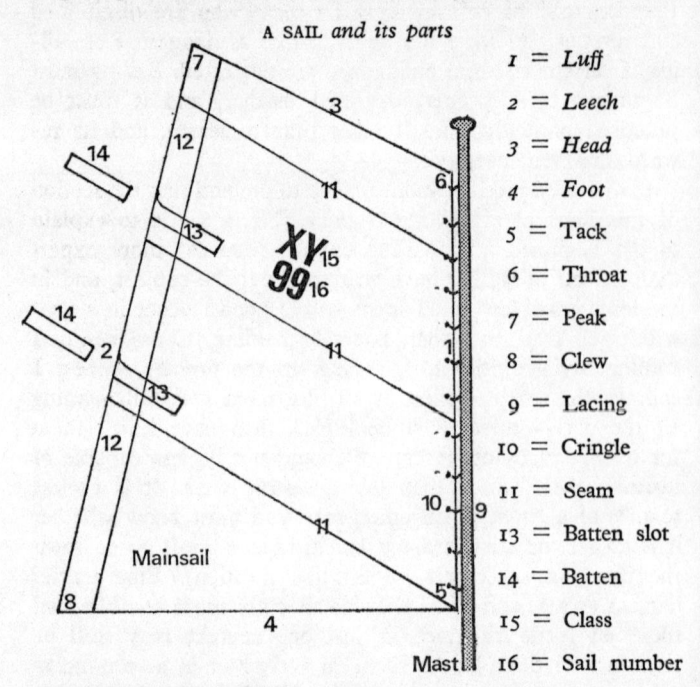

A SAIL *and its parts*

1 = Luff
2 = Leech
3 = Head
4 = Foot
5 = Tack
6 = Throat
7 = Peak
8 = Clew
9 = Lacing
10 = Cringle
11 = Seam
13 = Batten slot
14 = Batten
15 = Class
16 = Sail number

HOLDING THE TILLER

The tiller is usually held with the hand nearest the rudder. In a dinghy the tiller is held firmly between thumb and index finger; this does not mean grasping it hard, very slight movements are sufficient to modify your boat's course. Violent movements may bring you into *stays* or cause gybing (even capsizing). Rough movements on a tiller act as a brake. Make sure you sit so as to keep the boat in good trim.

**To go to the left –
Push Tiller to the right**

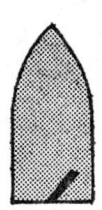

**To go to the right –
Push Tiller to the left**

WATCH THE BURGEE

Whether your burgee is a smart pennant or a strip of your girl-friend's dress tied to the shrouds you must spend a lot of time watching it. It reacts more quickly than the sail (being smaller) the idea is to angle the sail according to the wind.

A SAILING WE WILL GO

The helmsman sits grasping the tiller in his right hand; he is slightly to port, the mainsheet (rope) held in his left hand. The centreboard is lowered half-way. The crewman undoes the painter (rope which ties the boat to the mooring ashore), gives a shove to the boat and jumps aboard over the transom. Crewman sits to starboard of boom. We assume the wind is coming from the portside; the mainsail is drawn in by the sheet until there is no flapping of that sail, crewman moves more to centre . . . see diagram for a suggested beginner's trip. Consult *Foyle's Handbook on Sailing*.

Sailing is not just lazing happily in a gliding boat and doing nothing, it involves a constant watch on the burgee (winds do not stay constant but shift slightly and sometimes violently), and a constant readiness to trim the sails to suit the wind. On a long-distance voyage across a wide stretch of sea with a proper seagoing vessel you will pick up a wind which will carry you for many nautical miles, but this section is not written for this type of cruising, only for sailing in rivers, estuaries and lakes, perhaps a little inshore sailing too (close to the coastline).

Some Parts of a Boat

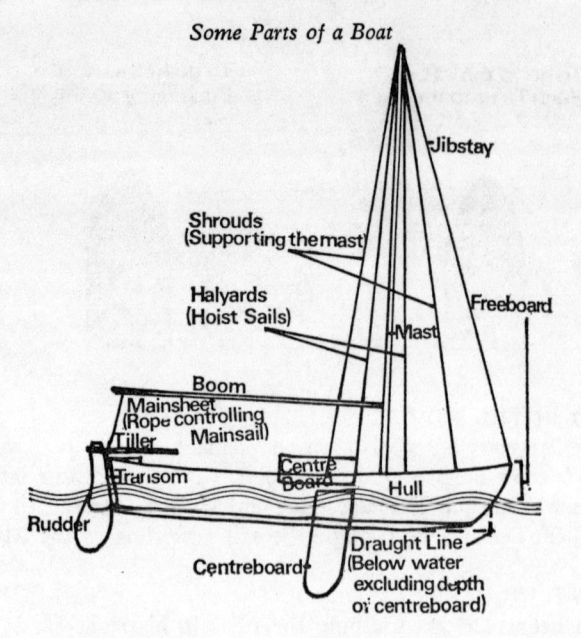

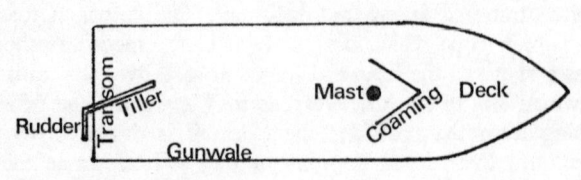

Labels on upper diagram: Jibstay, Shrouds (Supporting the mast), Halyards (Hoist Sails), Mast, Freeboard, Boom, Mainsheet (Rope controlling Mainsail), Tiller, Transom, Centre Board, Hull, Rudder, Centreboard, Draught Line (Below water excluding depth of centreboard)

Labels on lower diagram: Transom, Tiller, Rudder, Gunwale, Mast, Coaming, Deck

GO ABOUT!

This is to turn the boat from one tack to another across the wind, usually passing through a complete right angle. When you wish to change the direction in which you are going, and return whence you came, push the tiller to the right of the boat; this is called *helm down*; mainsail and jib must be quickly drawn to the centre line of the boat. You must have a good speed before you complete the manoeuvre, or you'll end up *in stays* (staying still) and lose the wind. You must *hold the helm down* until you catch the wind again. The art is not to lose the speed you have built up while coming up to the turn. As the boat starts her turn sheet the sails to get the correct angle of the wind (from 90 degrees to 45 degrees). It is essential that the crewman should keep hold of the jib sheet (rope holding the jib sail) keeping it in the direction of the wind before the turn until the turn is through the *eye of the wind* (direction from which the wind is blowing), so the jib is changed a slight second or so after the mainsail. If helmsman and crewman do not learn to duck quickly as the boom swings over to the new tack they can get a bump to remember!

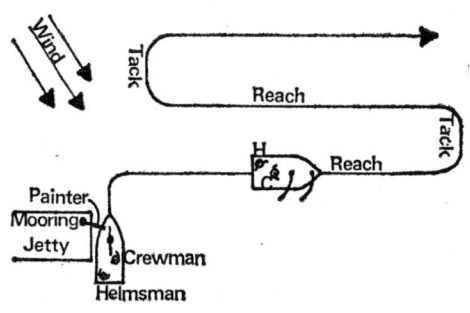

A beginner's first sail

The crewman will feel a change of wind pressure on the jibsail as soon as the turn has been completed; this is the signal to let go the jib sheet being held and pull the other jib sheet through.

IN STAYS
The trouble is that you will not really stay put for long but suffer the humiliation of being blown backwards slowly whence you came because the wind catches the resistance of your boat's bows! Hold out the jibsail to one side or the other to swing the bows round, once you get some movement of the wind it is easy enough to correct direction. Do not expect to get out of it by thrashing the tiller from port to starboard. In *Irons*—boat thoroughly out of control in *stays* during high winds.

HOW TO USE THE CENTREBOARD

Lower fully to increase resistance to pressure of wind on your beam. Remember light sailing dinghies need intelligent use of the centreboard for efficient sailing.

FREE RUNNING

It is an old maxim that you get nothing for nothing. When you have the wind behind you coming directly over the transom you must make sure that the helmsman and crewman do not overbalance the boat because (here is the catch) the boat is more difficult to control at this point of sailing than at any other point, and all trimming of sails is slower to show

Wind

Sails flutter uselessly 'in stays'

You need from 90° to 45° angle of wind to sail

effect when the wind comes from behind.

Raise the centreboard. The sails are placed in the *goosewing* position so that fullest use of the wind is made (and fast you will sail with it). It is a good practice to tie a stop-knot in the mainsheet to limit the amount which the mainsail may travel out, this lessens the likelihood of capsizing. The jibsail is usually held by a temporary, light boom called *jib-boom* or jib-stick.

If you can manage to sail at a slight angle rather than have the wind directly behind the transom you will lessen the chance of gybing suddenly, because if the wind veers the main boom can swing viciously across the boat, cracking a skull or two in passing.

Dropping the centreboard down fully will slow your speed down. Do not try running free if rough weather is about—not until you are a really experienced sailor; do not try it with a clumsy crew! Experienced sailors often use a special spinnaker sail to capture more wind speed, this is definitely not suitable for beginners. During a planned gybing remember to remove the jib-boom first, turn tiller to the left,

Hold the sheet (rope) as close to the boom as you can, haul boom and sail to opposite side - change sides as you do so.
Pull tiller towards you until wind is astern BEFORE you change boom and sail over.

helmsman and crewman to centre line of boat, duck heads, haul mainsheet, swing boom across to opposite side allowing mainsheet to extend until stopped.

REACHING

I suppose we may call this any course other than running before the wind, it is easy to think of it as having the wind on your beamside. Watch the burgee all the time. Check the luff of the sail, if it shivers you must haul on the sheets until the shaking stops. As a general rule aim at the wind coming on to the sail about 90 degrees. Avoid letting the sails ever become flattened out, this will loose your boat's direction (increase *leeway*). Boat's crew both tend to move astern, fasten the kicking-strap to keep mainsail steady.

I would emphasise that the information here is simplified especially for beginners, to give them the feel of sailing with as little detail (beyond the essential) as possible. According to how seriously you take the sport and how far you intend to sail (e.g. out of sight of land etc.)—so there is a great deal more to learn.

RETURN TO MOORINGS

Plan your course far ahead! Do not rely upon an angel to bring you in! Start about 100 yds. or metres offshore. If the wind is blowing your boat towards the shore (*onshore wind*) turn her head into the wind, lower mainsail, cruise in slowly by jibsail which is either dropped or allowed to swing freely for the last few yards—especially if entering a crowded yacht marina! An *offshore wind* presents a different approach to moorings. The boat must be tacked, usually close-hauled, up towards the jetty or landing stage. At the last minute the helmsman heads her round up into the wind, and as she drifts you jump ashore and make her fast with a painter (rope, not

Rembrandt!). If the wind is blowing along the jetty you circle in until by loosening jibsail, then mainsail, you turn her until she is virtually in stays alongside!

All of these manoeuvres are easier after practical experience than they sound on paper!

CLOSE HAULED

Is sailing as near into the wind as possible. The natural curve of the sails is flattened to squeeze the boat at an angle against the wind. To all intents and purposes your minimum angle is 45 degrees to take your boat forward, but this means an angle across the line of your direction, so you will have to tack (make zig-zag movements).

LAYING YOUR COURSE

If you sail even across an estuary or round a wide bay you must study navigation, using such works as G. G. Watkins' unrivalled *Coastwise Navigation* (Kandy Publications) and similar publications. The attached diagram will explain some of the difficulties to be mastered. Expert tuition from an experienced sailor is advisable.

Leeway is due to the action of the wind on the boat; it is the difference in the angle between the course steered and the actual line your boat really takes. Look at the wake in reference to the position of the boat and you can make a rough guess at the leeway you are making, checking this by compass, of course. The more shallow the draught of the boat the more leeway you'll make.

Tidal force. If the tide is against your direction of sail you will need proper instruments and charts to estimate and correct the position of the boat.

EMERGENCIES

Many are the emergencies which may occur at sea. If the wind freshens (blows from 17 to 21 nautical miles per hour) you would be well advised to shorten the sail by reefing. Small dinghies often lower the sail and roll part of it around the boom; most sails have reef points in lines so that the sail may be shortened (making it more manageable, lower and less liable to be torn to shreds by a gale etc.), the sail is folded

Laying your course

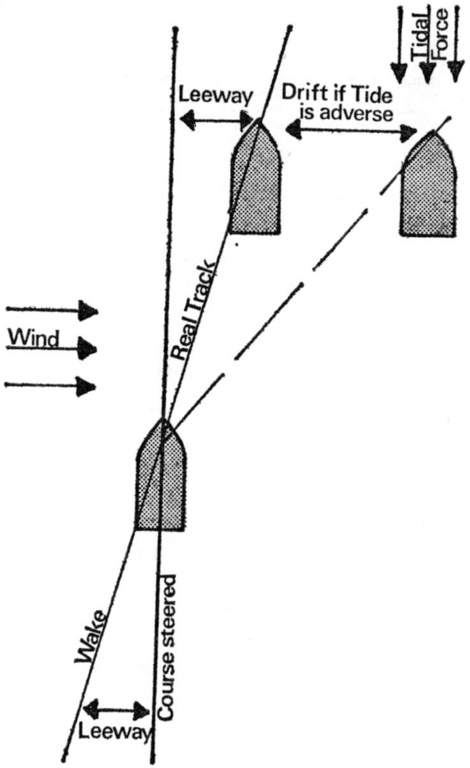
Tidal Force
Leeway
Drift if Tide is adverse
Real Track
Wind
Wake
Course steered
Leeway

down and the knots can be tied—hence reef-knot.

Make certain that the centreboard is down if you wish to lessen the likelihood of a capsize etc.

Distress signals, flares, lifejackets and common sense are a MUST for every sailor who ventures into an estuary or beyond.

If you capsize never leave your boat—it is bigger to spot and easier to find than a bobbing, small woollen-capped head in a vast sea.

Make sure you have a bailer with you to clear out any water shipped during a heavy sea.

Fishing and Subaqua

A FEW WORDS ABOUT FISHING

I think too much has been written about fishing, and too often people make it a sheer routine instead of a pleasant relaxation. For most men this is the last remaining vestige of our primeval hunting instincts, but in the words of Izaak Walton (1593-1683) *God did never make a more calm, quiet, innocent recreation than angling*. My advice is given in a few words, hoping your recreation may be quieter and the more enjoyable for them.

As a general rule, always buy the best equipment you can afford, suited to your height, muscular power etc. A boy with a rod and line suited for his size and physique will catch twice the haul that a man with luxurious but ill-chosen equipment would.

As a general rule, try to give any other fisherman up to 30 yards of river bank.

Remember there are two kinds of fishing—for the supper frying-pan and for the sport of catching them; be careful to throw back any fish you are not going to eat. Exposure to the air will not harm a fish as much as being handled by your bare hands which to the fish (cold-blooded creature) will seem hotter than boiling point to us. If you handle a fish use a wet cloth. If you want to retain the catch until somebody else sees it, put the fish gently into a keep-net. When you put a fish back into water do not throw it but lower it gently—holding it head pointing upstream! If you have to take a fish off a hook without a special disgorger press the hook downwards in the mouth first, and then push it backwards before pulling it out.

If the place you fish requires a licence, do not begrudge paying a few pence which contribute to the preservation of the fishery.

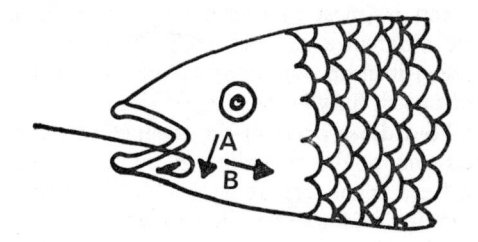

How to take a hook out

Check that your line is not too heavy for the rod; that is one of the main causes of getting those terrible knots in it. Never throw discarded line away on the river bank or in the fields—it can choke birds and small mammals to death.

Oil the reel and dry the rod before putting it away after your expedition.

Unless you wish merely to feed the fish, remember to bait your hook correctly. Maggots are used in two, threes or even fives. Do not burst them open, just pass the barb of the hook beneath their skin. For worms a size 6 or 8 hook may be necessary, a large worm can wriggle off of a small hook. The object is to arrange that the said worm has opportunity to wriggle.

How to fix bait to your hook

Remember that your rods must be well-balanced. Some cheap rods are top-heavy, not following the mere flick of the wrist which is the mark of a good cast (by which baited hook and line are thrown out on to the water). Whatever your rod is (most fishermen keep one type of rod for each of the different aspects of angling they follow) wipe it well and keep it clean, especially before putting it back into a cupboard to wait for your next expedition.

If your head doesn't reel at the thought of the arguments about reels you might as well face up to the virtues and vices of a fixed spool reel. It is less likely to let the thread of wound-in line twist and become uneven, less likely to allow the line to be entangled in knots, and it is certainly less trouble for a beginner to handle. Sea-anglers frequently prefer an open reel as these tend to take longer lengths of line.

A fixed spool reel (left hand winder)   *A typical sea-reel*

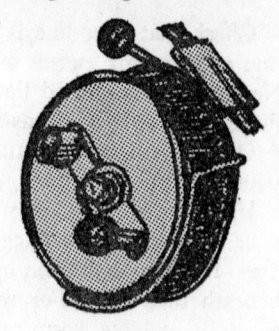

The average line today is nylon, perlon or dralon monofilament. Breaking-strains range from 3 lb. to 15 lb. Heavier lines can be had if needed.

The size of the hook is universally numbered, and it is best to talk to your supplier (who is almost certainly an angler himself) about which is the best size for the fish you plan to catch in the stream, pond or river you intend to fish. The same advice can be got about which float to use. These come in a wide variety of shapes and sizes, but it is more important to make certain that the angle of the line to the float is correct. (See diagram.)

Lead sea weights are common for deep sea fishing, and instead of using a simple hook, a paternoster on a boom wire is popular.

For sea angling some knowledge of tides is advisable, for

GUIDE TO SWIMMING AND WATER SPORTS

(i) Correct Line to Float angle

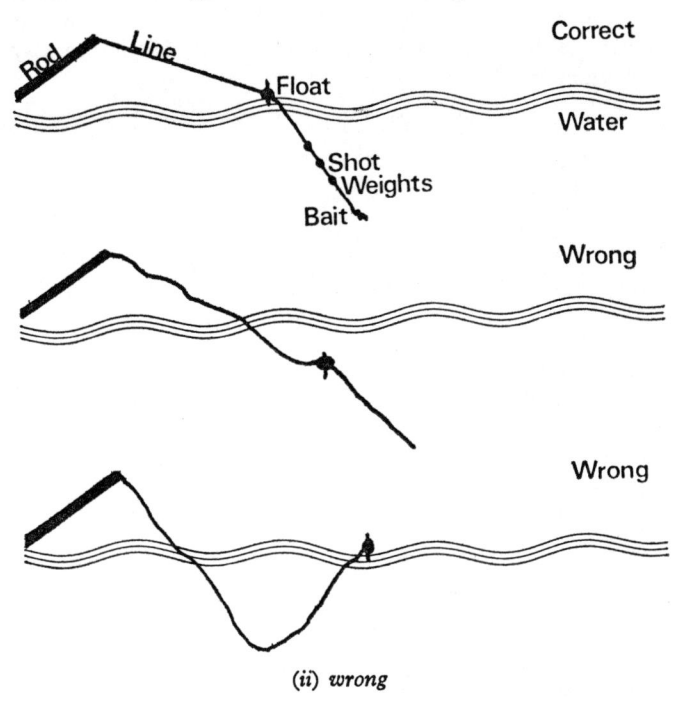

(ii) wrong

fish move with the tide and are often influenced by rough weather. Braving the elements may mean a better fish supper that night!

If you have a mind to build your own rod, remember that it should be whippy. You are advised to stick to nylon or similar monofilament lines, professional hooks etc.

A friend of mine who lived for a long time in Guiana, South America, described how the Indians of the forest there shoot fish with bow and arrow! If you try it, be careful not to shoot at your own foot.

In general, fishing is not a sport with widely applicable rules, but rather one with thousands of different local conditions. What some fish think is a tasty bait will be wholly rejected by others. Do speak to local fishermen to learn more about your local fishing.

202 GUIDE TO SWIMMING AND WATER SPORTS

For salmon, trout and sea trout fishing the reader should refer to Tom Ravensdale's book *Understanding Salmon and Trout*, as this is a highly specialised subject, and not so easy for beginners.

DIVING

DIVING FOR ADVENTURE AND PROFIT (*with schnorkel and scuba*)

The world under the sea is full of mystery and adventure. Centuries before Christ the Ancient Greeks used divers with strong lungs to clear a hidden boom from the harbour of Syracuse.

Japanese and Kanaka pearl divers learnt to remain so long under water in search of pearls that few people can credit their abilities without having seen them.

Man has been fascinated with the depths of the ocean; indeed some scientists maintain that our physical forms, if not our intangible minds, had their origins in the oceans.

The German invention of Scuba, underwater breathing apparatus was but a development of an idea of Leonardo da Vinci (1492-1519) and was the first step forward from the clumsy, but still often essential, massive, cumbersome, helmeted rubber-suited diver with a pipeline for air which had developed during the 19th century and later.

Do not take up skin or scuba diving unless you have a certificate for at least 880 yds (800 m) swim, can tread water for five minutes using no hands but feet only, float for 10 minutes without an aid and can tow another person as big as yourself for 100 yds (100 m) swimming on your back. You should be able to swim 20 bodylengths under water without any air-supply except what is in your own lungs. You *never* dive alone, and should not even practice alone. If you have any bronchial, cardiac or pulmonary illness you should not dive. All diving makes lungs and heart work much harder than breathing fresh air on land requires. Excitable, nervous or epileptic people should never dive . . . below the water is the last place to panic!

Ten metres down in the depths the pressures exerted

against all parts of the body are twice as strong as on surface level.

SWIMMING STROKES UNDER WATER
(i) A simple front crawl legs thrash, enhanced by wearing flippers. Do not use the front crawl arm movements.
(ii) Breast stroke leg movements; the arms are rarely used.
(iii) Arm movements are something approaching a dog-paddle movement; reduce the front crawl to a fin-like pull underneath the body.

Fish have no arms but they swim very well flicking fins and tail. Practise diving from the surface of the water, lowering the head, bending the hips and shooting the legs up 90 degrees to the surface, this carries you down very quickly.

EQUIPMENT
Never dive without the right equipment or with faulty equipment or with second-hand equipment you have not tested. Your life may be at stake, and you must be realistic about this. I am strongly opposed to the general use of a spear gun under water unless the diver is going into water which is suspected of harbouring dangerous creatures. Although, as both Jacques Cousteau and Hans Hass have written in their books, many of the sharks, sting rays and moray eels would not attack a man, sharks are temperamental so do not take chances with them.

WHAT CAN YOU DO ONCE YOU ARE DOWN BELOW?
There is always the lure of buried treasure. It is astonishing how many ships have been victims of the waves or of battles.

Many freebooters found their treasure an encumbrance. Banks were scarce. Gold and jewels worth many thousands of millions of pounds were hidden on the coasts; many hundreds of millions never reached their goal and lie on reefs or at the bottom of a coral strand.

Collecting shells; a friend of mine made a good living for himself when he was younger by diving for *abalone* shells (that was in Australia). The seabed is full of wonderful shells, and collecting them is a most exciting hobby.

Seaweeds can be collected too, there are so many different sorts. They can be pressed and dried.

There is quite a lot of money in recovering industrial metals and objects from the seabed . . . lead, copper, iron (even if rusty). Exploration of the seabed is another exciting activity; much of the bed is unmapped.

Archaeology has become one of the favourite occupations of divers, and under the inspiration of Jacques Cousteau and Frédéric Dumas men have begun diving for the treasures of the past. Golden vases of ancient Rome, statues from ancient Greece, hoards of silver, marble columns (usually covered by barnacles), and a host of curious but valuable antiquities can be dragged up. In Sweden a 300-year-old ship was raised complete with the vast treasure she carried—all through the devoted, enthusiastic efforts of the sub-aqua divers who made it possible.

The amateur detective may discover things which will aid the police in their heroic battle against crime. A murder weapon may have been cast into a river; a case full of smuggled watches recovered. By intelligent co-operation with the forces of law and order you can become a public benefactor.

Many newspapers and magazines pay high prices for good underwater photographs, and the efforts and time spent in mastering the techniques (you must have a special underwater camera) are often well-rewarded.

THINGS TO BE CAREFUL ABOUT

You are strongly advised to train with the help of an instructor to make sure you are safe to dive, because this is a real life adventure, and there are some dangers present if you are careless.

(a) *Schnorkel.* Make sure the mouthpiece supplied is comfortable in your mouth, that the tube is unblocked and that any valves are in working condition.

(b) *Scuba.* Alternatively you should use one of the systems of underwater self-contained air containers (aqualung). These work on the basis of compressed air in a metal cylinder which will release oxygen to the diver at a controlled (and adjustable) amount. It is essential that the equipment is fitted with a quick-release gear so that you can dump it whenever an emergency demands it. You should practise the quick release in a shallow swimming pool, and master the mechanism of the regulator hose which controls the amount of air released during use of the aqualung. After use wash the mouthpiece carefully, hang up hose parts and then dry them with talcum powder to preserve the long-life of the rubber parts. When you get your aqualung make certain that there is a special arrangement allowing for an *emergency reserve*, which will guarantee that if you have over-run your time below there will be enough air left for you to return to the surface. *Only buy aqualung equipment from a recognised dealer*, and get refills of compressed air from your supplier.

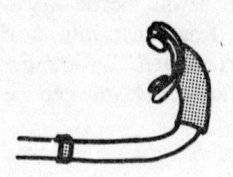

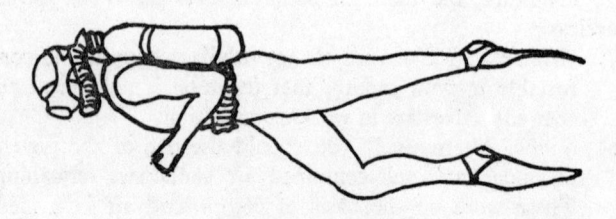

Diver using Aqualung

GUIDE TO SWIMMING AND WATER SPORTS 207

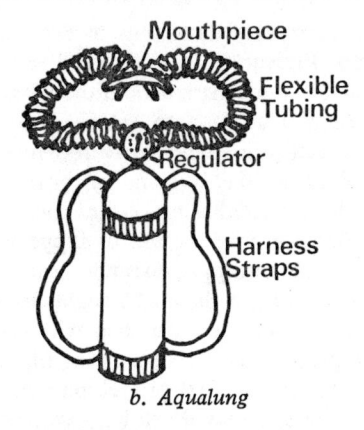

b. Aqualung

(c) *Mask.* Having made sure you can breathe under water safely here is how you see under water clearly. Human eyes cannot see adequately under the water without a mask; try picking up a small coin from the bottom of a swimming pool. Without a mask on you may succeed at 1 metre but not at 3 metres depth. Some of the water you explore may be 10 or 20 times as deep as that. The mask must fit closely without being too tight; it must be comfortable around the nose. If water gets in your vision will blur. The fittings (buckles etc.) should be of brass or some alloy which will not corrode with constant contact with salt water. You can use your own spit to smear the inside of the glass to prevent condensation, it is better than almost any of the commercial preparations unless you plan a long, deep dive. Dry the mask after use and dust it with talcum powder to care for the rubber parts.

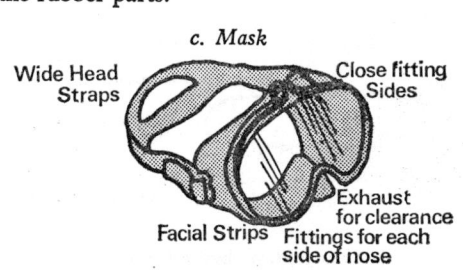

c. Mask

(d) *Ear plugs.* It is very dangerous to use ear plugs when diving deep. Pressurised air can get behind them, then the force of the water hammers in the plugs so deep that you may need a surgeon to get them out again. The chances are that you would *never* recover your hearing.

(e) *Flippers.* Because the amount of arm movement in swimming is restricted a great deal more attention has to be paid to the effective use of flippers worn on the feet. The size of the flipper does not mean a faster stroke. The width and length should be commensurate with the length of your own legs; the shop will advise you here (do go to a proper sports shop), wrong flipper size means exhausted muscles and less propulsion than you ought to get. If the flipper is wholly stiff it can bring on a nasty attack of cramp. Do not accept any sales line about a stiff flipper becoming softer after use, as like as not the salesman (anxious for his commission) does not have to go down 90 feet or so wearing them. A flipper should not be too supple or easily bent or you will not get any help from it. Test them for springiness and strength before buying. Keep them dry, and dust with talcum powder to preserve the rubber.

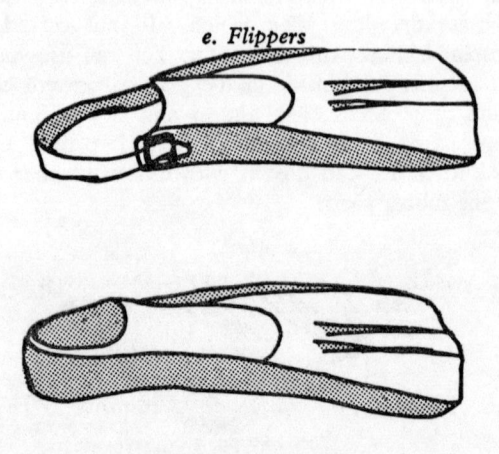

e. Flippers

A shoe with a duck's fitting!

(f) *Gauge and compass.* You must wear a gauge to tell you how deep down you are, and it is wise to wear a compass to tell you in which direction you are going, and where the boat or coastline lies. Under water (most diving is done at sea) there is little to tell you where you are until you are familiar with a location. Both instruments should be in waterproof housings. A watch should also be worn. This should have a luminous dial and preferably coloured sections showing the diver how long he has been down. This is often done with a coloured ring which swivels round the outer part of the watch, and is set at the time when he starts, and at a glance tells the diver whether he has been down the maximum time suitable for him (depends on how long you have been diving; beginners take less strain than experienced divers). Occasionally one may find an underwater watch with *an audible alarm signal which can warn you when your supply of oxygen is likely to run low.*

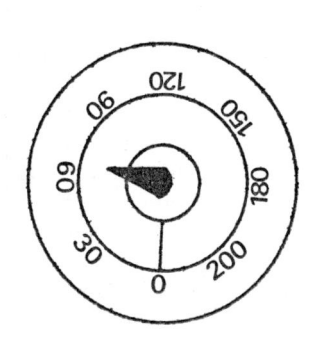

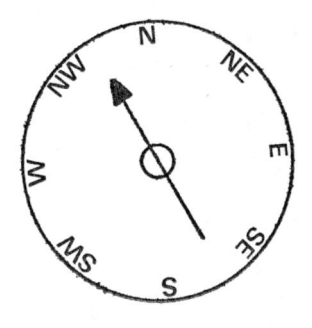

Depth Gauge   *Compass*

ALSO REQUIRED

A special knife, in case you get tangled up with old, abandoned nets, wrecks etc.

A strong torch for underwater use; it must be waterproof and have batteries which will give up to an hour's uninterrupted light. No good finding golden *pieces of eight* on the seabed if the torch gives out at that moment.

A belt which is weighted down with pieces of lead, usually about 5 lb. each, should be worn. *It must be fitted with a simple quick-release* for emergency (such as meeting a shark you are not on speaking terms with).

A wet suit is commonly worn. Small amounts of water may seep inside but the suit is insulated so well that it keeps body heat in. Cold is the danger—not the wet. Expensive wet suits are, despite their name, almost entirely water-insulating.

SAFETY—THE ESSENTIAL FACTOR

To all intents and purposes the pressure of water is 15 lb. per square inch per 10 metres (33 ft.) depth descended; the human body's average surface area is over 2,000 square inches, and the pressure at 10 metres below is about 34,500 kilograms or 76,000 lb!

What effect can this have? Well, in the body there are gases other than oxygen, and the effect of depth-pressure on them can produce ill-effects if certain precautions are not observed.

Never dive alone—even during a practice! (I cannot repeat this too often.)

As long ago as 1660 a famous scientist Robert Boyle (1627-1691) established that the volume of a given mass of gas at a given temperature is inversely proportional to its pressure . . . this means that when coming up from a depth a diver must breathe out consciously, because if he holds a breath while coming up into a different pressure level the air in his lungs will expand and damage the lungs. The opposite —breathing in continually whilst descending—comes naturally, but nervous tension often make a beginner try to hold his breath . . . this must be avoided by training and practice under a proper instructor. It is blithely assumed that we breathe in oxygen from the air about us. Pure oxygen is poisonous to us—especially at a depth below surface level. Air contains 21 per cent oxygen, 78 per cent nitrogen; carbon dioxide varies from 0.03–0.06 per cent and there is 0.9 per cent argon and traces of other gases.

Different components of air exert various pressures in the

compressed air the diver breathes. Jaques Cousteau related how one of the early divers drank champagne under water, when he came to the surface the carbon dioxide bubbles expanded enormously, and the unhappy man had to be rushed to hospital! An excess of nitrogen in the air breathed produces a hallucinatory effect on the diver. Some have been known to tear off their masks and offer them to passing fish! This is why your cylinders must be refilled by a proper supplier.

THE BENDS

This is a nasty affliction which some divers suffer from; it was identified by a French scientist, Paul Bert (1833-1886). The nitrogen in the air absorbed by a diver from his compressed air supply is not entirely dissipated when he breathes out again, so if a diver surfaces too quickly from a dive the retained oxygen can expand and froth like the bubbles you see when you open a can of *Coke* or beer. These bubbles can clog up the veins (cutting off blood from the heart), press with devastating pain upon nerves (hence the screwed-up, bent positions of divers who suffer this way) and may even cause death. This condition results from prolonged dives at depths greater than most amateurs are likely to descend. *Always surface slowly and breathe out all the time.* It takes up to 12 hours for a body to correct over-exposure to nitrogen. Do not dive the next day if you have symptoms of suspected bends or nitrogen hallucination (*L'ivresse de grands profondeurs*—Cousteau).

Before diving always get local information about tides, currents, possible poisonous creatures etc.

Many locations have small creatures, such as the sea urchin, weever fish, jellyfish and sting ray which have poisonous spines or tentacles—most of them are afraid of Man, and you are unlikely to have trouble from them unless you are careless. With reference to sharks, you are unlikely to get near their hunting grounds unless you (or a diver with you) are experienced, and advice and help should be at hand. Octopuses are mostly friendly and by no means the terrible monsters that Victor Hugo made them out to be.

Be careful where you poke your head; some caves are respectable dwelling places, and the owners such as moray eels may bite! (Do you like burglars in your home?)

The more common sense you use the more you will feel at home in the water. You may know the thrill that the great pioneers of the West knew as hitherto unknown landscapes unfolded before them, you may see the world as the very first men saw it . . . there is always the chance that you, like Cousteau, may find a beautifully marked road, forgotten, buried cities resting in peace for millenia beneath the waves.

Rowing, Punts and Rafts, Outboard Motors

ROWING

Ever since my first lesson in rowing on the lovely lake of Zürich—long, halcyon years ago when springs were always sunny and filled with the scent of magnolias and lilacs, I have enjoyed a turn at the oars. There is something very satisfying about a long pull and the gentle hiss of blades feathering across the waters.

Firstly, you always get into a boat when it is pointing against the current. In all rowing boats you normally sit down with your back to the direction in which you wish to travel. Always put your foot deliberately into the centre of the boat. Always seat yourself in the centre of the boat, and in the middle of the rower's seat.

Make sure the oars are securely fixed in the rowlocks (see illustration) this gives you a better resistance against which to pull on your oars.

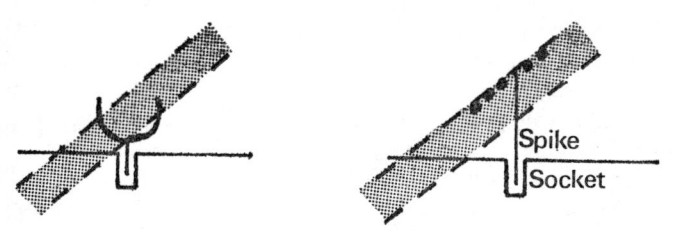

Types of ROWLOCKS (pronounced ROLLOCKS) to hold the oars

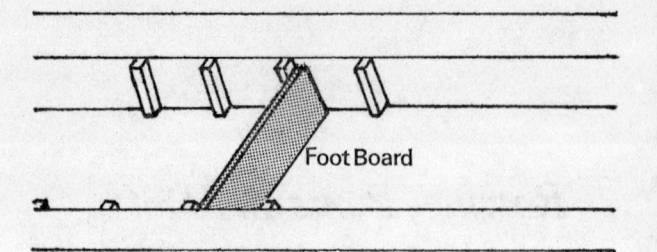

Alter the footboard to suit your length

Where your feet come you will see a series of grooves, and a stretcher-board against which you place the feet to make the movements of the body more rhythmic and precise. Alter this board until you find which grooves are most comfortable for you. You'll never get a good, easy, rhythm if you are not comfortable. Most oars have a line of brass nails holding the leather where the oars cross the rowlocks; this leather should be well greased or you will tire too soon. (Also dry leather makes a most annoying squeak.) You swing the oars forward (this is in the direction you are going) and dip them in the water so that just the blade is below the waterline—both blades must be the same depth below the water; to get one blade much deeper than the other impedes recovery of that blade, makes the boat lose course (headway) and spin, you will then tend to fall back . . . this is known as *catching a crab*!

As you swing the oars backward towards the wake of the boat you raise the wrists slightly upward and pull the oars into the chest . . . this upward movement of the wrists makes the oars turn in the rowlocks so that the broad, flattish blades *feather* (turn to avoid the wind). Only if you are a beginner will you doubt what a big difference an opposing wind can do to oars turned against it. In the part of this book dealing with canoeing I described how a wind can use blades as a sail and be very dangerous; although a rowing boat is heavier the effect is the same. Now a word about oars. Technically an *oar* is the heavier and a *scull* is the lighter version of the same thing. Sculls are usually shorter and used more for pleasure trips; they have a blade which looks more like a big spoon (sawn across its middle) and the shaft is usually flat on one side. Oars proper are usually flattish, especially for rowing at sea. Often sea oars are very short.

If a friend comes with you as passenger he or she will sit astern, and as likely as not lay claim upon the rudder and endeavour to steer with it. In my youth I used to take a very beautiful Indian girl, descendant of the emperor Aurangzeb, out rowing. Her steering was disastrous (still, she played tennis much better than I). Experienced oarsmen prefer to steer with the oars. It is so simple. You pull on one oar and the boat swings to the opposite side (60 seconds are all you require to find that out). Another way is to slow down and hold one oar in the water while rowing on the opposite side only. If you row at the seaside you are advised to row parallel to the shore and not out to sea . . . unless you are rowing a dinghy out to a yacht etc.

If you encounter a current you will have to cross it in an exaggerated sweep to allow the current to correct your movement and drift you on to the true course you really want.

Sometime you should take out a skiff with a rolling seat, which gives your pull on the sculls very great pressure. It is not for beginners, and should not be used until you can really handle a boat alone confidently. The skiff is extremely narrow, barely as wide as your own rump, long, thin and of very light construction, the rowlocks are mounted on outriggers leaning out over the water, not being in the boat at all. If you enjoy this type of rowing (and it can be fast and exciting) you should try to join a rowing club.

If ever you experience a capsize hang on to the boat, not the oars; it is larger, more easily seen, and help will come the sooner. If you have to climb into a rowing boat from the water always climb in from the stern; hold it with both hands, give a strong kick, and drag yourself up until you lie with your stomach across the transom (rear cross planking of the stern), from which position you can fall in without upsetting the boat. If you dive out of a rowing boat (to rescue somebody perhaps) always leave from bows or stern, never from the sides.

In racing the sculls are lightly held with the fingers and not gripped, and more effort is made by the movement of the legs against the footrest and the swing of the roll-seat. Wrist-rolling for feathering is essential. Keep the elbows well tucked in to the body as you raise the sculls from the water otherwise they may flip across the water; pretty as this looks it slows you down.

Never wet your hands if you think you are getting blisters, grease them with olive oil or a little soap.

Racing is for single skiff, a double (two rowers), a four or an eight boat.

Technically to scull is to use two oars (each rower) but in larger boats each man pulls only one oar. It is an exhilarating sport.

PUNTS AND RAFTS—A NEGLECTED FORM OF ENJOYING THE WATERS

A friend of mine who had lived in Guiana first drew my attention to rafts and punts.

A punt is a flat-bottomed boat with square ends, and is propelled by using a pole which is pushed against the bottom. Although probably the oldest system of crossing rivers it is clearly not suitable for deep rivers.

Punts and Rafts

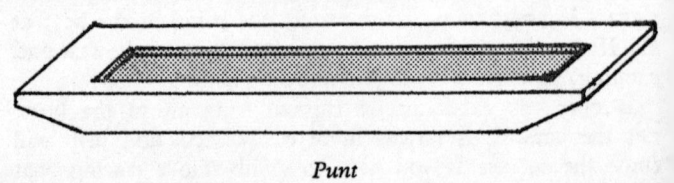

Punt

A raft is virtually any construction that floats. A wooden platform lashed together with ropes or cords, and attached to oil-drums is often used by youngsters on a local pond or river. Do make sure that the oil has been thoroughly boiled out of the drums so as to avoid pollution of the water.

GUIDE TO SWIMMING AND WATER SPORTS 217

Raft

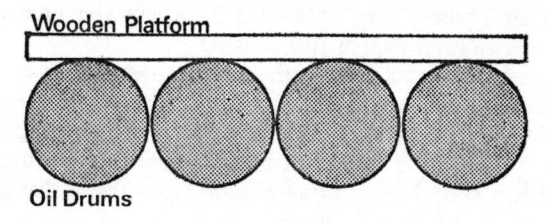

Punting sequence

Never venture on either unless you can swim 200 metres (220 yards). Both craft can be poled across the waters.

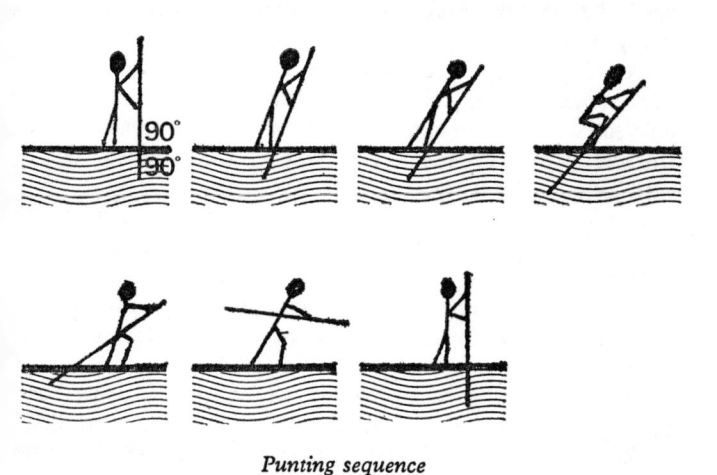

The technique of using the pole is set out in the illustrations (A—G). Poles are usually 15 feet long, some as little as 12, made either of metal alloy or of wood. Hold it upright with your right hand level with your own height (head), left hand about the height of your waist. The art is to touch the bottom of the river bed lightly—you press too hard the punt or raft will not wait for you, it will go on with the

H

current and leave you hanging on to the pole midstream. In an emergency hang on to the boat, not the pole ... cunning men keep a spare pole aboard!

I assume that you stand with one foot pointing forward in the direction you would go, the other at 45 degrees towards one side of the punt. Hold the pole lightly (not tightly), throw it straight down as near 90 degrees as possible; it should just slide loosely through your hands, raise the hands to the top of the pole by sliding them up, push so that the punt moves forward and the pole slides through your hands; as it does so pull the pole and tug it, sliding the rear foot a couple of steps back—as you do so the pole lifts and your hands gripping it come to the middle of your chest, the rear foot is swung forward again, the pole swings up until it is as vertical as it was before you slid it down at 90 degrees. This is a gentle rhythmic movement, the body sways and swings. *Never* thrust the pole far forward into a point ahead of the punt, otherwise the current and your weight will force the pole so deep into the mud that you may get marooned! You will easily pick up the feel of tapping the riverbed (don't drill for oil, a tap is enough).

Punting is done standing up; you must have a good balance, self-confidence, a sense of rhythm and a cool head.

Steering is clearly influenced by the movements of the body. Do steer very gently; the punt (or raft) has a will of its own and will swing all too readily (it has no keel to hold it on course).

You must practise using the pole on the left side as well as the right. Never make wide, large strokes; short, controlled strokes will get you there more safely, more quickly and with more fun.

Punting reached a heyday in Edwardian England when all the bright young men of the day took their girl-friends out for a lazy afternoon adventure on a punt, strawberry jam and cream with tea and shrimp paste sandwiches under the willows ... *and is there honey still for tea?* as Rupert Brook the poet asked in *Grantchester*.

For *messing about in boats*, as Kenneth Grahame's Ratty called it, there are few pastimes so cheaply and easily followed as punting and rafting.

OUTBOARD MOTORS

The outboard motor is so universally used as to need no description. It is probably the most widely used of all motors, and a source of great pleasure on rivers, lakes, canals and seas.

This section deals solely with some advice as to what to do if the motor goes wrong.

STARTING TROUBLES

Manual starter

(i) Unscrew and look at the large spring; is it greased? If not, grease it; a common cause of trouble!

(ii) If the cord has snapped, check the top of your flywheel which may have an emergency starter sleeve; you can wind a cord round this, jerk hard—behold a miracle—she starts!

(iii) Did the automatic rewinder function properly? Maybe it jammed, unscrew the assembly and check it.

90 per cent of all troubles are electrical, the others are usually fuel troubles; ignition problems are most common.

Ignition

(i) Check the sparking plugs; the electrodes may need a simple clean up. Check for cracked insulation.

(ii) Check for leaky washers or gaskets—change them.

(iii) Clean off any oil deposits.

(iv) Are spark plug leads connected? (Wear rubber gloves when checking—water on your hands may induce a shock.) Hold a lead almost touching the engine, start up the engine and look for a spark—if there is none the fault is purely one of broken wires, broken magneto or a dead battery. Check each plug.

(v) Check the condenser.

Fuel etc.

(i) Is the fuel tank clean?

(ii) Are fuel pipes broken or clogged up?

(iii) Check filter; is it clogged up or worn out?

(iv) Check gaskets for leaks.

(v) Check whether oil is smothering the petrol.
(vi) In cold weather the cold may be the cause of fuel not evaporating from the carburettor.
(vii) Is the propeller fouled?
(viii) Is the bearing assembly properly lubricated?
(ix) Is spray seeping into the powerhead?

Sounds of engine note
(a) Barking = mixture too thin.
(b) Purrs with smoke billowing behind = mixture too rich.
(c) Tapping sound = Check ignition timing; check oil (too little or too much). Maybe a rod is loose, check nuts on propeller.
(d) A spluttery stop = No fuel, fuel pipe blocked, carburettor trouble.
(e) Low thumping = Propeller damage, screws loose on transom, mixture too rich.
(f) Racing engine = Clutch, gears, check propeller sheering pin.

Overheating
(a) Leaking gaskets.
(b) Engine not properly angled in water.
(c) Blocked cooling system.

GENERAL NOTES

Do be consistent and careful about the oil and petrol you use for your engine. However difficult, do keep to the exact quantities and grades the manufacturers recommend.

Maintain your engine and service it regularly—this is so much cheaper than repairs.

Always carry a spare propeller, spark plugs, sheer pins, propeller nuts—and tools.

Life jackets, a fire extinguisher—even a spare sail or paddle would never come amiss.

Keep your engine and filters clean, never allow dirt or water to get into the fuel tank.

Check condition of sparking plugs at least once a month.

Remember to lift the propeller up if you are coming into land on a sloping beach.

Check the mountings of the engine on the transom, make sure they do not get worn down and change the angle at which the engine operates (cavitation). This usually occurs only on racing power boats. One of its many effects is that the prop creates a cavity and runs in air bubbles instead of water. It is a phenomenon not fully understood.

Always clean and dry the engine before storage for winter.

Water Polo, Water Skiing, Diving for Delight

WATER POLO

If you can swim you can play water polo. But in few games have there been so many different rules. In fact, it is not certain how long any set of rules can remain in force. It is extremely difficult to detect fouls under water; it is a man's game, and to many it seems at times a unique combination of swimming and all-in-wrestling, but that is the game at its worst; well-played by self-disciplined players it is a good, clean and very exciting game.

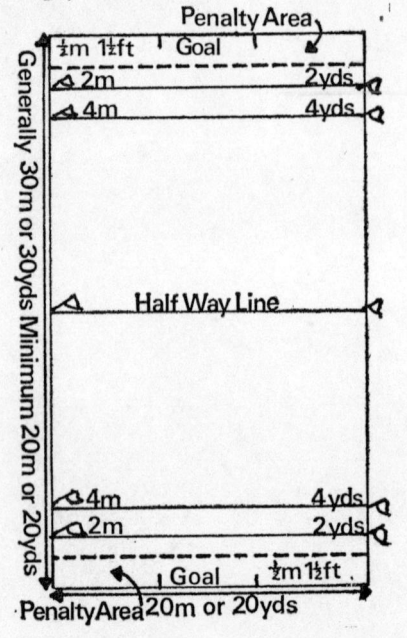

The field (bath size) must not exceed 30 yd. (30 metres usually in Europe) and must not be more than 20 yd. (20

metres) wide. A middle line is marked, and marks must be made to show a goal-line, a line two yards from each goal, a line four yards from each goal (4 metres). One foot (½ metre) behind the goal is out of bounds. Goalkeepers may not go over the 4-yard line.

Water polo shall not be played in less than 3 ft. (1 m.) of water. Space should be made in the centre of the pool for a referee to supervise the entire area of play, and preferably there should be walking room along the side of the bath for him to follow the game.

It is impossible to play in an area where there is any water weed, or possible unseen obstructions (broken glass, metal scrap etc.) below the water.

Goal-posts are 10 ft. 3 m.) apart, and the top of the goal 3 ft. (1 m.) above the line of the water surface, but if the water is less than 5 ft. (1½ m.) deep the goal crossbar must be at least 8 ft. (2½ m.) above the floor of the bath. Nets are loosely attached to the goal-posts. The ball weighs about 16 oz. (450 grams) and is the same size as a football.

Opposing teams must wear different-coloured swimming caps (these are often numbered but must clearly indicate the colours of the club in a club match).

Absolute obedience to the referee's whistle (start or stop play) is an essential of all rules.

Teams change ends halfway through the agreed time of the play (generally two periods of five minutes, but 7 or 10 are also used). Teams consist of 7 players: 1 goalkeeper, 3 defenders, 3 attackers; or 5 players: 1 goalkeeper, 2 defenders, 2 attackers. Nobody is allowed to wear rings, straps or to grease his body. The game starts when the referee throws in the ball to the middle line, and both teams swim for it.

If a player is injured a substitute is normally allowed. A goal is scored by the ball being cast fully into the goal area. *Nobody except the goalkeeper may touch the ball with two hands!* All throws and passes must be made with one hand only.

It is a Foul:
 To begin before the referee blows his whistle.
 To handle the ball with two hands; (unless goalie).

To duck opponents who are not holding the ball.

To put your feet to the bottom while play is on.

To hold the ball under water when the opposite side tackle you to get the ball.

To hold on to an opponent, to prevent him swimming.

To stop between the 2-yard line and goal when the ball is not in play in that area.

To change places with another player of your team during a match.

To hit the ball forward with a clenched fist.

To go over the 4-yard line if you are a goalkeeper.

To hold on to the ball and not swim with it or throw it.

Penalty for a foul is a free throw (the ref will blow his whistle and wave a flag showing the colours of the club (team) to whom the free throw is being awarded). One player of that team throws on the ref's further signal whistle, from the approximate position where the foul occurred. He must throw directly at the opposing goal; passing or dribbling the ball to his own team is not allowed.

If a player uses an unfair advantage in a tackle by holding on to the side bars, goal-posts, or places his feet on the floor he will be sent off in disgrace.

Disobeying the ref's instructions also means you will be sent off.

WATER POLO

1. How to hold and balance the ball

Illustrations

1 Shows how to hold the ball in a comfortable, balanced position with one hand. Some practice is needed.
2 Shows a method of throwing. Remember to drop the shoulder of the arm which is not throwing; this improves your leverage and throwing power.

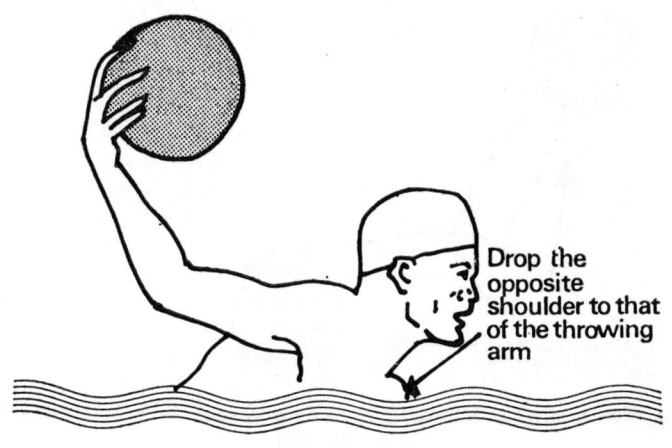

Drop the opposite shoulder to that of the throwing arm

2. How to throw the ball

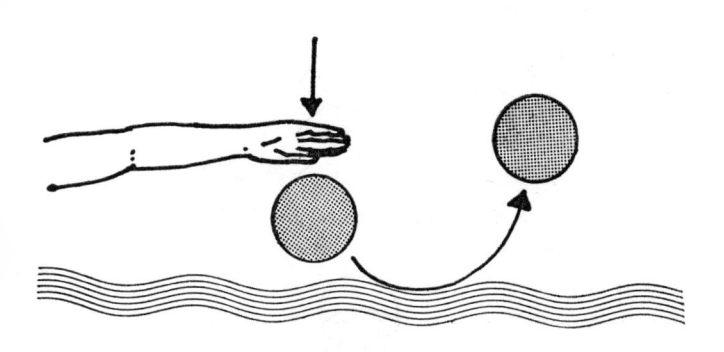

3. Slap the ball down into the water so that it bounces up into your hand

3 Shows us how to control the ball when it is on the surface; slap your hand down exactly on top of it, and the water makes it bounce back up into your hand, ready for a throw or a pass to another team-mate.

H*

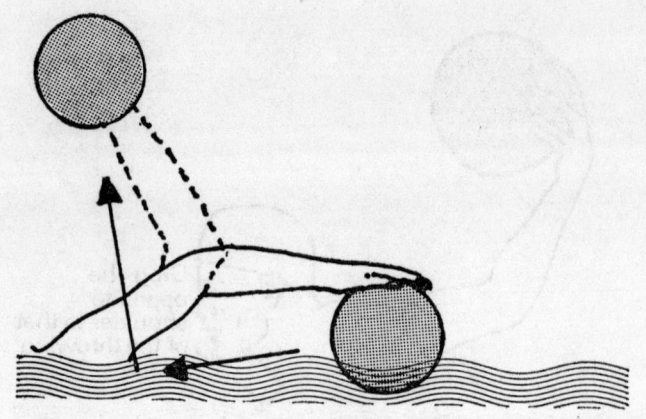

4. How to use a widespread finger grip to control the ball and edge it towards you

4 Shows how to spread the fingers wide, flick the ball in towards you, when you suddenly raise the hand, force the elbow down, the ball leaps up ready for throwing.

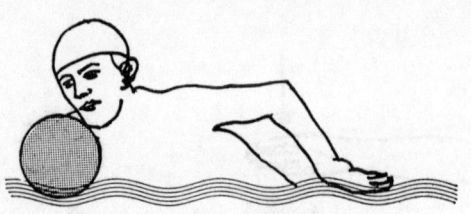

Swimming and controlling the ball

Sideways

5 Shows how to swim with the ball.

i. Straight arm — from behind head

ii. forward throw facing front

6 Shows the two principal methods of casting the ball.
N.B. Feet off of floor of bath.

THREE LAST PIECES OF ADVICE

Always try to keep your neck muscles relaxed when you throw the ball.

If you do get a few knocks take it as part of the game and don't moan about it.

Always have a referee, even in a friendly match or a *muck-about*; a bath attendant will often oblige you if no friend or relative is at hand.

I have enjoyed water polo and even got a couple of badges for it once, so I hope some of you will find it as much fun as I did.

WATER SKIING

This is a delightful sport which gives endless pleasure to the spectators. It requires skill, courage and a really athletic sense of balance and movement.

Obviously, it is essential to be able to swim 400 m. (440

yd.), and manoeuvre your body easily in the water before you try to learn this sport. Safety first!

REQUIREMENTS

1 A boat which can do between 16 and 20 mph.
2 A driver who can control the speed of a boat calmly, regularly and efficiently (sudden jerks, speed-ups, slow-downs etc, ruin the skiing).
3 A nylon or other strong artificial fibre rope with a breaking strain of not less than 850 lb.
4 Handles at the skier's end of the rope. Skiers tend to prefer one broad handle of 30–45 cm. (12–18 inches). The handle must have a soft lining internally to avoid fraying the rope. Length 75 ft.
5 Skis vary in length and weight according to the weight of the skier.
Skis 4 ft. 6 in. long and 5 in. wide are suitable for up to 6 stones weight.
Skis 5 ft. 6 in. long and 6 in. wide are suitable for up to 14 stones.
Skis 6 ft. long and 8 in. wide are suitable for up to 20 stones.
Very expert skiers will tend to work more in precise half-inches etc. It is not widely known that water skis each have a small keel which gives them a better *grip* on the water, and lessens their tendency to topple over.
Beware of skis with adjusting binders; they will not do much harm for a beginner moving at comparatively slow speeds, but for anybody moving fast they are a nuisance, a danger and almost useless.
The size of the binder, the emptiness of toe and heel holders must be built for the individual skier.
Types of Ski
(a) Fairly wide, curling upwards at front end; squared off rear; parallel sides. This is best at slower speeds, does not react well at fast speeds, popular for beginners.
(b) Slalom skis, thinner, suitable for fast use, less stable; slimming down towards the front. Curled front and back.

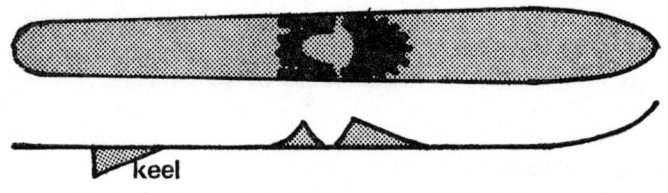

a. General purpose ski

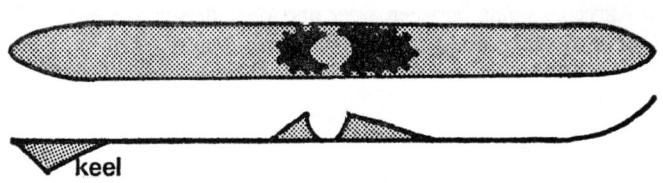

b. Slalom ski

(c) Jumping skis. From 5 to 6 ft. long, never thicker than an inch. About 15 cm. wide (6 inches) or a little more. Very strongly built, they must also be whippy, able to spring and take shocks. If the ski is thicker it jolts the skier when he lands on the water from the jumping ramp.

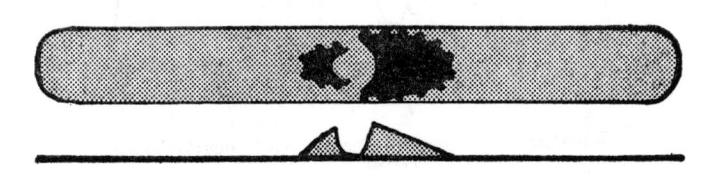

c. Jumping skis

230 GUIDE TO SWIMMING AND WATER SPORTS

6 Beginners are advised to wear a properly-padded life-saving belt covering the kidneys (lower back) around the waist. Then any fall backward would be less of a shock, and the skier would stay afloat if he let go of the rope.

7 A wet suit may be recommended by your trainer.

FIRST STEPS

There should always be an observer in the boat looking back at the beginner (and sometimes at the advanced); his job is to give a message immediately to the driver.

The driver should be experienced enough to keep a specific speed and an agreed straight line over as smooth a course as possible.

Agreed signals between skier and boat driver are essential. One arm only raised means I am in difficulty.

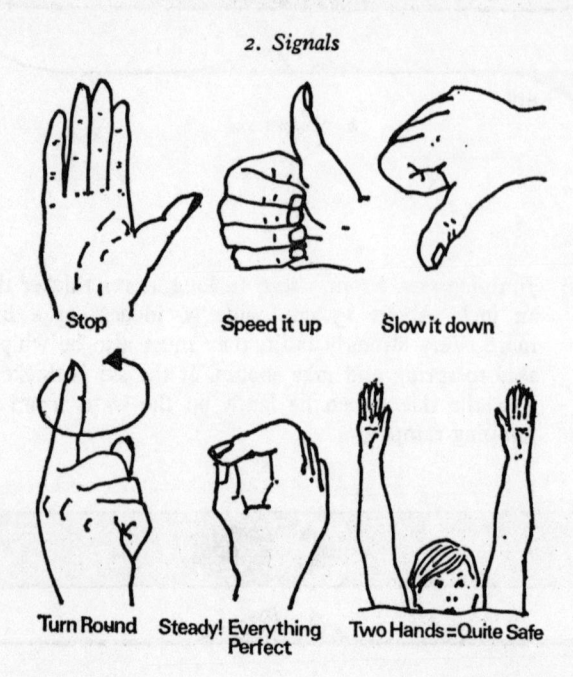

2. Signals

Stop   Speed it up   Slow it down

Turn Round   Steady! Everything Perfect   Two Hands = Quite Safe

Of the handholds the beginner should use the double grip with both hands holding over the bar (as illustrated).

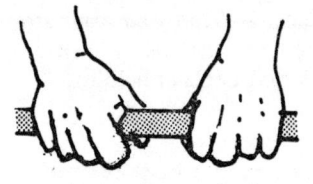

3. Theory   *i. Handholds on the bar*

a. both grip over the bar

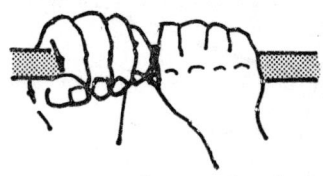

b. one over and one under the bar

If a beginner (or skiing during chilly weather), it is most advisable to wear a wet-suit which not only keeps the body at an even temperature but lessens the shock if for any reason you fall back slap into the water.

Check the ski-binders before you put them on, make sure there are no sharp pebbles, seaweed etc. in them—just a little water should be used to make them feel easier on your feet. Practise putting them on several times.

You will keep the two skis slightly apart and your task is to maintain *a balance between them*; if one ski is allowed to wander away distorting the sense of balance you'll be swimming for it! *Control the skis with your knees*, this means using the thigh muscles. Do not try to control the skis only with your feet. Crossed skis means loose knees.

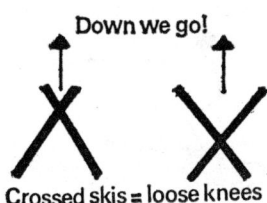

Good knee control

Down we go!

Crossed skis = loose knees

GUIDE TO SWIMMING AND WATER SPORTS

Before starting in the water get a friend (or two) to haul you over a stretch of wet foreshore (using manpower, not boat power). Start crouching down on the skis, and as you feel the rope pull, straighten up at once, taking the strain with your knees. Beginners—*Keep your arms straight*. Never bend them, this destroys the triangle of control (see illustration), arm ache means wrong angle of holding.

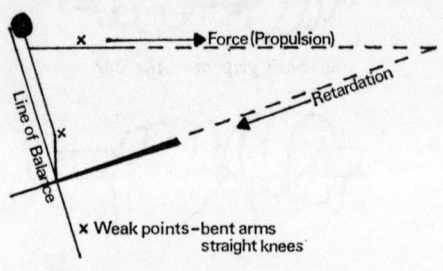

Imagine invisible lines (in green)

Start next from a sloping beach, get a friend to hold you the first few tries. Practise starts from sitting on a small jetty.

Beach start with help from a friend

Overbalancing is done easily enough, and by using the law of opposite pressures you can break the circular motion of a coming fall and restore the balance—provided you have not gone too far.

Law of opposite pressures: Press heavily on the ski that rises up to restore balance.

Techniques

Law of opposite pressures

If one ski rises you tend to fall to the opposite side. Press more heavily on ski that rises as you fall — this restores your balance

All overbalancing is circular in motion!

Reduce the line of balance to ride safely over difficulties, waves, rough waters, emergencies etc. By crouching down you lessen the line of balance between propulsion and drag, in this position you minimise the effect of shock on your body.

Having mastered balance you use the same effects to steer a course across the wake of your boat, crisscrossing as you wish. All crossing over the wake should be tried at 90 degrees or as near that as possible, otherwise the wake may force your skis out of parallel and you will be swimming instead of skiing.

The slightest change of weight over the centre of gravity will tend to tilt the skis slightly and change your direction of travel.

Crossing the boat's wake

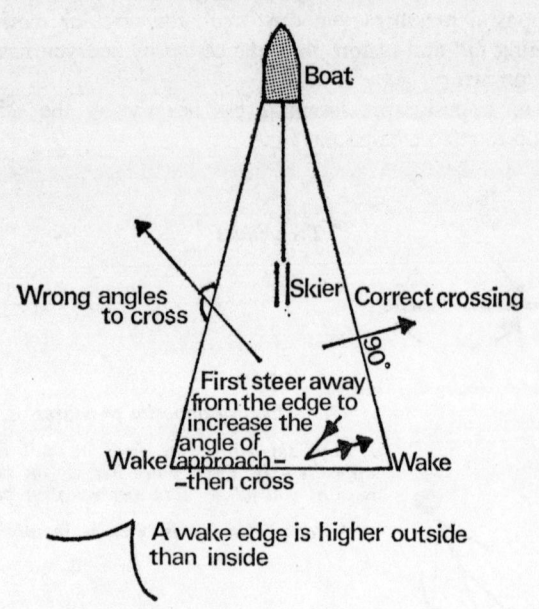

[Diagram: Boat at top with wake spreading outward. Skier shown with "Wrong angles to cross" on left and "Correct crossing" at 90° on right. Labels: "First steer away from the edge to increase the angle of approach — then cross", "Wake" on both sides. Below: "A wake edge is higher outside than inside"]

SOME SIMPLE STEPS IN WATER SKIING

Crossing the wake is done by first steering away from the edge you plan to cross over; this means that when you turn in towards that edge you have a sharper angle and can cross about 90 degrees. Bend the knees deeper down as you cross, lean more forward at your waistline, stretching the arms out forward (otherwise you'll react to the changing lines of force by falling backward).

More advanced skiers learn how to jump across the wake edge. Remember that having crossed the wake going outward from it, you must sooner or later return into it. The inward turn must be made with a fighting, tough quality of mind, the slightest hesitation can result in a spill; you must aim at it, be resolute and as precise as possible in the angle (90 degrees) because the outside of a wake edge is higher than the inside, so tilt the tips of your skis more upward as you come back in.

Do not try this when your boat is turning until you are very expert.

Learning to control the rope with one hand only is not too difficult, and the free arm, apart from making signals to your boat-driver from time to time, can be used for a wave or artistic movement which adds to the impression you can make on the watchers ashore.

If you are quite at ease doing this, you may try to balance one one ski only, and then experiment with removing one ski (don't let the wind blow it away!)—this may be held a while and then replaced. The technique of this is to loosen the heel of the binder first, and fasten this back again only when the ski is back on the foot, and the foot gliding back on the water—for the toe part of the binder ensures that the direction of the water prevents the ski from coming off.

At places such as Cypress Gardens, Florida, USA, wonderful displays of talent on water skis are given; whole towering pyramids of skiers glide across the sunlit waters, and a common feat there is to place the handlebar behind the thighs at the back and to ski with both arms outstretched. This alters the balance slightly but by the time you try this you should be in good command of your balance.

The more tricks you try the more you must insist that your driver keeps the same speed for every outing.

When feeling very confident you may take a friend riding on your shoulders (make sure he or she is an extremely good swimmer first). The girl carried (they are lighter) tucks her feet under the shoulders of the boy and keeps them steady (not fidgeting) behind his back; she will soon learn to make graceful, balletic movements to enhance the pleasure spectators will get from the ski show.

When you feel able to try more difficult manoeuvres you should consult *Introducing Water Skiing* by P. Felix and P. Rivers (Foyles Handbooks) and *Water Skiing* by Al Tyll (John Gifford)—a must for would-be experts.

SURF RIDING

Probably one of the least energetic means of enjoying the fun that the sea can offer is to let the sea do half the work for you. You lie down on the board and paddle yourself to catch a good wave, and then the wave obligingly carries you hurtling in at up to 20 miles per hour to the beach—some waves pound in at that rate on almost any shore!

How to get out

Lie full length on your surfboard, your nose is about one hand's width above the water; this position is deemed important because any further inclination or declination will alter the board's buoyancy, and if you will forgive the pun it is a *handy* distance to measure. From this position, keeping quite relaxed and still, you paddle yourself out by stretching the arms forward and using the Dolphin/Butterfly arm movement described in the swimming section. No other arm movement will serve your purpose, so make sure you know it before you try surfing. A Crawl arm movement would distort the course (the sea is moving against you while you paddle out).

Surf riding

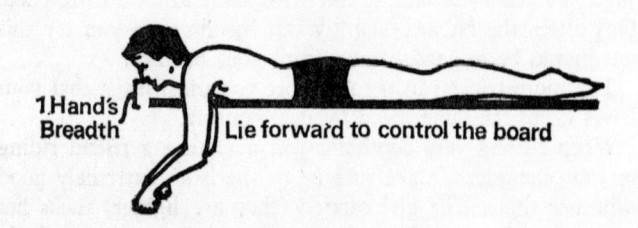

1 Hand's Breadth Lie forward to control the board

It is a mistake to be far down along the board; that is a bad distribution of weight, the first big wave will throw you backward and that might hurt you badly.

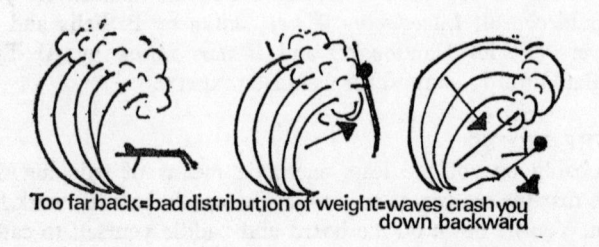

Too far back = bad distribution of weight = waves crash you down backward

The surfboard is entirely at the mercy of the waves, if you overbalance you'll never get out.

Paddle with the Dolphin arm movements, speeding up as you approach an incoming wave (if you do not speed it up the wave will have greater momentum than you . . . and backward you will go). Very experienced surfers tackle huge incoming breakers by clasping their surfboard, rolling round, holding the board on top of them. The heavier the board the easier it is to get through the waves.

How to learn the art

You start with nice, easy waves, coming in, perhaps, on a wave that has already crumbled. At first you will probably prefer to come in on the board *sitting down,* this will give you a better sense of balance which is the critical art of surfing.

The next stage is to come in on easy waves in a crouch position, knees bent loosely (if you are too stiff you'll swim for it sooner). Then it is a simple matter to extend the newly-found balance to coming in fully erect, balanced, and the envy of your friends and all who watch you. It is an extremely thrilling experience to ride a foaming white comber, sliding along the direction of its break. Another way to master the art of surfing is to follow the wake of a small launch or cruiser. A lot of the technique is related to the mental attitude and the amount of self-confidence and determination the surfer shows. It may well be said to be character forming, like most other water sports.

Where are the brakes?

As the city boy said when he got on a horse for the first time, *where are the brakes?*

You are your own brakes! You may glide one foot backward; this depresses the rear of the board, lifts the front, alters the balance and produces a gliding-motion stop. For the less expert there are two other methods: You can drop down bodily into a position on the front of the board, or just throw the entire length of your body towards the side of the board (do not forget to hold on to it) and the result is that you have become your own anchor—everything stops (except the wave).

238   GUIDE TO SWIMMING AND WATER SPORTS

Steering

When you have balanced yourself enough to stand up erect you will find it advisable to keep one foot about two foot-lengths ahead of the other; the foot in front points roughly to the centre of the board, the foot to the rear is at 45 degrees roughly to the foot in front (see diagram). Foot movements turn the board left, right etc.

General position of feet on board.

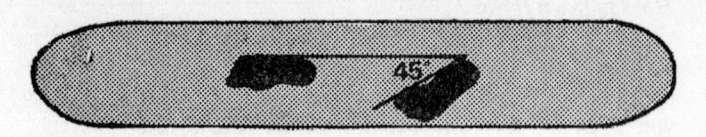

If the front of the board rises up, lean forward.
If the rear side comes up, lean backward.
If the left side comes up, lean left.
If the right side comes up, lean to the right.

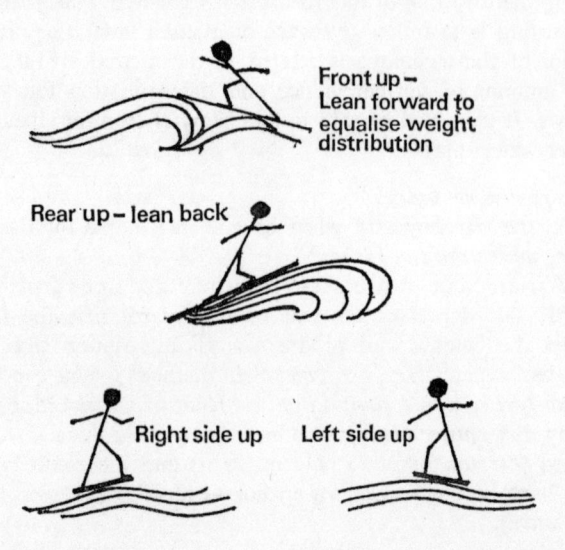

Front up – Lean forward to equalise weight distribution

Rear up – lean back

Right side up   Left side up

Most of this comes naturally with practice and experience.

Frankly speaking, this is about all any book can tell you about surfing techniques, the rest is the result of experience. I cannot put into writing exactly how to judge when the peak of a wave is forming, and how to recognise the moment when you twist your feet left, right and so on to come on to that peak. Try not to come straight in on a wave, but always on an angle to the shore, otherwise the surfboard moves more quickly than the wave and you will tumble down to the shingle below.

Surfboards

Many types of board are in use. A cheap one is good enough to begin with; make sure it is suitable to the weight and length of your own body . . . in a word, be sure you can practise on it in comfort and can really balance on it.

A professionally-made board bought from a proper sports suppliers shop will give you far more sense of control, expertise and has a better gliding action on the water, due mainly to a plasticised surface.

Always polish your board with paraffin wax; it will give you a better grip on it!

DIVING FOR DELIGHT

Diving is a higly complicated sport quite remote from Swimming, although it is true that every diver must be able to swim a little. There is no connection other than that. Most swimming pools have one or more diving boards, and it would be unusual if man's questing nature did not encourage the swimmer to experiment.

This section limits itself to describing some simple dives which anybody can perform for his or her own delight. Anybody who has seen the sheer artistry and technical ability of such divers as Johnny Miles, Brian Phelps, Alun Roberts, Betty Slade and 'Spider' Webb, all of whom I have known personally, will not regard this introductory work as true diving.

Diving is the nearest that man comes to flying without wings, electronics or anything else. All good divers began with an innate curiosity and a fascination for the sport, so if the reader achieves ability and grace in the elementary work, that will be the time to contact a good diving club.

Rule 1. Don't go into the water head first until you can go in successfully feet first.

  (a) Stand to attention on the bath side, toes slightly over the edge of the bath. Achieve a good balance before taking off, then you can control your entry and not fall into the water like a sack of potatoes.

  (b) Keeping both arms stiff, bring them straight up roughly at shoulder width apart, keeping them above but in front of the face. At the same time spring *from the ankles* outward and forward into the water, keeping the legs stiff on entry, toes pointed downward. Do not move head, arms, back or legs while in mid-air—this will change your direction and the jump will end in an uncomfortable splash.

  (c) Repeat this but try to jump up higher.

Rule 2. The diver needs height from whatever surface the jump or dive is made, *take it up!*

  (a) Repeat the same jump described above but face inward to the side. Have a friend or instructor near to push your face away if you lose control and come down too near the hard surface of the bath side. In this jump the arms carry further upward and slightly to the rear.

  (b) Repeat this jump but learn to raise the arms up and then lower them before entering the water. This is not quite so simple as it sounds. The movement of up then down must be made with stiff, fast moving arms.

  (c) Repeat the up and down arm technique for the first forward jump. Do not proceed further until this technique is good.

Rule 3. Controlled movement is safe. Hesitation is fatal.

  (a) Perform the forward jump but while in the air hold arms and legs in an X position. This is known as the *Star* jump. *Legs and arms must close before entering the water.*

  (b) Only when the above exercise can be performed well

proceed to master the technique of jumping backwards, facing the bath side. If the jumper is not jumping up there will not be time to make the movements.

Rule 4. Precise movements are vital. Careless movement can lead to painful 'landings' in the water. Do not attempt the following until all the previous jumps can be performed well.

(a) Stand on the bath side, well back from the water, do not try to enter the water until you have mastered this on land. Throw the right arm up so that the biceps brushes the ear, keep the right arm stiff, fingers pointed. At the same time jump up as high as possible and *throw quickly and decisively* the left arm across the chest so that the hand tucks in under the right armpit. Turn the head smartly to the right. The movement of the left arm should carry you in a complete circle; the position of the stiff right arm exactly above the head should keep you balanced. Practise this several times, then change arms and learn how to do it in the other direction.

(b) Having mastered the above technique on dry land, try it from the bath side, and jump in the water, keeping the toes pointed as you jump downward, do not relax until below the water.

Rule 5. Whether jumping or diving do not relax in mid-air, it can be painful. For a soft substance water can sometimes feel quite hard.

(a) This must be practised over the water, and with the help near. The take-off is as for a forward jump, but at the acme of the 'flight' the legs are raised forward to make a big 'L' shape, the top half of the jumper's body staying more or less still, except for a slight inclination as the jumper brings his arms forward for the hands to touch the toes briefly. The slightest and shortest visible touch is needed then the jumper lowers the legs into a vertical position, hands and arms swinging back to vertical; the jumper should enter the water in a vertical straight line.

(b) Take off as for a forward straight jump but at the acme of the flight the jumper brings his legs smartly up to the chest, gripping them with both arms, trunk bending slightly frontward, but head keeping still. After the position has been clearly shown, the legs and arms are straightened, and a vertical entry is made.

(c) The same as before but made as a backward jump. Keep head slightly more to the rear.

DIVING: JUMPS

a. Plain jump.

b. Star jump.

c. Tuck jump.

d. Backwards jump.

GENERAL

Do not lean forward if you are jumping forward, keep vertical.

Do not lean backward if you are jumping backward, keep vertical.

If jumping backward you may have the back of the heels just over the edge of the bath instead of the toes projecting as in forward jumps.

All of these jumps when mastered from the bath edge can be taken from the one-metre board, then the three-metre board.

Many pools wisely prohibit jumping from a five-metre board, and the author does not recommend jumping from that height.

Mastery of jumps speeds up the capacity for learning simple dives for delight, and builds up confidence in the learner.

Do not look downward when jumping; this will destroy the balance of the body and the chances are that you will land on your face.

If you fail to control your arms or legs you will slap them hard as you land—don't say you haven't been warned.

The water is softer to 'land' on than is the bath side so never, repeat *never*, jump for the bath side—always out into the friendly water.

Jumpers who look downward while doing the tuck jump usually end up by doing their first somersault dive . . . in which case tell them to go ahead, they've graduated higher than they expected.

Any jumper is controlled mainly by his arm movements and secondly by his head movements.

The technique of head-first entries is different to that of the jumps but jumping builds up confidence.

SIMPLE DIVING FOR ADULTS

Strange as it may seem in many ways it is easier to control the human body in flight while moving head first than when going feet first.

A world-famous champion springboard diver once told me that he detested going into the water feet first.

With nervous individuals it is wiser to sit them down on the side of the bath, put their feet on the scumrail below the edge, stretch their knees wide apart, bend the body forward and downward between the parted knees, stretch their hands in a straight line, hands stiff and pointed and then encourage them to dive down for one of the black lines (racing lane markings) on the bottom of the pool. Keep the head between the arms. Keep a pole handy if you have a very nervous class. The basic error of beginners is that they insist on raising their face at the last moment and land flat on it! Tell the novice to breathe out slowly through the nose and keep the mouth shut while entering the water.

The next stage of progress is to dive from the *Squat* position; the diver squats on his heels on the edge of the bath side, places arms out in front as before, keeps head between arms and enters by a spring from ankles and knees.

This is followed by the same dive from a *Bend* position. The diver stands on the bath edge, bent over at right angles, arms pointing downward, head between them. The spring is effected through the ankles and the knees.

The sequence is completed by the *Standing Header* for which the diver stands fully upright on the bath side, with the toes overlapping and gripping the edge of the bath (or later the end of the diving board). The heels should be touching but the toes may be either apart or together as the individual diver may find more comfortable. The body is erect, the head straight with the eyes level (never looking downward), the chin is tucked in, the chest slightly pulled out, stomach drawn inwards. The arms stretch upward to give the body the appearance of a large letter 'Y'. Thumbs and fingers are close together. The diver springs making the fullest possible use of the ankles, and upon reaching the acme of his flight upward he slightly drops the head forward but keeps the arms straight. The object is for the body to achieve an entry at 90 degrees to the water and enter in a perfectly straight line; the diver should try to keep his body straight until the water has closed over his toes.

Later on the dive can be done from a one-metre board. Later the enterprising diver may wish to try the dive with a *Star* leg action, a Tuck or Piked leg action etc.

g. Sit dive.
h. Crouch dive.
i. Bend dive.

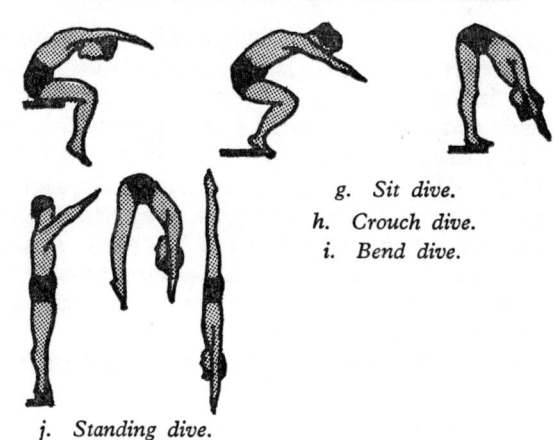

j. Standing dive.

SIMPLE DIVING FOR CHILDREN

It is not always advisable to teach children anything but the straightforward jump before instructing them in the following techniques. Some teachers would not even teach the straightforward jump.

(1) Hold on to the rail with one hand only and duck the head quickly right down under the water, keeping the eyes wide open ('Have you ever seen a fish swimming with it's eyes shut?'). We don't hold our noses because we are breathing out through our nose all the time we are under water.

(2) *Ring-a-ring of Roses.* All the children join hands and play the old children's game, when we come to 'Atishoo, atishoo, we all fall down' they put their heads under water holding each other firmly by the hand.

(3) Two children hold their hands outstretched, standing face to face, their arms form a little bridge, and all the children have to walk under the bridge, ducking their heads deep in the water to avoid bumping their heads on the low bridge.

(4) Several children make a chain, holding hands on the bath side; on the word 'go' they all jump in together.

(5) Jumping in one by one, breathing out through the nose.

(6) Jumping in one by one and picking up the standard rubber brick which is available at most baths if you ask for it. Any other large object will serve, provided it sinks and a child can easily pick it up from the bottom of the bath.

(7) One child stands about six feet from the bath edge and keeps his legs as wide open as he can. The other children then bend down and glide through. It may be advisable to have another responsible person to catch them and pull them to the surface quickly if the children get stuck or have difficulties.

(8) The same exercise as in 7, but the child starts from a position of sitting on the top of the steps leading out of the bath.

Notes Avoid wiping the face ('Your face won't get dirty in the water'). Keep the hands slightly apart; if they are close together the would-be diver can lose balance and control.

(9) *The Humpty-Dumpty Dive.* Sit on the edge of the bath. Place the feet on the rail or scumrail; keep the knees wide apart; the body bends forward; the arms are stretched out with the biceps by the ears, and slightly pressed against them. The diver 'falls off the wall' like Humpty in the poem by pushing the head downward and springing from the ankles. Eyes stay open, breathing out through the nose, the diver turns the hands up to the surface and comes up at once. Surprisingly perhaps, even untrained children have this instinct to surface well developed.

(10) The *Otter* dive. The child kneels with one knee only, the other leg has the foot with the toes over the edge of the bath and slightly gripping it, the knee is bent up by the crouching position of the diver. The arms and head are in the same direction as before (9) but slightly more acutely downward pointing to the water. Then on the word 'Go' the child enters the water like an otter about to catch a fish.

(11) The *Ballet* dive. The diver stands on the edge of the bath, leans forward with both arms stretching outward and straight, the left leg comes up behind slowly,

GUIDE TO SWIMMING AND WATER SPORTS 247

toes pointed, at the same time as the trunk leans forward and the arms begin to go downward. Before complete balance is lost the diver uses the firmly-anchored right leg to give a little spring. Although very simple this can be a very graceful dive, and *is often used at school galas* as follows: All the competitors start lined up along the entire length of the bath edge and at the blow of a whistle each one after another all down the line enters the water with a *Ballet* dive, swims across the width and climbs out. It is possible to achieve an effect like a wave or a ripple. A further improvement is to have each diver carry a lit waterproofed torch in one hand and switch the bath lights out just before the competitors dive in. After the *Ballet* dive the learner can proceed with the *Standing Header* dive as described above in the section on adult diving.

WHAT CAN GO WRONG WITH A SIMPLE DIVE?

(a) A negative movement without a positive direction of thought and body often ends in disaster. If you are going to dive make up your mind that it will be as planned, do not allow doubts and dismays to distract the mind from the things it must remember to make the dive a success. Don't fall—Dive!

(b) Don't lift your face up to see where you're going!

(c) Make the tips of your fingers like spearheads to pierce the water. If they are loose like bunches of wet seaweed the slap you get on the arms may hurt.

(d) Never loosen the body up after the dive until it is completely submerged in the water; keep the arms well in front of the head otherwise a careless dive may result in a nasty bump . . . ('Please be careful not to crack our nice pool open with your heads').

(e) failure to lower the head at the acme of the dive leads to that squashed-nose feeling.

(f) Look straight ahead if going off a board, make sure you are balanced.

248 GUIDE TO SWIMMING AND WATER SPORTS

(g) The object of any dive or jump is to go *up* before going down. Go up well, gravity will ensure you come down. Several easy dives are illustrated below.

k. Diving under legs.   *l. Surface dive.*

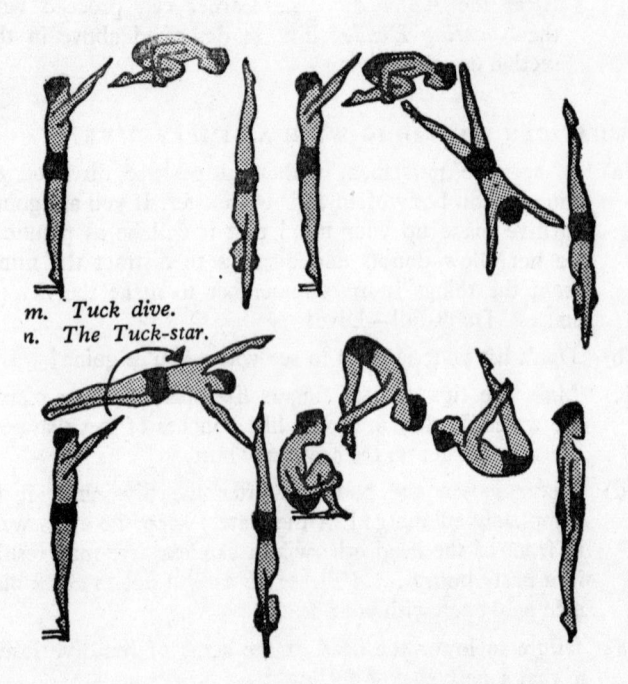

m. Tuck dive.
n. The Tuck-star.

o. Sideways roll.   *p. Forward tumble.*

THE END